"Atonement theologies have fo
ror culture wars. Atonement theologies have become obse
mechanics of atonement, that is, how God accomplished atonement—how
justice was dealt with, how sin was erased, how God's wrath was pacified.
Far too often atonement theologies have focused on what is less known and
ignored what is known. Michael Gorman in *The Death of the Messiah and
the Birth of the New Covenant*, has accomplished keeping our eyes on what
is known: that in the death and resurrection of Jesus, God has formed a new
covenant people."

—SCOT MCKNIGHT
Professor of New Testament, Northern Baptist Theological Seminary, Lombard, IL

"This book, what a gem! Gorman situates atonement in the new messianic
cruciform covenant, fulfilling OT visions of peace. Reorienting standard
atonement theories, Gorman grounds atonement where it belongs, in Jesus's gospel of peace, love-driven death, and new covenant! Virtually all
NT writings bear witness. Salvation, politics, and spirituality shine in new
light. The bibliography is rich. This is an *essential* read and resource for New
Testament theology-ethics."

—WILLARD M. SWARTLEY
Professor emeritus of New Testament, Anabaptist Mennonite Biblical Seminary,
Elkhart, IN

"With this biblically and theologically mature study, Michael Gorman shifts
our focus away from fascination with the how of the atonement and toward
reflection on the what: What does Jesus's death accomplish? The result is
a richly textured statement of how the atonement reaches deeply into the
scriptural story of God's mighty acts in order to present the consequences
of the cross for the church's faith, hope, and love."

—JOEL B. GREEN
Dean, School of Theology, Fuller Theological Seminary, Pasadena, CA

"Traditional atonement theories, often historically unmoored from the
large narrative of Scripture, try their best to articulate what we are saved
from. Gorman's book sounds the clarion call of the New Testament found
in Jesus Christ—that ultimately we have been saved for and called to

spirit-empowered, cruciform discipleship in Christ as children of God's new covenant of shalom. As the New Testament atonement metaphors rest within the grand scope of God's covenant of salvation, we hear afresh the truly astonishing good news of the gospel!"

—CHERITH FEE NORDLING

Professor of Theology, Northern Baptist Theological Seminary, Lombard, IL

"Spread the word! The New Testament demands that Christ's atonement on the cross must bring forth a holy witness in the very practices of each and every Christian parish and congregation. Thanks to Michael Gorman for taking us beyond endless discussions of the 'how' of Christ's atonement to its visible end, Christ's atonement as manifest in the life of the church for the sake of the world!"

—JOHN W. WRIGHT

Professor of Theology and Christian Scripture, Point Loma Nazarene University, San Diego, CA

The Death of the Messiah
and the Birth of the New Covenant

THE DEATH OF THE MESSIAH
and the Birth of the New Covenant

— A (Not So) New Model of the Atonement —

MICHAEL J. GORMAN

CASCADE *Books* · Eugene, Oregon

THE DEATH OF THE MESSIAH AND THE BIRTH OF THE NEW COVENANT
A (Not So) New Model of the Atonement

Cascade Books
An Imprint of Wipf and Stock Publishers
199 W. 8th Ave., Suite 3
Eugene, OR 97401

www.wipfandstock.com

ISBN 13: 978-1-62032-655-8

Cataloguing-in-Publication Data

Gorman, Michael J., 1955–

The death of the messiah and the birth of the new covenant : a (not so) new model of the atonement / Michael J. Gorman.

xii + 278 p. ; 23 cm. Includes bibliographical references and index(es).

ISBN 13: 978-1-62032-655-8

1. Atonement. 2. Jesus Christ—Crucifixion. I. Title.

BT265.2 G65 2014

Manufactured in the U.S.A.

In memory of my father,
Peter J. Gorman (April 3, 1922—December 25, 2012),
in gratitude for his life and his support
and
with thanks to
Rev. Thomas R. Hurst

Contents

Acknowledgments

THIS BOOK HAS BEEN in process for quite some time, and many people—knowingly or unknowingly—have contributed to its conception and birth, to borrow the metaphor from the title.

I am extremely grateful to Wipf and Stock publishers for their extraordinary flexibility and assistance in the publication of this book. Special thanks go to Chris Spinks, Jim Tedrick, Dave Belcher, and Ian Creeger. Thanks are also due to John Barclay, Bill Campbell, Stephen Chester, Mark Gorman, Kathy Grieb, Nijay Gupta, Richard Hays, David Horrell, Brent Laytham, Troy Martin, Peter Oakes, Chris Skinner, Klyne Snodgrass, Paul Seaton, Tom Stegman, Drew Strait, Sarah Whittle, Tom Wright, and Gordon Zerbe for their scholarly feedback to earlier versions of the material in various parts of the book, or to specific passages. As always, Andy Johnson has read versions of nearly the entire book in various stages and made extraordinarily helpful comments.

I also wish to thank my former student and research assistant, Kurt Pfund, as well as my former student and present research assistant, Daniel Jackson, for their help with various aspects of the book. Daniel, in particular, did much of the leg work involved in bringing the book to its final form.

As the thesis of this book has evolved over the years, I have taken several opportunities to lecture and/or write on aspects of it, or on its thesis as a whole. One of those opportunities was the inaugural lecture for the Raymond E. Brown Chair in Biblical Studies and Theology at St. Mary's Seminary & University. The lecture, which was also the annual Dunning Lecture of St. Mary's Ecumenical Institute of Theology (of which I had previously been Dean for eighteen years), was entitled "The Death of the Messiah: Theology, Spirituality, Politics" and delivered in November 2012. I am enormously grateful to St. Mary's President Rector, Fr. Thomas Hurst, and to the U. S.

Acknowledgments

Province of the Society of St. Sulpice and its Provincial, Fr. Thomas Ulshafer, for the privilege of being named the first occupant of the Raymond Brown chair. The title of the inaugural lecture and of the book reflect my debt to and respect for Fr. Brown, whose two-volume book *The Death of the Messiah* was just one of his many significant contributions to the field. Although my primary interests in this book differ from those of Fr. Brown in that book (the subtitle of which is *From Gethsemane to the Grave: A Commentary on the Passion Narratives in the Four Gospels*), both works recognize the absolutely critical need to understand the death of Jesus. I am grateful as well to Brent Laytham, the current Dean of the Ecumenical Institute of Theology, for his support in combining the inaugural lecture with the Dunning Lecture.

My gratitude extends as well to Dean Laytham's former institution, North Park Theological Seminary, and to the colleagues and friends there who invited me to participate in the 2010 North Park Symposium on the Theological Interpretation of Scripture that focused on the atonement. Klyne Snodgrass and Stephen Chester courageously agreed to present and interpret my paper in my absence due to a family emergency. Chapters 1 through 3 of this book, and part of the conclusion, are based largely on that paper, which was published in the journal *Ex Auditu* 26 (2011). It is used by permission of the editor, Klyne Snodgrass, and the publisher, Wipf and Stock. Chapters 4 and 5 have been developed from a paper published in a collection of essays for Frank Matera. It is used by permission of the editors, Chris Skinner and Kelly Iverson, and the publisher, the Society of Biblical Literature. Chapters 6 and 7 grew out of a paper delivered at the British New Testament Conference at St. Andrews University in Scotland, and from an expansion of that paper published as an article in the *Journal for the Study of Paul and His Letters*. I am grateful to Peter Oakes and Sarah Whittle for the invitation to deliver the original paper, and I am equally grateful to the publisher, Eisenbrauns, and to the editors, Michael Bird and Nijay Gupta, for permission to adapt the published article.[1] In every case I have significantly revised and expanded the original lectures and publications.

Expansion, indeed, has been the order of the day for this book. Troy Martin, my respondent to the earliest public display of its basic thesis,

1. The articles mentioned are "Effecting the New Covenant: A (Not So) New, New Testament Model for the Atonement," *Ex Auditu* 26 (2011) 26–59; "Cruciformity according to Jesus and Paul," in *Unity and Diversity in the Gospels and Paul: Essays in Honor of Frank J. Matera*, edited by Christopher W. Skinner and Kelly R. Iverson, SBLECL 7 (Atlanta: SBL, 2012) 173–201; "The Lord of Peace: Christ our Peace in Pauline Theology," *Journal for the Study of Paul and his Letters* 3 (2013) 91–126.

complained (in agreement with the author) that it was both too short and too long. Some may now think it is *far* too long. Others may think it is *still* too short. The more I study and think about the New Testament texts, however, the more interconnectedness I perceive along certain key beliefs, values, and practices. I therefore needed to stop writing (and reading—the literature on the atonement is voluminous) before this book squashed all other projects and approached the length of recent books by some of my esteemed colleagues and friends. That said, I know there is still much more to be said, and I hope others will join me in that investigation and conversation.

Unfortunately, two important books related to the thesis of the present work appeared too late for me to integrate them with my own thinking. Grant Macaskill's *Union with Christ in the New Testament* examines the interrelated themes of incarnation, atonement, participation, new covenant, and Spirit in ways that seem quite compatible with what I argue in this book, despite his disapproval of the term "theosis." In addition, Edward Keazirian's book *Peace and Peacemaking in Paul and the Greco-Roman World*, with special emphasis on ecclesial conflict resolution, agrees with this book that peace is much more important to Paul than is generally thought.[2]

As always, my family has been very interested in and supportive of my writing projects. I am especially grateful that my children (Mark, Amy, and Brian), now adults, have always taken the subject of this book with the utmost seriousness, not just academically but personally. They have become in their own way theologians, both practically and—in the case of Mark—vocationally. That would not have happened without the inspiration of my wife, Nancy, who has been by my side through every project, and through much more. My gratitude to and for her is too deep for words.

Finally, I have dedicated this book to the memory of my father, Peter J. Gorman, who passed away on Christmas day of 2012 at the age of 90. The first drafts of much of the book were written during the last phase of his life, when he was frequently critically ill. These situations sometimes prevented either him or me from attending conferences or other events that were associated with the drafts of these chapters. Nonetheless, his love and support were part of what encouraged and sustained my work, and I am grateful

2. See Grant Macaskill, *Union with Christ in the New Testament* (Oxford: Oxford University Press, 2013); Edward M. Keazirian, *Peace and Peacemaking in Paul and the Greco-Roman World* (Studies in Biblical Literature 145; New York: Peter Lang, 2014).

both to and for him. This is the first book I have published since his death, and it seems altogether appropriate to dedicate it to him.

I have dedicated the book as well to Fr. Thomas Hurst, whom I admire as a President Rector and as a colleague in biblical studies, with thanks to him for the privilege of sitting where I do—in Fr. Raymond Brown's chair.

Holy Week, 2014

Introduction

Refocusing the Atonement

FOR MOST CHRISTIANS, FROM professional theologians to lay women and men, the word "atonement" refers to the means by which Jesus' death on the cross saves us and reconciles us to God. Was that death a punishment? a sacrifice? an example? a victory over powers? Some people have insisted strongly on one of these perspectives, often over and against the others. Recently, some discussions of the atonement have tended to be more generous, incorporating multiple theories, models, or images from the New Testament and Christian tradition into a more comprehensive—and therefore less precise—account of the atonement.

However, the fact that there is no theory or model of the atonement called "covenant," "covenant-renewal," "new-covenant," or something very similar is, or should be, rather surprising. These terms refer, after all, to a biblical image connected to Jesus' death—originating, it appears, with Jesus himself at his Last Supper[1]—and the source of the term "the New Testament." The latter fact rightly suggests, indeed, that "new covenant" is what the New Testament is all about. The neglect of the new covenant in discussions of atonement is likely due to an over-emphasis on the theological question of *how* Jesus' death brings about atonement, salvation, etc.—the

---

1. Matt 26:28; Mark 14:24; Luke 22:20. There has been some scholarly debate about the authenticity of the synoptic account of Jesus' interpretation of his death in terms of the (new) covenant, but the point for now is that the Gospels certainly report Jesus interpreting his death this way, as does Paul (1 Cor 11:25) and, Paul implies, early Christian tradition more generally.

mechanics, so to speak. But this is not, I would submit, the focus of the New Testament.[2]

To put it a bit differently, I would suggest that most interpretations of the atonement concentrate on the *penultimate* rather than the *ultimate* purpose of Jesus' death. This ultimate purpose is captured in texts like the following[3]:

> James and John, the sons of Zebedee, came forward to him [Jesus] and said to him, "Teacher, we want you to do for us whatever we ask of you." And he said to them, "What is it you want me to do for you?" And they said to him, "Grant us to sit, one at your right hand and one at your left, in your glory." But Jesus said to them, "You do not know what you are asking. Are you able to drink the cup that I drink, or be baptized with the baptism that I am baptized with?" They replied, "We are able." Then Jesus said to them, "The cup that I drink you will drink; and with the baptism with which I am baptized, you will be baptized; but to sit at my right hand or at my left is not mine to grant, but it is for those for whom it has been prepared." (Mark 10:35–40)

> "And I, when I am lifted up from the earth, will draw all people to myself." (John 12:32)

> Do you not know that all of us who have been baptized into Christ Jesus were baptized into his death? Therefore we have been buried with him by baptism into death, so that, just as Christ was raised from the dead by the glory of the Father, so we too might walk in newness of life. For if we have been united with him in a death like his, we will certainly be united with him in a resurrection like his. We know that our old self was crucified with him so that the body of sin might be destroyed, and we might no longer be enslaved to sin. (Rom 6:3–6)

> And he died for all, so that those who live might live no longer for themselves, but for him who died and was raised for them . . . For our sake he [God the Father] made him [Christ] to be sin who knew no sin, so that in him we might become the righteousness of God. (2 Cor 5:15, 21)

2. On the source and problem of fixating on the mechanics of atonement, see Green, "Must We Imagine?," 164.

3. Unless otherwise indicated, all scriptural citations are taken from the NRSV. Translations marked "MJG" are those of the author.

He it is who gave himself for us that he might redeem us from all iniquity and purify for himself a people of his own who are zealous for good deeds. (Titus 2:14)

To him who loves us and freed us from our sins by his blood, and made us to be a kingdom, priests serving his God and Father, to him be glory and dominion forever and ever. Amen. (Rev 1:5b–6)

In texts such as these, we see that the ultimate purpose of Jesus' death was to create a transformed people, a (new) people living out a (new) covenant relationship with God together. Moreover, this people will not simply *believe in* the atonement and the one who died, they will eat and drink it, they will be baptized into it/him, they will be drawn to him and into it. That is, they will so identify with the crucified savior that words like "embrace" and "participation," more than "belief" or even "acceptance," best describe the proper response to this death. (Even the words "belief" and "believe" take on this more robust sense of complete identification.) But most models of the atonement stop short of this goal, focusing on absolutely necessary but nonetheless penultimate issues, such as forgiveness of sins or liberation from evil powers. To put it even more starkly, some discussions of the atonement may be compared to arguments over which type of delivery is best in dealing with a difficult birth situation—forceps, venthouse (suction), C-section, or whatever—when the point is that each of them effects the birth of a child, each solving the problem from a slightly different angle. But it is the result (a healthy child) that is most important, and it is the child, not the delivery process, that ultimately defines the word "birth."[4]

Building in part on that analogy, I have chosen as the title for this book *The Death of the Messiah and the Birth of the New Covenant*. Jesus' death and the inauguration of the new covenant are explicitly linked in 1 Cor 11:25 and Luke 22:20, with similar links in the parallel gospel texts. The birth imagery is not present per se in these texts, but the metaphor is not without New Testament roots (e.g., John 3; Rom 8:18–25; Gal 4:19). In certain liturgical traditions, the connection of the new covenant and Jesus' death to a "birth" is made explicit: "By the baptism of his suffering, death, and resurrection, you [God] gave birth to your church, delivered us from slavery to sin and death, and made with us a new covenant by water and the

---

4. This is not meant to underestimate the value of carefully exploring the meaning of Jesus' death from various angles, but to urge a proper ultimate focus.

Spirit."[5] This liturgical tradition for the celebration of the Lord's Supper has it right, and it serves as a rather perceptive, if unintended, summary of the thesis of the present work.

In this book, therefore, I aim in a modest way to help in correcting the problem of penultimate models of the atonement by proposing a new model that is really not new at all—the new-covenant model.[6] In fact, this model may legitimately lay claim to being the oldest interpretation of the atonement in the Christian tradition, going back to Jesus, the earliest churches, and the earliest Christian theologians (i.e., Paul, the evangelists, etc.).[7] I will argue that this is not merely an ancient model in need of re-discovery, but also a more comprehensive, integrated, participatory, communal, and missional model than any of the major models in the tradition. It overcomes the inherent rift in many interpretations of the atonement between the *benefits* of Jesus' death and the *practices of participatory discipleship* that his death both enables and demands. I contend throughout the book that in the New Testament the death of Jesus is not only the *source*, but also the *shape*, of salvation. It therefore also determines the shape of the community—the community of the new covenant—that benefits from and participates in Jesus' saving death.

The purpose of this book, then, is not to develop some new theory about the mechanics of Jesus' representative, sacrificial, nonviolent, and/or victorious death "for us." There are plenty of those around, and many of them have great merit. Rather, the purpose of this book is to show some of the connections between the themes of atonement, new covenant, participation, and discipleship in the New Testament, focusing especially on the participatory practices of faithfulness, love, and peace. At first, this trio sounds like a new version of the Christian tradition's three theological virtues of faith, love, and hope. It is, rather, the same triad articulated in a new (but not really new) way. What I will argue is that, throughout the

5. Present in the United Methodist services of Word and Table I and II, and sometimes used in other traditions or settings as well.

6. I have no connections with the developing theological movement within some parts of evangelicalism (especially Reformed Baptist circles) that calls itself "New Covenant Theology" as a via media between "Covenant Theology" and "Dispensational Theology." See, e.g., Swanson, "Introduction to New Covenant Theology."

7. Its origin in Jesus is (like everything else involving "the historical Jesus") debated. The major focus of this book is not the historical Jesus but the New Testament documents and their implications for Christian theology, though I will offer some theses, and arguments, regarding Jesus himself.

New Testament, *faith*, as a practice, is about faithfulness even to the point of suffering and death; *love*, as a practice, has a distinctive, Christlike shape of siding with the weak and eschewing domination in favor of service; and *hope*, as a practice, means living peaceably (which includes nonviolently) and making peace. Thus the summary triad "faithfulness, love, and peace" is appropriate.

The surprising part of this interpretation of the theological virtues to some readers will be the notion of hope as a practice, and specifically hope as practicing peace. But a moment's reflection on the theo-logic of this idea should reveal its inherent plausibility. The greatest form of hope in the Bible is for a new creation in which violence, suffering, tears, and death will be no more. We see this expressed in such lovely, inspiring texts as Isa 65:17–25 and Rev 21:1—22:5. Those who have this hope for a new creation and, more to the point, those who believe that this new creation has already been inaugurated by the life, death, and resurrection of Jesus, will begin to practice its vision in the present. Accordingly, the practice of hope is the practice of peace. This sort of practice may be referred to as *anticipatory participation*. Such participation, however, stems not only from hope about the future (a purely proleptic participation), but also from participation in the death of Jesus that makes such hope possible by creating peace.

With this emphasis on participation, and thus transformation, I will claim that the New Testament is much more concerned about *what* Jesus' death does for and to humanity than *how* it does it. The New Testament employs a wide range of images and metaphors to portray God's gracious action in Christ's death. Yet this stunning array is part of a remarkably coherent picture of his death as that which brings about the new covenant (and thus the new-covenant community) promised by the prophets, which is also the covenant of peace. Many of the traditional and more recent models of the atonement related to the New Testament's various metaphors can be taken up into the more comprehensive model I am proposing as *penultimate* aspects of the *ultimate* purpose of Christ's death: the birth of the new covenant. Life in this new covenant is life in the Spirit of the resurrected Lord that is shaped by the faithful, loving, peacemaking (and therefore hope-making) death of the same crucified Jesus. Of course there is no Christian hope (or reason for faithfulness and love) without the resurrection of this Jesus from the dead. At points the resurrection will emerge explicitly, but even when it does not, we will assume its reality and significance throughout the entire book.

Along the way, we will intuit various implications of this model of the atonement for contemporary Christian theology and practice, and some of them will be noted explicitly, especially in chapter 8. The goal of this book, however, is not to present a complete, fully developed model of the atonement with all of its ramifications in place; that would require a much larger volume, and probably a different author. (Nonetheless, if given more years and energy, I may one day develop the arguments and implications of this book more fully. In the meantime, I leave that task to its readers.) Rather, the goal of this book is to present some of the basic New Testament foundations of, and its framework for, a new-covenant model of the atonement.

This is not to say that the New Testament (or even a single author, such as Paul) speaks with a single voice about these matters. As with other topics in New Testament theology, we will not find uniformity but unity in diversity. Yet, I will argue, the New Testament contains both sufficient raw material and a sufficient number of recurring themes—patterns, if you will—to justify discerning and describing a new-covenant model of the atonement. (Readers, in fact, will notice a number of lists and tables that display some of the various textual parallels and thematic patterns that express the new-covenant model of the atonement for which I am arguing.) Nevertheless, my approach to utilizing the New Testament writings is deliberately eclectic, as my goal is not merely, or even primarily, to survey the New Testament on a particular topic, but to develop a biblically informed model of the atonement that draws on the New Testament in its unity and its diversity. Not every New Testament writing will contribute equally to that project.

The significance of Jesus' death, both in terms of theology and in terms of existential consequences, has been the focus of my professional and personal life for many years. I have given many lectures and written many essays, and authored more than one previous book, on this topic. The present book builds on other treatments of the New Testament that I have published, but it moves in new directions and is much broader than simply a consideration of one particular author, such as Paul, or one individual book, such as Revelation. Paul does, however, receive a significant amount of attention, as does Luke.[8]

The most obvious reason for emphasis on these two writers is that together the Pauline and Lukan writings constitute a little more than half

8. Soon to appear also is a book solely on Paul that takes up some of the themes in this book: *Becoming the Gospel: Paul, Participation, and Mission.*

of the New Testament, and each author uses the phrase "new covenant." If further justification with respect to Paul, who receives quite a bit of attention, is needed, I would simply say three things. First, Paul has been the source of a great deal of the discussion about the atonement in the Christian tradition; he needs to be heard again and again, and he needs to be heard afresh. Second, all models of the atonement are necessarily selective, because the New Testament writers did not set out to write a theology of the atonement, and certain perspectives and themes emerge in particular writers and writings more than in others. In that respect, this book is within the range of "normal." Third, Paul is my own primary area of expertise. All of that said, however, I am convinced that the new-covenant model being proposed here is not restricted to Paul but is, on the contrary, widespread in the New Testament, even if Paul (by virtue of the quantity and variety of his canonical writings) preserves and develops the model more fully than others.[9] Hebrews, which also uses the term "new covenant," will also figure in the discussion, of course, as will New Testament writings that do not use the term per se.

The explicit and ostensible subject of this book is the death of Jesus, and the book's genre a kind of thematic treatment of a central New Testament theme that is simultaneously a constructive theological proposal for a new (actually, not so new) model of the atonement. It may seem rather brash or even foolish to attempt to offer a new, even a not-so-new, model of the atonement. Yet, as we will see in chapter 1, numerous new models have recently been suggested, and the new covenant has begun to emerge as something in need of renewed consideration in connection with the atonement. In reality, moreover, this book is also a broader contribution to New Testament theology and ethics. (It may be the closest thing to a "New Testament theology," which some people have urged me to undertake, that I will produce.) In fact, I intend it to be a contribution to Christian theology and ethics more broadly still. This is not really due to the original intention or the expertise of the author as much as it is to the nature of the subject. What I have discovered, and now offer as the working assumption of this book, is that the death of Jesus is itself an extraordinarily comprehensive reality and topic. At the same time, I also wish to register my conviction and assumption that without the incarnation (as well as the resurrection, noted above),

---

9. This claim will surprise some readers, as there are some Pauline scholars who argue that the theme of the new covenant is of minimal importance to Paul. I, obviously, think otherwise.

the death of Jesus has no salvific value. That conviction will also emerge explicitly from time to time in various ways and various places.[10]

My intended audience is also quite broad: any and all who are interested in the significance of the death of Jesus for Christian theology and life. Although the book is quite heavily footnoted and is, at times, somewhat technical, I am hopeful that these aspects of it will not discourage non-specialists from engaging its claims. From initial reactions to earlier versions of these chapters presented orally and in writing (including some blog posts by non-academics), the book should be of interest to, and accessible to, not only theologians and biblical scholars, but also pastors and lay people (among whom I am one). I of course do not intend or expect this book to be the last word on atonement, covenant, and participation, but I do hope that it will help to contribute to an emerging sense that these interconnected themes are worthy of exploration as the Christian tradition continues to think carefully about the meaning of Christ's life and death on our behalf.

10. Mark Gorman, in personal correspondence, has reminded me of two important things to note here. First of all, although the doctrine of salvation (soteriology) is important to all Christians, atonement, and models thereof, is a peculiarly Western Christian phenomenon going back to Anselm in the Middle Ages. At the same time, secondly, even Anselm was concerned about the incarnation. His work, *Cur Deus Homo?—Why the God-Man?* or *Why did God become Human?*—raises the fundamental question "Why did God become incarnate in Jesus Christ in order to accomplish salvation?" (See also, e.g., Spence, *Promise of Peace*, 1, 118.) The answer this book will propose in the next eight chapters is, at least in part, that God did so to enter into intimate, covenantal relations with a people so that they could share in the divine life revealed in the crucified Messiah and made available by the Spirit. For a constructive theological proposal about participation in relation to divine desire and the Holy Spirit, see Mark Gorman, "On the Love of God."

−1−

The Promise of the New Covenant

As NOTED IN THE Introduction, that there is no theory or model of the atonement called "covenant," "new-covenant," or something very similar is one of the great wonders of the theological world. This book aims to address that lacuna, that theological hole, so to speak, by proposing a new model of the atonement that is really not new but is often overlooked and always underexplored: the new-covenant model. In this chapter we consider the promise of the new covenant. The chapter title is a deliberate double entendre: it refers both to the promise of the new covenant made by the biblical prophets and to the theological promise of considering the new covenant as fundamental to our interpretation of the atonement.

The chapter begins by noting the curious overall absence of new-covenant language and theology from discussions about the atonement, as well as hints that atonement and new covenant are inherently connected to each other. This leads to a case for a new, more comprehensive model of the atonement focused on the new covenant. The chapter concludes with an overview of the new covenant promised by the prophets and of the resulting new-covenant model of the atonement being proposed in this book.

THE ABSENCE OF THE OBVIOUS

How many images of the atonement are there in the New Testament? In most recent interpretations, from precise exegetical studies like those of John Carroll and Joel Green in *The Death of Jesus in Early Christianity* to more synthetic, theological treatments like Scot McKnight's *A Community Called Atonement*, the answer is "many."[1] Based on these various images, how many major models or theories of the atonement have developed in the course of the Christian tradition?[2] A standard answer is three—*Christus Victor*, satisfaction (often associated with sacrifice and/or punishment), and moral influence—though some prefer to separate sacrifice from satisfaction and call it a separate model, yielding four basic models or, by omitting moral influence from the list of true models, retaining three.[3]

These major models have been supplemented in recent years by a variety of new models and by recognition of older models that are not as prominent as the "big three." A volume called *The Nature of the Atonement: Four Views*, edited by James Beilby and others, contains essays treating the *Christus Victor*, penal substitution, healing, and "kaleidoscopic" views, the last being the name given by Joel Green to his proposal that no one model or metaphor suffices to articulate the meaning of the atonement. He refers vividly to "the church's glossolalia with regard to the soteriological effect of the cross."[4] In his book *Triune Atonement: Christ's Healing for Sinners, Victims, and the Whole Creation*, Andrew Sung Park prefaces his own contribution (summarized in the subtitle) with a review of eight theories, five traditional and three recent. The five traditional theories are ransom, *Christus Victor*,

1. See Carroll and Green, *Death of Jesus*; McKnight, *Community Called Atonement*.

2. Like many others, I use the term "model of the atonement" as a generic reference to major interpretations of the salvific death of Christ, without committing to a particular understanding of that death (e.g., a substitutionary or expiatory sacrifice for the forgiveness of sins). Two major traditional models, *Christus Victor* and moral influence, for instance, do not really understand Christ's death as an atonement (atoning sacrifice), but they are still called models of the atonement.

3. The typology of three is due in large measure to the influential book by Aulén entitled *Christus Victor* and published in 1931, in which Aulén describes these three ("classic" = *Christus Victor*, "objective" = satisfaction [Anselm], "subjective" = moral influence) while arguing for the one summarized in the book's title. Fiddes (*Past Event and Present Salvation*) acknowledges many images but focuses on four main models: sacrifice, justice, decisive victory (*Christus Victor*), and act of love (moral influence). Gunton (*Actuality of Atonement*) similarly separates sacrifice and justice but omits moral influence, treating three main models, or metaphors: battlefield, justice, sacrifice. McKnight (*Community Called Atonement*, 48) names the "five big metaphors" as incorporation into Christ, ransom or liberation, satisfaction, moral influence, and penal substitution. For a readable "history and assessment" of the models, see Baker and Green, *Recovering the Scandal of the Cross*, 142–91.

4. Green, "Kaleidoscopic View," 157–85, esp. 165. See also Baker and Green, *Recovering the Scandal of the Cross*, who speak of a "mélange of voices" about the atonement in the New Testament (52, 90). McKnight would be sympathetic to this approach.

satisfaction, moral influence, and penal substitution, while the more recent additions he calls "last scapegoat" (proposed by René Girard), nonviolent narrative *Christus Victor* (J. Denny Weaver), and symbolic (i.e., "the symbolic power of Jesus' blood"—Paul Tillich).

David Brondos, in his *Fortress Introduction to Salvation and the Cross*, considers the role of the cross in ten more general soteriological models, both from the ancient church (e.g., redemption/recapitulation and the union of divine and human natures) and from more recent discussions about such themes as the kingdom of God (Albrecht Ritschl), reconciliation (Karl Barth), proclamation (Rudolf Bultmann), and liberation (Jon Sobrino, Rosemary Radford Ruether). "Covenant" is absent.[5] Peter Schmiechen, in *Saving Power: Theories of Atonement and Forms of the Church*, also surveys ten "theories of atonement" under four rubrics, but, again, none of the rubrics or theories contains the word "covenant."[6] With emphasis on soteriology and relying largely on the church fathers, Ben Myers proposes a fascinating "alternative typology" to Gustaf Aulén's (in his *Christus Victor*). Myers identifies six types of early Christian soteriology, with Christ as the second Adam, sacrifice, teacher, brother, life-giver, and healer, suggesting that the death of Christ alone is not sufficient for soteriology and that a focus on Christ's salvation as teaching and as healing was prominent in the patristic era.[7] In none of these surveys or others with which I am familiar, however, is there a chapter called something like "the new-covenant model of the atonement."

The recent work of two prominent theologians, however, does suggest that there is hope and promise in pursuing this kind of model. The work of the late reformed theologian T. F. Torrance (d. 2007) comes close to the development of such a new-covenant model.[8] Torrance argues that Christ's

5. As we will see below, Brondos identifies the creation of a new-covenant community as the main New Testament understanding of the atonement, but he does not develop this thesis or attempt to integrate it with the claims of the traditional or recent models he considers.

6. The four rubrics are Christ died for us (sacrifice, justification, penal substitution); liberation from sin, death, and demonic powers; the purposes of God (renewal/restoration of creation); and reconciliation. Of these, "the purposes of God" rubric may come closest to the model being proposed in this book.

7. See http://www.faith-theology.com/2013/09/how-does-jesus-save-alternative.html, accessed September 17, 2013.

8. Torrance, *Atonement*. Torrance's work is quite compatible with many of the directions pursued in this book; among other strengths, he deftly ties together atonement and participation. The recent development in certain evangelical circles of something

life and death effect both the fulfillment of the covenant—God's desired relationship with a people—and its transformation into the new covenant. For Torrance, Christ's atonement encompasses his entire life (with a strong emphasis on the incarnation), not only his death, but it culminates on the cross. "Christ fulfills the covenant in that he is the embodied communion between God and man, and in that he is himself the instrument whereby the covenant is established . . . The Son offers his life and death in a covenant sacrifice for the remission of sins and the establishment of covenant communion between God and humanity."[9] This basic thesis and framework allow Torrance to explore and incorporate a variety of New Testament atonement metaphors into his overall perspective, especially redemption, justification, and reconciliation. Torrance also stresses that the giving of the Spirit, and thus the existence of the church, is the completion and "actualizing" of the atonement.[10] That a reformed theologian would stress covenant comes as no surprise. However, although covenant is highly significant for Torrance's understanding of atonement, it is apparently not sufficiently developed or stressed to be recognized by others as constituting the core of a model.

Echoing some of Torrance's interests, theologian Kevin Vanhoozer has developed a "canonical-linguistic," or "theo-dramatic," approach to theology in which God as dramatic covenant-maker and -keeper is center stage.[11] He argues that Scripture tells us that God has "one overarching purpose: to communicate the terms, and the reality, of the new covenant."[12] In this approach, the cross is seen, not in narrow terms, but as that which "recapitulates the through line of God's covenantal action and, as such, is oriented to the theo-drama's superobjective, namely . . . the creation of a people with

---

called "New Covenant Theology," as noted in the Introduction, is not connected to the work of Torrance or other major theological voices, to the thesis of this book, or to the atonement per se.

9. Torrance, *Atonement*, 22.

10. Ibid., e.g., 129, 189–90.

11. Vanhoozer, *Drama of Doctrine*. Vanhoozer's work, among recent theologians, may come closest to mine in overall approach. I would not, however, say that it is Scripture that creates the new-covenant people (176). It is more properly the cross, as he says in "Atonement and Postmodernity." My work on a new-covenant model of the atonement was carried out independently of Vanhoozer's, whose writing on the atonement I happily discovered rather late in the game, so to speak.

12. Ibid., 67.

whom God can fellowship and enjoy right relations."[13] Vanhoozer, in fact, anticipates one of the main conclusions of the present book:

> While the sundry conceptualities championed by the various atonement theories do not, strictly speaking, cohere, they are nevertheless *compatible* thanks to the integrative framework of the covenant—a complex, multilevel reality that combines the judicial and relational aspects of Jesus' death "for us" in a garment as seamless as the one for which the soldiers cast lots.[14]

In his particular theological approach, Vanhoozer seeks to bring together "judicial" and "relational" models of the atonement in an understanding of Jesus' death as *"the climax to a covenantal drama."*[15]

Nevertheless, apart from an occasional voice like that of Torrance or Vanhoozer, and an additional, fairly narrow, strand of reformed theology, covenant is largely a missing ingredient in the recipe for atonement.[16] There, is however, one book-length exception to the lacuna we have identified, a 2006 book by Wesleyan theologian R. Larry Shelton entitled *Cross and Covenant: Interpreting the Atonement for 21st Century Mission.*[17] Shelton has two main goals in proposing covenant as the key to atonement: greater faithfulness to the biblical witness and greater effectiveness in communicating the faith in the postmodern context. Shelton's proposal is in many ways quite similar in substance to the one in this book, though his work

---

13. Ibid., 391. This is part of Vanhoozer's meta-thesis that "what God was doing in Jesus Christ ultimately makes sense only according to the biblical script that places the person and work of Christ in the Old Testament context of creation and covenant"; "[t]here is a cosmic stage and a covenantal plot" (39). See also Vanhoozer's "Atonement in Postmodernity," esp. 396–401, where he articulates atonement in terms of divine covenant and self-gift, specifically in the form of the Spirit.

14. Ibid., 391. This is not to say that I agree in every detail with Vanhoozer's proposal.

15. Ibid., 387; emphasis his. Cf. 391, where Vanhoozer draws on Hosea to say that the marriage metaphor nicely captures the spirit of covenantal relations as both legal and relational. Johnson ("The Cruciform Bridegroom") offers a fascinating study of the atonement theology of St. John of the Cross, who sees Jesus' death as "a romance—a marriage" (395). We will return to both Vanhoozer and St. John of the Cross in chapter 8.

16. This more conservative reformed approach may focus on the extent of the atonement ("limited" or "definite") and/or an entire approach to theology with covenant(s) as the overarching rubric.

17. For a summary of his proposal, see 19–35. Shelton had earlier written an article outlining his proposal: "A Covenant Concept of the Atonement." He has also summarized the book in a paper delivered at the American Academy of Religion called "Relational Atonement: Covenant Renewal as a Wesleyan Integrating Motif," delivered ca. 2008.

does not appear to have received much attention to date.[18] Nevertheless, the very existence of Shelton's work suggests that the intuition that atonement and new covenant belong together is not idiosyncratic.[19]

Torrance's theology, Shelton's volume, Vanhoozer's approach, and other hints at the emergence of covenant notwithstanding, the lack of a theory or model of the atonement called "new-covenant" is remarkable. After all, according to all three Synoptic Gospels, this appears to have been Jesus' own interpretation of his death on the night before he died, with Luke probably making explicit ("new") what is implicit in Mark and Matthew:

> This is my blood of the covenant, which is poured out for many." (Mark 14:24)

> "[T]his is my blood of the covenant, which is poured out for many for the forgiveness of sins." (Matt 26:28)

> "This cup that is poured out for you is the new covenant in my blood." (Luke 22:20b)[20]

18. Shelton argues for an "interpersonal, relational covenant concept of atonement" that is "transcultural" and "community-oriented" (*Cross and Covenant*, 5). Covenant becomes for him the hermeneutical lens for interpreting and incorporating other models and metaphors of the atonement. The project, like this one, understands atonement in deeply participatory, Trinitarian, and missional categories. The lack of attention to Shelton's book may be due in part to its mode of argumentation, which is at times somewhat popular and/or dated. (This is less true of the summary article "Relational Atonement.") The thesis itself is significant and worthy of further development by others.

19. In "Relational Atonement," Shelton draws attention to a paper for the 2009 meeting of the American Academy of Religion by feminist theologian Marit Trelstad, "Atonement through Covenant: A Feminist, Process Approach."

20. Some manuscripts of Luke lack v. 20 and thus the phrase "new covenant," but the RSV, NRSV, NIV, TNIV, NAB, and ESV all retain the verse. (In addition, a few manuscripts of Mark and Matthew include the word "new," probably the work of scribes aiming for consistency in the gospel accounts.) Though the issue remains debated, throughout the book I will assume that v. 20 is part of the original Gospel of Luke. See especially the discussion in Green, *Death of Jesus*, 35–42. My interests do not require us to settle the question of the genuineness of this saying attributed to Jesus, which some have questioned because he does not appear to develop the covenant idea. What matters for this discussion is that the evangelists claim that Jesus pronounced these kinds of words. In chapter 4, we will consider the authenticity of the passion predictions in Mark as an example of how the question of authenticity both is and is not critical to the concerns of this book.

The scriptural overtones in these accounts are rich and plentiful. The references to blood are obviously echoes of the Passover sacrifice and the Exodus, an event of liberation. Linked with "covenant," they are probably also an echo of the covenant-renewal blood in Exod 24:6–8. Furthermore, the implicit or explicit (in Matthew) connection to forgiveness of sins suggests that Jesus' death both fulfills the Day of Atonement in Leviticus 16 (plus perhaps the atoning sacrifices more generally [e.g., Lev 4:1—6:7]) and inaugurates the new covenant promised in Jer 31:31–34, which (as we will see below) includes liberation and forgiveness. James Dunn has argued that the gospel tradition accurately reflects Jesus' own belief that his coming death would be a covenant sacrifice (and probably also an atoning sacrifice)—"the sacrifice which would bring into effect" the "long-promised" new covenant of Jer 31:31–34.[21] That is, Jesus' death is the means by which the people of God are liberated, forgiven, and brought into a new covenant with God. My main point now, however, is that despite its apparent significance to Jesus and the evangelists, (new) covenant is not very significant to the Christian theological tradition on the atonement.

This need not be the case. Joel Green, in his "kaleidoscopic" approach to the atonement, briefly emphasizes the Last Supper as "a point of entry into our understanding of Jesus' death"[22] and rightly states that Jesus "developed the meaning of his death in language and images grounded in the constitution of Israel as the covenant people of God (Exod 24:8), the conclusion of the exile (see Zech 9:9–11) and the hope of a new covenant (Jer 31:31–34) so as to mark his death as the inaugural event of covenant renewal."[23] In continuity with the theological tradition, however, Green does not develop these observations in his subsequent discussion of the atonement.

In the only canonical account of the Last Supper outside the Gospels, Paul passes on the same kind of tradition we find in the Synoptic Gospels, especially Luke, indicating that both the Last Supper and the present act of its remembrance, the Lord's Supper, narrate an interpretation of Jesus' death centered on the establishment of a new covenant:

---

21. Dunn, *Jesus Remembered*, 816. Dunn rightly insists that "[t]he point does not hang on the presence of the word 'new,'" for if early participants in the tradition added "new" to Jesus' actual words, "they would no doubt have claimed that they were simply making explicit what was implicit" (816n252).

22. Green, "Kaleidoscopic View," 165n16.

23. Ibid., 165. This view is consistent with Green's treatments of Jesus' death and the new covenant elsewhere (e.g., *Gospel of Luke*, 763–64): it is perceptive but not developed at length.

> For I received from the Lord what I also handed on to you, that the Lord Jesus on the night when he was betrayed . . . took the cup also, after supper, saying, "This cup is the new covenant in my blood . . ." (1 Cor 11:23, 25)

Thus, given the interpretation of Jesus himself (or at least Jesus as remembered and narrated by the evangelists), as well as what is probably a very early, pre-Pauline Christian tradition rooted in Jesus' own interpretation ("I received from the Lord"; 1 Cor 11:23),[24] the theological inattention to atonement and new covenant is curious indeed: not merely the lack of covenantal language in the "names" of the standard theories of the atonement, but also, more broadly, the near-absence of such language from standard expositions of their content.[25]

New-covenant language appears in Paul not only in the context of the Last Supper but also in 2 Cor 3:6, as Paul interprets Exod 34:29–35. There it seems to serve as a summary of the reality to which Paul's mission is dedicated: he and his team are "ministers of a new covenant." Paul describes this new covenant as one characterized by the Spirit and glory, but references to Christ's death are not far away. Second Corinthians 4 and 5 make it clear that the ministry of the new covenant is in a profound sense a re-presentation of the death of Jesus, both in lifestyle and in words. It can only be such if the new covenant itself is inaugurated by the death of Jesus.[26]

Then, of course, there is one book in which covenant is the central theological concept, namely Hebrews. There the word "covenant" appears seventeen times (just over half of the thirty-three occurrences of "covenant," Greek *diathēkē,* in the New Testament), with Jesus described as the "mediator" of a "better" (8:6), "new" (9:15; 12:24), and "eternal" (13:20) covenant, which is effected by his blood/death (10:19; 12:24; 13:20; and many other texts). This new covenant is what Jeremiah promised, a promise that

---

24. Although "received from the Lord" could possibly refer to a direct revelation, the language of receiving and handing on is the vocabulary of tradition, not revelation, and therefore more likely refers to the teaching of Jesus received via the Jerusalem apostles.

25. It is likely that more time has been spent in recent decades discussing the tradition history of the two forms of this tradition—the Markan/Matthean ("covenant"), on the one hand, and the Pauline/Lukan ("new covenant"), on the other—than their common theological content and its theological significance.

26. We will explore this topic in chapter 3. I will suggest there that Paul assumes the Corinthians will understand the phrase "new covenant" as a reference to Jesus' death and its consequences, as the apostle had earlier instructed and then reminded them (1 Cor 11:25).

Hebrews quotes twice (8:8–13; 10:16–18), the first of which is the longest scriptural quotation in the New Testament. Atonement and new covenant are inextricably linked in Hebrews.

These facts alone, it would seem, justify a theory—or a model, which is the language I prefer[27]—of the atonement that we could call "effecting the new covenant," "birthing the new covenant," or simply "new-covenant." But that model is generally missing, both from the traditional accounts of the atonement and from most recent revisions of, and additions to, them. As we will see especially in the next two chapters, I do not think that this is because covenant "is not a common category through which the New Testament writers, apart from the writer of Hebrews, processed their thinking."[28]

IS ATONEMENT THEOLOGY ITSELF THE PROBLEM?

Before we proceed to our consideration of a new-covenant model of the atonement, one additional recent model of the atonement needs to be mentioned: what we might call the anti-atonement, or the non-atonement, model. An important representative of this (non-) model is Ted Grimsrud's *Instead of Atonement: The Bible's Salvation Story and Our Hope for Wholeness*. Grimsrud argues that "salvation in the Bible is not dependent upon atonement—that is, dependent upon adequate sacrifices being offered (including the ultimate sacrifice of God's Son, Jesus) as a condition for salvation. I also mean to suggest that in the overall message of the Bible. God's response to sin is not violence."[29] He goes on to speak of the "merciful, shalom-oriented story of salvation the Bible tells," a story of "'restorative' justice rather than retributive justice."[30] For Grimsrud, because

L eg,perek f100b

27. My use, and even preference, for this term is hardly original or unique. It is preferable to others for two principal reasons: it conveys something less speculative than "theory" but more concrete than "image" or "metaphor," and it suggests a holistic, more comprehensive approach to atonement—we might say an architecture of atonement—that moves beyond the more narrowly focused traditional theories. In other words, the standard dictionary definition I have in mind for "model" is not "pattern," but "description of a complex reality."

28. McKnight, *Community Called Atonement*, 74. McKnight rightly suggests, however, that the new-covenant theme is significant as an outgrowth of (or is at least inseparable from) the early-Christian experience of the Spirit. Peterson (*Transformed by God*) rightly contends that new-covenant themes are present throughout the New Testament even when the language of "new covenant" is absent. So also Macaskill, *Union with Christ*.

29. Grimsrud, *Instead of Atonement*, 4.

30. Ibid., 4, 19.

God is the covenant God who is always ready to save and always merciful, the cross is therefore not necessary for salvation; it is not a soteriological event: "the Bible's portrayal of salvation actually does not focus on Jesus's death as the basis for reconciliation of humanity with God."[31] Rather, the cross is a revelatory event, illuminating the idolatry of the various Powers (cultural exclusivism, religious exclusivism, and political authoritarianism, as Grimsrud sees them, building on the work of Walter Wink) that oppose God and humanity, revealing the consequences of embodying God's non-discriminating mercy, and manifesting God's way of nonviolent peacemaking as Jesus faithfully embodied that form of merciful salvation.[32]

There is much to commend in Grimsrud's book, including his rejection of divine retribution and violence, his focus on salvation as restorative justice and the establishment of shalom, his concern to see the cross as a revelatory act of mercy and nonviolence and as a paradigm for faithful discipleship, and his insistence on the resurrection as God's vindication of Jesus' life and death. I espouse these same beliefs, and I am especially grateful for Grimsrud's appreciation of my own work on both Paul and Revelation.[33] At the end of the day, however, Grimsrud's solution to the crisis in atonement theology will likely strike many readers as a classic case of throwing out the baby with the bath water. What he affirms does not necessarily lead to what he denies.

The witness of the New Testament does not, in my view, allow us to conclude that Jesus' death is first and foremost the consequence of evil Powers to which Jesus appropriately responds. Rather, the death of Jesus is first and foremost the work of God and God's Son; it is a divine and christological initiative, not merely a response. To be sure, Jesus' death is, in part, what Grimsrud says it is, and his interpretation helps us see a side of Jesus'

31. Ibid., 226.

32. On the cross as illumination, see, e.g., 90, 95–96, 110, 201, 233. For helpful summaries of various aspects of Grimsrud's thesis, see 86–88, 89–90, 91–96, 226–27, 233.

33. It is rather ironic that on p. 206 Grimsrud approvingly quotes from the section of my book *Inhabiting the Cruciform God* that argues for the necessity of highlighting peacemaking and reconciliation in order to "develop a faithful construal of Pauline thought" (my words; *Inhabiting*, 143) when he does not discuss at all—anywhere—the two key texts in Paul's soteriology on which this claim is based: 2 Cor 5:11–21 and Rom 5:1–11 (the latter being only very briefly noted in *Instead of Atonement*, 189, as focused on God's salvific intent). In both texts, the death of Christ as both God's initiative/act and Christ's initiative/act is absolutely central to the argument. In effect, what the book offers as an interpretation of Paul's soteriology is a construct uninformed by many of the key soteriological texts in Paul.

✓ death that is often neglected. But Grimsrud does not tell the whole New Testament story. New Testament texts stressing God's and Christ's initiative in the cross—including what are probably some of the earliest texts of the Christian faith—are either omitted or downplayed.[34] Even more, significant texts about the *necessity* and/or the *sacrificial character* of Jesus' death (whether in the Gospels, Paul, or Hebrews) are either omitted from the discussion or interpreted in ways that highlight neglected aspects of such texts while, ironically, neglecting the normally highlighted aspects. The result is a necessary corrective that, at the same time, unfortunately creates a distorted composite picture.[35] Jesus' death is not merely an act of accidental illumination in the New Testament; it is a *deliberate self-revelation* and an *effective salvific act*.

Our contemporary theological task is to discern and articulate precisely what that means, and to construct theologies that neither misinterpret the cross in misguided or poorly thought-through traditional categories nor eliminate any of the fundamental perspectives of the biblical witnesses.

THE NEED FOR A NEW, MORE COMPREHENSIVE MODEL

Even for those whose reaction to the atonement debate is less radical than Grimsrud's, there are at least four major problems with the traditional models of the atonement as a group. We will consider each of these problems briefly.

- The first problem is the isolationist, or sectarian, character of the models. Each one is constructed as a kind of stand-alone theory that supposedly tells the whole (or at least the most important) story and requires the exclusion (or at least the marginalization) of other versions of the story. In sympathy with certain postmodern complaints about the very idea of a doctrine of the atonement, Kevin Vanhoozer says, "The problem is that theologies of the atonement seem unable to articulate a theory that explains the saving significance of Jesus' death

---

34. These include the various forms of the surrender and self-surrender formulae such as Rom 8:3, Gal 2:20, and John 3:16, to name just three—none of which appear in the Scripture index or the book.

35. Grimsrud asserts that Jesus died willingly (e.g., *Instead of Atonement*, 86) and self-sacrificially (e.g., 202)—that is not at issue—but only in response to the forces of evil. I want, with the New Testament itself, also to stress God the Father's and Jesus' initiative in his death.

without betraying the rich testimonies to the event of his death."[36] Only rarely, as in the case of Colin Gunton (*The Actuality of the Atonement*), does a theologian try to appropriate and integrate various traditional models.[37]

- The second problem derives from the first: the atomistic, or non-integrative, character of the traditional models. They do not naturally pull other aspects of theology into their orbit. "Atonement," however interpreted, often stands apart, separated from ethics, spirituality, ecclesiology, pneumatology, and missiology. In some cases atonement becomes a narrow branch of theology that is almost irrelevant to the actual life of Christian individuals and communities.[38]

- The third problem is individualism. The traditional models have a nearly exclusive focus on the individual, rather than on both the individual and the community, as the beneficiary of the atonement. Scot McKnight (in *A Community Called Atonement*) and others have, of course, also recognized and begun addressing this problem.[39]

- The fourth problem we might call "under-achievement." That is, the models do not *do* enough. We may summarize a model of the atonement in terms of its understanding of the fundamental effect of the cross on a person (or on humanity). In the satisfaction-substitution-penal model(s) the effect is propitiation, expiation, and/or forgiveness; in the *Christus Victor* model the effect is victory and liberation; and in the "moral influence" model the effect is inspiration. As I suggested in the Introduction to this book, the under-achieving character of these models means that, on the whole, they focus on the *penultimate* rather than the *ultimate* purpose(s) of Jesus' death.[40] In the new-covenant

36. Vanhoozer, "Atonement in Postmodernity," 369.

37. See also, however, though much more modestly, McKnight, *Community Called Atonement*; Spence, *Promise of Peace*; Flood, *Healing the Gospel*. That is, others perceive the problem.

38. Spence (*Promise of Peace*) notes the same problem and has explicitly, if briefly, sought a "unified" (from the book's subtitle) and "overarching" (66) theory as preferable to the "comparatively self-contained" (18) theories in existence.

39. See also Green, "Must We Imagine?," 164–65.

40. This should not be mistaken merely for a distinction between focusing on the efficient cause (traditional theories) versus the formal cause (my proposal) of the atonement, as Martin does in a response to an earlier version of this argument (Martin, "Response to Gorman," 61–62). Rather, I am arguing that the traditional theories underestimate the effects—the final cause, to use Aristotelian language—of Jesus' death and therefore also

model I am proposing, the purpose (and actual effect) of Jesus' death is all of the above and more, but that effect is best expressed, not in the rather narrow terms of the traditional models, but in more comprehensive and integrative terms like transformation, participation, and renewal or re-creation.[41] The inclusion of terms like these in a discussion of atonement will seem odd to some readers, but I will introduce them because they capture the spirit of the new covenant promised by the prophets and inaugurated by Jesus' death. It is precisely certain elements of the promised new covenant (which we will consider in the next two chapters), such as the coming of the Spirit and empowerment to fulfill the law, that are generally not considered to be aspects of atonement per se in traditional theories. This is, in part at least, why the traditional theories fall short of a fully biblical interpretation of the atonement.

I am not so naive as to think that my proposal is completely comprehensive or new. Regarding the issue of comprehensiveness, a truly comprehensive new-covenantal model will need to incorporate aspects of other models that are not addressed in any detail in this book. That is another project for another day, though we will refer to those models briefly in the last chapter. As for newness, in addition to Shelton's work from a Wesleyan perspective, I am happy to report (as an Anabaptist Wesleyan) that Anabaptist Caleb F. Heppner has seen the lacuna and made an initial attempt to address the problem in a brief online article entitled "A Covenantal View of Atonement."[42] Interestingly, David Brondos, in *Salvation*

---

underestimate the significance of the efficient cause (the death itself), even, ironically, as they focus narrowly on it.

41. So also Shelton, *Cross and Covenant*. Green similarly complains about understandings of the atonement, especially penal substitution, that produce "anemic salvation" ("Must We Imagine?," 166–67). McKnight (*Jesus and His Death*, 349–50) contrasts Paul's theology of the atonement as "an actual recreation and empowerment" with Anselm's dominant view (in the Christian tradition), saying that "Paul's indissoluble connection of death and resurrection . . . shatters the cultic and quantitative reductionism in Anselm's theory." Whether or not he is right about Anselm, he is right about Paul.

42. See http://www.thepaulpage.com/a-covenantal-view-of-atonement/, last accessed October 14, 2013. He writes in the first paragraph: "In this view Jesus' primary role was not as a substitute or example, but as mediator of a new covenant. If there is a unique theology of atonement that supports an Anabaptist perspective of peace and justice, then this is it." And in the last: "Jesus is the mediator of a new covenant where justice (or righteousness) apart from the law has been revealed. It means that we also become mediators of this justice for all the downtrodden and outcasts of society, for they too have full standing under the New Covenant as God's people."

and the Cross (referenced above) argues that we need the variety of atonement models in the tradition but also that the basic New Testament model, which he derives from an analysis of Luke and Paul, is new-covenantal.[43] He contends that the reactionary emphasis in certain theological circles toward a less "objective" understanding of the atonement (i.e., what Christ's death, etc., actually accomplishes), in favor of a focus on the (allegedly) redemptive value of what Christ's life, death, and resurrection *reveal* about God, humanity, and the world, is an inadequate interpretation of the New Testament's witness. In the New Testament, Brondos claims, "Christ saves human beings not merely through the revelation he brings but by *serving as God's instrument to found a new covenant community* in which people may now find salvation, redemption, forgiveness, and reconciliation with God through him as their Lord."[44] This way of describing the new-covenant community as the place where salvation is a possibility ("may now find"), rather than a dynamic reality, may itself not be quite adequate, but the main point is spot-on: in and through Jesus God has created, and is creating, the community of the new covenant.

Various new interpretations of the atonement have recently been proposed by those who have seen similar, or other, problems with the traditional models—hence the proliferation of models noted above. Although this is not the place to offer a review of these proposals, to the degree that they offer a more comprehensive, integrative, transformative, participatory, and/ or missional interpretation of the atonement, they will likely be compatible with the new-covenant model being offered here.[45] Furthermore, I will later suggest that there is a close relationship between the new-covenant model of atonement and the soteriological model of theosis (or deification: the primarily Eastern-Christian term for becoming like God by participating in the life of God), which has been much neglected but which is now rightly enjoying renewed attention.[46]

---

43. See his summary of the book on 182–84. I disagree with some of the particulars of his interpretations but agree with the overall point. Unfortunately, Brondos does not connect these two basic claims (the necessity of variety and the centrality of covenant) about atonement theology.

44. Brondos, *Salvation and the Cross*, 184; emphasis added.

45. For two quite compatible interpretations that stress a cruciform, missional understanding of the atonement, see Belousek, *Atonement, Justice, and Peace*; and Flood, *Healing the Gospel*.

46. So also Shelton, *Cross and Covenant*, though he does not use the language of theosis.

There are, however, some people who will hesitate about the language of new covenant, finding it theologically problematic rather than promising. At least two basic, related reasons for this exist: new-covenant language sounds supersessionist or anti-Jewish, and it sounds unrealistic (in the sense of "out of touch with reality"), if not arrogant. An entire book could be written about this subject, but we will limit ourselves to brief statements that are the tip of an iceberg of serious theological reflection about these matters.

With respect to the concern about supersessionism or anti-Judaism, the first thing to be said is that the idea of a new covenant does not make sense except, first of all, as a category of Jewish identity and theology, as we will see shortly. The appropriate perspective of Christian faith, therefore, is that the new covenant in which it claims to participate is not a *replacement* covenant but a *renewed* covenant, even if it has been quite drastically renovated by the reality of a crucified and resurrected Messiah. This renovation is such, in fact, that it can appear that the old has been *replaced* by the new rather than that the old has *become* the new for those who believe Jesus to be God's Messiah. The difference is subtle but significant.

Second, with respect to the concern about unrealism or arrogance, it can be said that those who affirm the arrival of the new covenant do not think—or should not think—that *they* have arrived, or that the new covenant has arrived in its eschatological fullness. In a way not unlike the kingdom of God, the new covenant is both now and not yet. When Christians realize this, and when they keep their appropriate connections to the Scriptures and people of Israel in mind, they will think and speak of their life in the new covenant joyfully but also humbly and self-critically, not arrogantly or triumphalistically.

With these important theological perspectives in mind (to which we will also return in the last chapter), we begin our consideration of the new covenant as promised by the prophets.[47]

---

47. It would be impossible for me to address all the possible concerns about new-covenant language without writing another, or a different, book. These concerns often emerge in connection with the letter to the Hebrews. My exegetical and theological conclusions in this book do not, in my view, further either anti-Judaism or arrogance; the conclusions' implicit critique, in fact, will be of deeply ingrained Christian theological traditions that are hyper-individualistic (and in that sense inappropriately unJewish) and fixated on one sort of theology of the atonement (which can be, though does not need to be, held with arrogance).

THE PROPHETIC PROMISE AND THE OUTLINE OF A NEW-COVENANT MODEL OF THE ATONEMENT

The phrase "new covenant" only appears in the Old Testament in Jer 31:31. This is clearly a classic case of the importance of *weighing* items rather than *counting* them when it comes to determining significance. If Paul is a reliable guide, it appears that at least one other prophet, Ezekiel, wrote about the same future reality, for in 2 Corinthians 3 Paul blends the language of Jeremiah 31 with the language of Ezekiel 11 and 36.[48] The book of Ezekiel, full of covenant language and the hope of a renewed people, implicitly sanctions this merger. We will therefore consider the relevant portions of these three chapters as guides to the prophetic promise of a new covenant, first articulated during the Exile.[49] The major relevant passages are the following:

> *Jer 31:31–34*: [31]The days are surely coming, says the Lord, when I will make a new covenant with the house of Israel and the house of Judah. [32]It will not be like the covenant that I made with their ancestors when I took them by the hand to bring them out of the land of Egypt—a covenant that they broke [LXX = 38:32: "in which they did not remain"], though I was their husband, says the Lord. [33]But this is the covenant that I will make with the house of Israel after those days, says the Lord: I will put my law within them, and I will write it on their hearts; and I will be their God, and they shall be my people. [34]No longer shall they teach one another, or say to each other, "Know the Lord," for they shall all know me, from the least of them to the greatest, says the Lord; for I will forgive their iniquity, and remember their sin no more.

> *Ezek 11:17–20*: [17]Therefore say: Thus says the Lord God: I will gather you from the peoples, and assemble you out of the countries where you have been scattered, and I will give you the land of Israel. [18]When they come there, they will remove from it all its detestable things and all its abominations. [19]I will give them one heart, and put a new spirit within them; I will remove the heart of stone from their flesh and give them a heart of flesh, [20]so that they

---

48. See especially Stockhausen, *Moses' Veil*, 42–71. Other Second Temple Jewish writers apparently made the same connections.

49. Lundbom (*Jeremiah 21–36*, 466) lists additional new covenant texts (without that precise term, but often with "everlasting covenant") in Jeremiah (24:7; 32:38–40; 50:5) and Ezekiel (16:60; 34:25; 36:27–28; 37:26), as well as (Second and Third) Isaiah (42:6; 49:8; 54:10; 55:1–5; 59:21; 61:8) and Malachi (3:1).

may follow my statutes and keep my ordinances and obey them. Then they shall be my people, and I will be their God.

Ezek 36:23–28: [23]I will sanctify my great name, which has been profaned among the nations, and which you have profaned among them; and the nations shall know that I am the Lord, says the Lord God, when through you I display my holiness before their eyes. [24]I will take you from the nations, and gather you from all the countries, and bring you into your own land. [25]I will sprinkle clean water upon you, and you shall be clean from all your uncleannesses, and from all your idols I will cleanse you. [26]A new heart I will give you, and a new spirit I will put within you; and I will remove from your body the heart of stone and give you a heart of flesh. [27]I will put my spirit within you, and make you follow my statutes and be careful to observe my ordinances. [28]Then you shall live in the land that I gave to your ancestors; and you shall be my people, and I will be your God.

Ezek 37:21–28: [21]Thus says the Lord God: I will take the people of Israel from the nations among which they have gone, and will gather them from every quarter, and bring them to their own land. [22]I will make them one nation in the land, on the mountains of Israel; and one king shall be king over them all. Never again shall they be two nations, and never again shall they be divided into two kingdoms. [23]They shall never again defile themselves with their idols and their detestable things, or with any of their transgressions. I will save them from all the apostasies into which they have fallen, and will cleanse them. Then they shall be my people, and I will be their God. [24]My servant David shall be king over them; and they shall all have one shepherd. They shall follow my ordinances and be careful to observe my statutes. [25]They shall live in the land that I gave to my servant Jacob, in which your ancestors lived; they and their children and their children's children shall live there forever; and my servant David shall be their prince forever. [26]I will make a covenant of peace with them; it shall be an everlasting covenant with them; and I will bless them and multiply them, and will set my sanctuary among them forevermore. [27]My dwelling place shall be with them; and I will be their God, and they shall be my people. [28]Then the nations shall know that I the Lord sanctify Israel, when my sanctuary is among them forevermore.

Similar themes are found as well in Deuteronomy 30, a text about covenant renewal:

The Death of the Messiah and the Birth of the New Covenant

> *Deut 30:1–6, 8*: [1]When all these things have happened to you, the blessings and the curses that I have set before you, if you call them to mind among all the nations where the Lord your God has driven you, [2]and return to the Lord your God, and you and your children obey him with all your heart and with all your soul, just as I am commanding you today, [3]then the Lord your God will restore your fortunes and have compassion on you, gathering you again from all the peoples among whom the Lord your God has scattered you. [4]Even if you are exiled to the ends of the world, from there the Lord your God will gather you, and from there he will bring you back. [5]The Lord your God will bring you into the land that your ancestors possessed, and you will possess it; he will make you more prosperous and numerous than your ancestors. [6]Moreover, the Lord your God will circumcise your heart and the heart of your descendants, so that you will love the Lord your God with all your heart and with all your soul, in order that you may live . . . [8]Then you shall again obey the Lord, observing all his commandments that I am commanding you today. . . .

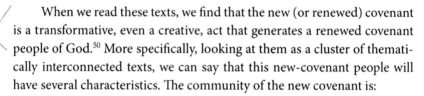

When we read these texts, we find that the new (or renewed) covenant is a transformative, even a creative, act that generates a renewed covenant people of God.[50] More specifically, looking at them as a cluster of thematically interconnected texts, we can say that this new-covenant people will have several characteristics. The community of the new covenant is:

1. liberated (having experienced a new Exodus);

2. restored and unified (Israel and Judah together; gathered from the peoples; returned to the land of Israel; one heart);

3. forgiven, cleansed from unholiness and idolatry/infidelity to YHWH;

4. sanctified;

---

50. On Deuteronomy 30 and covenant renewal/new covenant, see Hahn, *Kinship by Covenant*, 78–79, and the resources noted there. A few other texts could be added, such as Isa 59:20–21: "And he will come to Zion as Redeemer, to those in Jacob who turn from transgression, says the Lord. And as for me, this is my covenant with them, says the Lord: my spirit that is upon you, and my words that I have put in your mouth, shall not depart out of your mouth, or out of the mouths of your children, or out of the mouths of your children's children, says the Lord, from now on and forever." Paul cites this text in Rom 11:26–27. On Deuteronomy 30 in Paul, see Whittle, *Covenant Renewal*.

5. existing in a mutual covenantal relationship with YHWH ("I will be their/your God, and they/you shall be my people"[51]) characterized by community-wide faithfulness, intimacy, and knowledge;

6. internally empowered and enlivened (law / new spirit / God's Spirit within; heart of flesh, not stone) to keep the Law/covenant;[52]

7. bearing witness to YHWH's holiness;

8. experiencing *shalom*: at peace with God and secured from enemies; and

9. permanent, i.e., partners in an everlasting covenant.[53]

We can summarize these in nine adjectives: liberated, restored, forgiven, sanctified, covenantally faithful, empowered, missional, peace-filled, and permanent.[54] (And in one text, Ezek 37:24–25, the people will be shepherded by David.) According to the exilic prophets Jeremiah and Ezekiel, this will be the nature of the new-covenant community, the transformed people of God. It is a comprehensive vision, to be sure.

There has been some debate about what precisely is new about the new covenant. Suggestions include its apparent unconditional character, its interiority, its gracious pronouncement of forgiveness, its intimacy, its universality, its permanence, and its requirements.[55] There can be little doubt that the images of interiority—new heart and indwelling Spirit/Law—and permanence are critical to both the prophets and the New Testament writers. Without minimizing either of those emphases, I would suggest that what is critical and new is not one particular aspect but the *total character* of the new covenant just outlined.

51. This is the fundamental "covenantal formula"; it appears in all four of our prophetic texts, and it is implied throughout Deuteronomy 30. See also Exod 6:7; Lev 26:12; Deut 29:13; Jer 7:23; 11:4; 24:7; 30:22; 32:38; 38:33; 39:38; Ezek 11:20; 14:11; 37:23, 27; Zech 8:8; 2 Cor 6:16; Heb 8:10; Rev 21:7.

52. This characteristic—the presence and empowering of God's Spirit to do God's will—is absolutely critical to nearly all of the New Testament witnesses to the fulfillment of the new covenant in the church. For the Spirit and the new covenant in Paul, see Whittle, *Covenant Renewal*, esp. chap. 5.

53. For similar analyses, see Stockhausen, *Moses' Veil*, 63; McKnight, *Jesus and His Death*, 312–14; and esp. Peterson, *Transformed by God*, 17–43. Permanence is implicit in these texts, more explicit in corollary texts.

54. See my *Apostle of the Crucified Lord*, 115–30, for somewhat similar language to characterize Paul's spirituality.

55. See the discussion in, e.g., Lundbom, *Jeremiah 21–36*, 466–71.

In one respect, this newness will also be continuity. James Dunn has argued that the main point about the new covenant (at least in Paul) is not its different content but its "more effective implementation" by virtue of the Spirit.[56] This is at least partially correct, and it means that the *new* covenant is actually in many ways the *renewed* covenant. But of course the understanding of this new covenant, and the community it calls into existence, will be dramatically affected by the story of Christ, especially by his death that brings about the new covenant. That is to say, the cross of Christ does

✓ not only *effect* the new covenant, it also *affects* it. It effects a "fracture" of traditional understandings of the new covenant.[57] For example, the work

✓ of the Spirit, and thus the covenant faithfulness and holiness the Spirit produces, will take on a cruciform shape, meaning, for instance, sacrificial self-giving, sometimes even to the point of death. So too with mission: it will be inextricably connected to both the death of Jesus and the transforming, empowering life of the indwelling Spirit. Moreover, the reconstituted community will unite, not merely Israel and Judah, but Jews and Gentiles. Nonetheless, the key elements of the vision of Jeremiah and Ezekiel will remain, even if reshaped. We will address these elements in later chapters, not one by one but—like the new-covenant vision itself—holistically.

We should note at this point that the New Testament writers may not have been alone in connecting their community with the fulfillment of the new covenant. The Qumran community near the Dead Sea may have seen itself similarly as the embodiment of the promised new covenant, the remnant of Israel in which divine forgiveness and eternal life are available.[58] Jintae Kim has argued that important Qumran scrolls name some of the key new-covenant features noted above as fulfilled in their communal life: knowledge of God, forgiveness (specifically by atonement), the presence of the Spirit, and obedience to the laws of God.[59] Kim suggests that the New

---

56. Dunn, "Did Paul Have a Covenant Theology?," 18.

57. For the great discontinuities caused by the cross, see Harrisville, *Fracture*.

58. Kim, "Concept of Atonement." Cf., e.g., Dunn, *Jesus Remembered*, 394n65, 512–13. Kim notes (99–100) that "the new covenant" (*haberith hadashah*) language is unique to Qumran in Second Temple Judaism (excluding the New Testament). Dunn (*Jesus Remembered*, 513n115) lists the following Qumran texts as expressing the new covenant image explicitly or implicitly: CD 6.19; 8.21; 19.33–34; 20.12; 1QpHab 2.3–6; 1QSb (1Q28b) 3.26; 5.21–23. Some scholars, however, deny a correlation between the Qumran language of new covenant and Jeremiah 31. See Koester, *Hebrews*, 113, and the literature cited there.

59. Kim, "Concept of Atonement," esp. 105–11.

Testament writers are indebted to this "Jewish eschatologizing of forgiveness as evidenced at Qumran."[60] This probably goes beyond the evidence, but his work certainly yields two important results: first, that the idea of embodying the new covenant was in the air and could be linked explicitly to atonement; and second, that the specific form of the new covenant's instantiation will be a distinctive expression of the particular community's founder, founding, and fundamental identity while remaining absolutely Jewish.[61] The latter point is clearly true for the New Testament writers and the communities they represent, as we have just noted.

Before exploring, in subsequent chapters, the ways in which the death of Christ both effects and affects the new covenant promised by the prophets, we need to pause to consider the content of the covenant obligations that a new-covenant community will be empowered to fulfill.

THE VERTICAL AND HORIZONTAL DEMANDS OF THE COVENANT[62]

In his *Theology of the Old Testament*, Walter Brueggemann says that for Israel the demands of covenant relations may be summarized in one requirement: love for people as the expression of love for God.[63] Perhaps Brueggemann goes too far in conflating love for God and love for others, but he is clearly right that both are fundamental to covenantal life and that they are inseparable. We may refer to these two inseparable categories of the covenant as the vertical (God-oriented) and horizontal (human-oriented) dimensions, the two tables of the Law given to Moses (Exod 31:18).[64] The covenant expectation, as summarized in Mic 6:8, is a practical symbiosis of vertical and horizontal love:[65] "He has told you, O mortal, what is good; and

---

60. Ibid., 101.

61. On this topic with respect to Qumran and its implications for reading new-covenant theology in the New Testament, see Johnson, *Hebrews*, 212–14.

62. The following two paragraphs draw from my discussion of this topic in *Inhabiting the Cruciform God*, 48–49.

63. Brueggemann, *Theology of The Old Testament*, 424; cf. 429 and the entire discussion of "Israel's Covenant Obligation" (417–34).

64. The spatial metaphors are imperfect but handy, and still rather commonly used. Thus I employ them deliberately but urge their metaphorical rather than literal interpretation.

65. See ibid., 460–61.

what does the Lord require of you but to do justice, and to love kindness, and to walk humbly with your God?"

According to the Synoptic Gospels (Mark 12:28–34; cf. Matt 22:36–40; Luke 10:25–28), Jesus understood the covenant obligations in this twofold way. In fact, while in Mark and Matthew Jesus enumerates them ("first . . . second"), in Luke he affirms an inquiring lawyer's perspective, which speaks of them as one inseparable obligation: "He [the lawyer] answered, 'You shall love the Lord your God with all your heart, and with all your soul, and with all your strength, and with all your mind; and your neighbor as yourself'" (Luke 10:27).[66] It may be more than coincidental that Luke has two Samaritan "heroes" in his gospel: one who displays the horizontal grace of love (the "Good Samaritan"; Luke 10:30–37) and one who evidences the vertical grace of grateful faith (a leper; Luke 17:11–19). Other Second Temple Jews viewed love of God and love of neighbor as the two fundamental, inseparable covenant mandates, including the author(s) of *Jubilees* and of the *Testaments of the Twelve Patriarchs*, as well as both Philo and Josephus.[67] Thus the covenant-keeping that the new covenant will effect can be summarized in two phrases: love of God and love of neighbor.[68] Since the love of God (i.e., human love for God) in the Bible means both loyalty/ obedience and intimacy/communion, we may use the word "faithfulness" to connote these senses in one word.

On the other hand, love for neighbor in the Bible includes also the establishment of justice; justice is love in the public arena. Justice, in turn, is one constituent part of *shalom*—peace, wholeness, God's intended harmony. Thus to love God and neighbor is also to be part of God's *shalom-* making activity. The Bible gives voice to this reality by referring also to the covenant of *peace*.[69]

---

66. So also Johnson, *Luke*, 172. This dialogue is the preface to the "parable of the Good Samaritan," which might be better (if less memorably) named the parable of the inseparability of love for God and love for neighbor.

67. See, e.g., *Jubilees* 20:2; *Testament of Issachar* 5:2; *Testament of Dan* 5:3; *Testament of Benjamin* 3:3–5. Early Christian tradition continued this understanding: *Didache* 1.1; Justin, *Dialogue*, 93.2; Theophilus, *Ad Autolycum* 2.34; see Aune, "Following the Lamb," 281.

68. As we will see, the neighbor-love prescribed by the cross and new covenant is especially favorable toward the weak, which is already a biblical mandate grounded in the character of God. See, e.g., Psalm 41:1–3; 72:12–14; 82:1–4; 146.

69. Num 25:12–13; Isa 54:10; Ezek 34:25; 37:26; Mal 2:4–5; Sir 45:24.

The claim of the Bible's new-covenant theology is that God aims to create a liberated and forgiven community, a faithful, loving, and peaceable people empowered by the Spirit to bear witness to the holy character of God, to God's own faithful love and *shalom*. This is the ideal that runs throughout the Scriptures of Israel; it is the promise of the new covenant to bring this ideal to realization. Another way to describe this new-covenant ideal is to say that God wants to form a people in his own image, which for the New Testament writers will mean a community that becomes more and more like Christ, the image of God, and, as Paul would say (joined later by Irenaeus and others), regains the glory of God that Adam lost. To become more Christlike will be simultaneously to become more Godlike and more human. The new covenant will therefore mean a new humanity and a new creation; the image of God will be restored, not just in individuals, but in a people. The question, of course, is, what does all of this have to do with Jesus' death?

CONCLUSION

In this chapter we have noted the surprising overall lack of attention to the theme of "new covenant" both in traditional and in most recent discussions of the atonement. We have also identified several problems with the main models of the atonement and made the case for taking new-covenant texts and themes more seriously in considering the atonement, as a few biblical scholars and theologians have also recently hinted. And we have mapped out some dimensions of the new covenant articulated by scriptural texts, especially God's desire to create a faithful people that practices horizontal and vertical love. All of this lays the groundwork for the rest of the book. In the next two chapters (chapters 2 and 3), we will consider several New Testament writings that bear witness to, and can help us articulate, a new-covenant model of the atonement that brings cross and new covenant together, and that thereby gives rise to participatory discipleship, to being "baptized" into the Messiah's death. In the subsequent chapters, we will examine key aspects of participatory discipleship: faithfulness toward God (chapter 4), love toward others (chapter 5), and peacemaking (chapters 6 and 7).

– 2 –

Cross and New Covenant in the New Testament

The Gospels and Acts

IN THIS CHAPTER AND the next, we survey various parts of the New Testament for their witness to the new-covenant model we began to propose in chapter 1. In this chapter we will look at Mark, Matthew, Luke-Acts, and John. In chapter 3 we will consider the writings of Paul, Hebrews, and Revelation. Our emphasis in both chapters will generally be two-pronged. We will note (1) the way in which the cross gives birth to the new covenant, as well as the various aspects of it (as discussed in chapter 1) effected by Jesus' death. We will also focus on (2) the nature of participation in that salvific and paradigmatic death as an integrated life of cross-shaped vertical and horizontal love, for according to the New Testament the signature of the living, resurrected Jesus on the life of his followers is the cross on which he died.[1] This second aspect of our discussion will provide the basis for a more detailed examination of participation in Jesus' death in the form of cruciform faithfulness and love, to which we will turn in chapters 4 and 5. In addition, in these chapters we will take some note of the theme of the

---

1. Throughout the book I will frequently use the word "cross" as shorthand for Jesus' death, even when texts do not specifically mention the cross or crucifixion.

cross and peace, though we will turn to the new covenant as the covenant of peace more fully in chapters 6 and 7.

CROSS AND NEW COVENANT IN THE SYNOPTIC GOSPELS AND ACTS

Cross and New Covenant in Mark

What is the significance of the cross in the Gospel of Mark? This is the Synoptic Gospel that most fully fits Martin Kähler's famous description of a gospel as "a passion narrative with an extended introduction," so there is much that could be said. The shadow of the cross reaches back from chapter 15 to at least chapter 2 of Mark. Although Jesus' healing and teaching dominate the first half of the gospel, his suffering and dying take center stage beginning in chapter 8.

Those looking for evidence of the New Testament's sacrificial or substitutionary view of the atonement have found a showcase text in Mark 10:45, which paradoxically combines the images of Son of Man (Daniel 7) and of Suffering Servant (Isaiah 53).[2] But this text is not merely, or even primarily, about the mechanics of atonement. Its christological claim is linked to a summons to discipleship. This is in fact the case in all four of the passion predictions in Mark (of which 10:45 is part of the third) and therefore in all of the Synoptic Gospels, since Matthew and Luke take them up. Jesus calls his disciples to a life of "taking up their cross" (Mark 8:34 and parallels in Matthew and Luke) that is analogous to his own death and can therefore be termed "cruciform existence" or "cruciformity." According to the corollaries of the three passion predictions, this cruciform existence consists of (1) self-denial—losing oneself as the path to finding oneself—in witness to the gospel (8:31–34 par.); (2) hospitality to the weak and marginalized, represented by children (9:31–37 par.); and (3) service to others rather than domination (10:32–45 par.), all with the possibility of suffering (13:9–13 par.). Discipleship will be a life of "danger and dishonor . . . shame and suffering."[3] We will explore this threefold cruciform participation more fully in chapters 4 and 5.[4]

---

2. See Marcus, *Mark 8–16,* 754–57.

3. Hooker, *Not Ashamed of the Gospel,* 54.

4. As we will see in chapter 4, a synoptic "passion prediction" is more appropriately linked with what follows and called a "prediction-summons."

33

The call to cruciform discipleship is, in fact, a call to covenant faith-fulness, a summons to embody, simultaneously, the two tables of the Law. We see this clearly in the story of the encounter of Jesus with the man who wanted to know what he had to do to "inherit eternal life" (10:17–22, short-ly before the third passion prediction). After Jesus replies with a recitation of the requirements of the second table of the Law and the man claims his compliance with them from his youth (10:19–20), Jesus informs him that he lacks one thing, and that to fulfill that one thing the man must sell his possessions, give the proceeds to the poor, and follow Jesus (10:21). The promise that the man would thereafter "have treasure in heaven" suggests that the thing he lacks, and will now gain, has something to do with his relationship with heaven, with God, and therefore with the first table of the Law. The fulfillment of that table takes place by following Jesus, as if Jesus functions in the role of God, the proper focus of life's commitments and direction. At the same time, this radical love for God is not separated from love for others; in fact, the two are inextricably interconnected, as giving to the poor and having treasure in heaven are here two sides of the same coin of discipleship. In fact, we could say that following Jesus is the way to simultaneously fulfill—really fulfill—both tables of the Law: love of neighbor, especially the poor, and love of God.[5] Moreover, in caring for the poor, Jesus' disciples become not only Christlike, but also, as the Scriptures of Israel make clear, Godlike, for God is the God who attends to the needs of the poor and oppressed (e.g., Psalm 82). Such covenant faithfulness also creates justice for the poor, at least for the poor who would benefit from this potential disciple's divestment, thus showing the link between covenant faithfulness and *shalom*.

Having heard the three summonses to cruciform discipleship, along with the story of the man seeking eternal life, the audience of Mark's gospel, whether ancient or contemporary, is more than likely overwhelmed by the cost of being part of the people of the covenant reconstituted around Jesus. Thus, upon finally hearing the words of Jesus at the Last Supper—"This is my blood of the covenant, which is poured out for many" (14:24)—the audience can breathe a sigh of relief. Why? Because Jesus' imminent death will create the covenant community that the entire gospel narrative has de-scribed: a community of missional, self-giving, loyal-to-God disciples who are able and willing to suffer and die for their commitment. To be sure,

5. For a recent theological examination of the connection between love for God and love for the poor, see Anderson, *Charity*.

Jesus' death will not create such a community apart from the resurrection (which Jesus has also predicted three times), but it is Jesus' death that is the covenant-creating and community-creating act. As Morna Hooker has written, "[Jesus'] reference to the covenant takes us back to the covenant made between God and his people on Sinai, which established them as his people . . . Jesus' blood seals a new covenant, and in doing so establishes a new community . . . [T]hrough Christ's death a new people of God is created."[6] Hooker continues: "The death of Jesus is the beginning of something new: it is the ransom which creates a new people, the means of establishing a new covenant."[7] At the same time, the setting of the Passover meal reminds us that before Sinai there was the Exodus, the event of liberation that inaugurated the original covenant.[8]

Mark 15:39 is the climax of Mark's story of the cross: "Now when the centurion, who stood facing him, saw that in this way he breathed his last, he said, 'Truly this man was God's Son!'" Of the many things that could be said about this crucial text, two are especially significant, one focused on soteriology and one on Christology/theology (though of course the two are inseparable). First, within the narrative of Mark, the cross is *salvific*, and it is so in a comprehensive way, offering "revelation to the blind, reconciliation to the estranged, and redemption to the outsider [i.e., Gentiles]."[9] Jesus is the new temple (see 15:38), the place where God and humanity meet, the place where "the blood of the covenant poured out for many that Jesus anticipated . . . has now ratified the binding relationship between God and humanity."[10] In other words, "the cross brings together the human and the divine in the person of Jesus and effects a new covenant binding them together."[11]

Second, the cross is *revelatory*: Jesus is God's Son. The cross as revelation of Christ's identity as Son of God is, at least implicitly, a profound theological statement of the inseparability of act and being. The Son of God did what he did in life and in death because that is what it means to be the

---

6. Hooker, *Not Ashamed of the Gospel*, 59.

7. Ibid., 67. According to Hooker (55), the ransom text echoes the redemption from Egypt and from Exile more than Isaiah 53, though others would see Isaiah 53 echoed in a significant way.

8. See below on Luke for more on the Passover—new covenant connection.

9. Gamel, "Salvation in a Sentence," 65.

10. Ibid., 75.

11. Ibid., 77.

Son of God. Thus, discipleship is not merely following the Son of God who accidentally or arbitrarily died, but following the one who has died because that is the fullest manifestation of the self-giving and reconciling nature of the Son of God, and thus of God himself.[12] Therefore, to follow Christ in the way of the cross is more akin to participating in the reality or life or story of God—God's narrative identity, we might say—than to following someone at a distance or even imitating a master. To be the new covenant people is truly a new experience of knowing, loving, participating in, and being like God.

Cross and New Covenant in Matthew

Matthew is the only gospel that specifically says that Jesus' blood is spilled for the forgiveness of sins: "Then he took a cup, and after giving thanks he gave it to them, saying, 'Drink from it, all of you; for this is my blood of the covenant, which is poured out for many for the forgiveness of sins'" (Matt 26:27–28). As noted earlier, in this dominical claim we should probably hear echoes of at least three scriptural texts and themes—the Passover/Exodus, the blood of the covenant (Exod 24:6–8), and the new covenant and its forgiveness (Jer 31:31–34)—plus, in light of Matthew's ransom text (Matt 20:28 = Mark 10:45), the suffering servant's death (Isa 53:12).

We would be wrong, however, to conclude that the covenant about which Jesus speaks in Matthew is reducible to the forgiveness of sins in some narrow (i.e., "vertical" only) sense. Rather, receiving God's forgiveness is part of existence as a community of salt and light (5:13–16) that is called and empowered to practice forgiveness (5:21–24; 18:15–20) and its associated virtues, such as deeds of mercy and compassion (9:13 and 12:7, citing Hos 6:6[13]) like those of their Master (9:36; 14:14; 15:32; 18:33; 20:34). These practices result in part from the reality that the covenant established by Jesus' death is the covenant of peace, of *shalom*.[14] Although the Last Sup-

---

12. Although I am using traditional Christian theological (even ontological) categories here, the argument works even if we take "Son of God" language primarily, or exclusively, to be messianic rather than Trinitarian. As God's appointed representative, the anointed one (king or messiah) acts representatively of God in such a way that what he does is what God would do—in fact it is what God does (e.g., judge the poor with justice).

13. Cf. 5:7; 23:23; 25:31–46.

14. So also Swartley, *Covenant of Peace*, 75, 89–90. We will return to the covenant of peace in chapters 6 and 7.

per text is an explicit statement of the purpose of Christ's death (like the "ransom" text), to limit that purpose to the vertical relationship would be to rip it out of its context, negating the message of the rest of the Gospel.

✓ This *forgiven* and *forgiving* new-covenant community embodies, indeed fulfills, the two tables of the law. As Richard Hays persuasively argues, the Matthean audience is being called to follow the one whose "hermeneutic of mercy" and claim to fulfill the law (5:17–18) yield for his disciples a mandate to love God and neighbor (22:34–40, based on Mark 12:28–34). Matthew's specific point is that "everything else in the Torah 'hangs' upon them [the two love commands]; everything else must be derivable from them. In consequence, the double love command becomes a hermeneutical ✓ filter—virtually synonymous with Hosea 6:6—that governs the community's entire construal of the Law."[15]

Matthew famously concludes with the Great Commission text (28:16–20). This too needs to be understood in connection with the covenant inaugurated by Jesus' death. Disciples, members of the new-covenant community, are sent out to make more disciples who similarly fulfill the Law by obeying Jesus. This missional activity, and implicitly the life of double-commandment discipleship as a whole, is not done alone but by means of the power of the always-present Jesus (28:20), the one who is the covenant-God-with-us (1:23).

Cross and New Covenant in Luke-Acts

The role of the cross in Luke-Acts has been warmly debated. Not only does ✓ Luke lack the phrase "poured out for many for the forgiveness of sins" in his account of the Last Supper, but he also famously omits (intentionally or not) the Markan/Matthean "ransom" text (Mark 10:45 = Matt 20:28) when he places the call to discipleship from the third passion prediction in the context of the Last Supper (22:24–30). These and other features of Luke have caused significant confusion and, in some quarters, consternation around the question of Luke's theology of the cross. Is it an atoning, sacrificial, redemptive event? Is his death a death for sins or only the death of a martyr and prophet?

---

15. Hays, *Moral Vision*, 101, in a section called "The Hermeneutic of Mercy" (99–101). Hosea 6:6 reads, "For I desire steadfast love and not sacrifice, the knowledge of God rather than burnt offerings."

The new-covenant model both alleviates some of our distress and re-focuses our interest. Luke is the only synoptic writer who uses the precise phrase "*new* covenant."[16] According to the prophetic tradition, the new covenant includes the forgiveness of sins; it is highly likely, then, that Luke's account implies forgiveness and thus an atoning death, especially in light of the word of forgiveness from the cross in 23:34.[17] But Luke's associating Jesus' death with the new covenant is more comprehensive than a word or act of forgiveness. As John Carroll and Joel Green have said, "The cup after the meal is a metaphor for a new covenant enacted through the blood Jesus spills 'on your behalf.' Jesus here interprets his death as an event enabling a new covenantal loyalty, a gift creating a new covenantal community (cf. also Acts 20:28). His self-sacrifice is a means of benefaction for the community of his followers."[18]

Here Carroll and Green point out at least two significant elements of a "benefaction" that is, in fact, a transformation: the creation of a "new covenantal community" and the enabling of a "new covenantal loyalty," two of the main features of the new covenant and of the proposal being advocated in this chapter.

In addition, the setting of the Passover meal, as in the other Synoptic Gospels, also suggests covenant and thus new covenant. The Passover meal was a time of remembering and participating in the deliverance of God's people from slavery, the start of the special covenant and the birth of the people of the covenant. It was an act of grace, of mercy, of liberation—all key dimensions of Luke's theology. Now, at this Passover meal, the Last Supper is really the First Supper, the first celebration of the new covenant. By Jesus' sacrificial and covenant-making death, the community of the new covenant, the people whose sins are forgiven, is born.[19]

16. On the assumption that Luke 23:20 is original to the gospel. See n. 20 in chapter 1. For new-covenant themes in Luke-Acts, see Peterson, *Transformed by God*, 45–76.

17. Although some early manuscripts omit the word of forgiveness from the cross, I find it nearly impossible to explain the words of Stephen in Acts 7:60 apart from the presence of the saying in Luke's original gospel. For compelling arguments that this is the case, see especially Brown, *Death of the Messiah* 2:975–81. For a succinct recent statement of the case for authenticity, see Carroll, *Luke*, 466, who includes additional bibliography. For a concise but compelling case for connecting new covenant and atonement here, see Green, *Gospel of Luke*, 763.

18. Carroll and Green, *Death of Jesus*, 69.

19. See the succinct but insightful discussion in Carroll, *Luke*, 435–36 (despite his suspicion—with which I disagree—that Luke himself did not include the new-covenant text).

For Luke, then, this means Jesus' death, as part of a whole divine event of deliverance (suffering, death, resurrection, ascension/exaltation), has a particular purpose that is not *less than* atonement (something that effects the forgiveness of sins) but is *much more* than that. The forgiveness of sins is certainly important; it is an integral sign of the new exodus and new covenant. But forgiveness is only part of the larger purpose of God in the Messiah's suffering and death; the larger purpose is to create a new people who will both be and bear universal witness to the new covenant—which is really a (re)new(ed) covenant—that means salvation for all.[20] This is, in part, why Luke is relatively un-preoccupied with the "mechanics" of atonement.[21]

At this point an important theological point about the very notion of a "new covenant" needs to be made. Commenting on its appearance in Luke's gospel, Joel Green wisely and rightly says this: "Setting the cup-word [Luke 22:20] within the larger framework of Luke's presentation of Jesus' ministry disallows any notion of a 'new covenant' discontinuous with the old, for Luke has emphasized the continuity between the ancient purpose of God and its fulfillment in the coming of Jesus."[22] The same is fundamentally true, it can be argued, for the rest of the New Testament writers who use or allude to the language of new covenant—even the writer to the Hebrews (see discussion in the next chapter).

Finally, we see in Luke's handling of the three Markan passion predictions and their corollary calls to discipleship the especially close connection Luke envisions between the death of Jesus and the countercultural cruciform and missional existence of disciples. Disciples need to (1) take up their cross *daily* (9:23; "daily" being present only in Luke); (2) follow Jesus and share his mission, even to Jerusalem, without hesitation or distraction (9:43b–62); and (3) remember *on the very eve of Jesus' death* that they are called to forsake the cultural norms of hubris and domination to

20. On this whole point, see Mallen, *Reading and Transformation of Isaiah*, 118–25, 132–33. Mallen goes back and forth between the language of "new covenant" and that of "covenant renewal."

21. That said, it still seems likely, despite the absence of the ransom text, that Luke understands Jesus' crucifixion not only as a sacrificial death for sin (see discussion above), but also as the death for sins of God's servant described in the fourth servant song (Isa 52:13—53:12). The narrative of Jesus' death corresponds in various details with aspects of that song (e.g., emphasis on innocence, interceding for transgressors), and in Luke 22:37 Jesus quotes Isa 53:12 ("counted among the lawless"). It is more likely that Luke is implicitly referring to the entire song rather than "weeding out" certain dimensions of it.

22. *Gospel of Luke*, 763.

embrace cross-shaped service (22:24–30).[23] This call to cruciform disciple-ship is then symbolized in the act of Simon Cyrene, who literally—and symbolically—takes up Jesus' cross on the way to the crucifixion, graphi-cally depicting the life of the new-covenant community (23:26).[24]

It is as such a Jesus-like community, empowered by the Spirit, that the apostles and those who respond to their message in repentance and faith will bear witness (24:48). The Acts of the Apostles, Luke's narrative of early Christian life and mission, will relate this witness-bearing existence in detail. Indeed, Luke's dramatic narrative of Pentecost itself is his way of stating (among other things) that the Spirit-filled community of the new covenant promised by Jeremiah and Ezekiel has arrived.[25] "Luke's point," writes Luke Johnson wittily, "is not the pyrotechnics of theophany, but spiritual transformation."[26] It is the age of Israel's restoration and resurrec-tion (Ezekiel 37), as well as the age of salvation for the nations (Luke 24:47),

23. In Luke the second Markan passion prediction and its immediate aftermath (Luke 9:43b–50) become the segue to the narrative of Jesus' journey to Jerusalem (9:51—18:14), which itself begins with another call to discipleship and a sending out (9:51—10:20). Luke actually splits the third Markan passion prediction and discipleship call into two parts, leaving the prediction in the Markan narrative context (Luke 18:31–34) but mov-ing the call to the Last Supper (Luke 22:24–30). See the discussion in chapter 5.

24. Bøe (*Cross-Bearing in Luke*, 198–220) rejects the idea of Simon as a disciple be-cause his cross-bearing is not voluntary. This misses the narrative and theological point, however; the question is not whether Simon is a disciple but whether his act symbolizes discipleship—a subtle but significant difference.

25. So also, e.g., Talbert, *Reading Acts*, 25; Parsons, *Acts*, 36–37; Parsons, *Luke: Story-teller*, 153–54; Thompson, *Acts of the Risen Lord Jesus*, 125–43. Acts 2 "unfolds with an ideal portrayal of the community of the new covenant" (J. Potin, cited in Bovon, *Luke the Theologian*, 259). Parsons notes the importance of the new covenant to Luke, but also that the most important covenant for him is the Abrahamic covenant (*Luke: Storyteller*, 153–54). It is unnecessary to play these two off each other, however, since for Luke the fulfillment of the Abrahamic covenant is in fact the new covenant effected by the blood of Jesus. Similarly, it is not necessary to argue for only one particular biblical image or tradi-tion behind Pentecost; it is a lovely merger of Sinai, temple, and new-covenant themes—and much more. The theophany (and its "fireworks") is temporary, but the presence of the Spirit, like the new covenant, is permanent. McKnight (*Jesus and His Death*, 312–21), traces the origins of the church's new-covenant hermeneutic, not to Jesus (in general or at the Last Supper), but to early Christian reflection on the meaning of the Pentecost event. It is more likely that the church reflected further on the new covenant in light of the coming of the Spirit.

26. Johnson, *Acts*, 45. Johnson does not relate Pentecost specifically to the new cov-enant, but he does suggest that Luke probably has covenant renewal in mind (45–46) and that the Spirit's arrival indicates once again for Luke that Jesus brings Israel's hopes to fruition—and to the nations (47).

brought about not by Jesus' death alone, but also by his resurrection and exaltation.[27] Nonetheless, in Acts Luke does not ignore or discount the salvific value of Jesus' death, as some have charged. The most important texts are Acts 8:32–33 and Acts 20:28.

The conversion of the Ethiopian eunuch (Acts 8:26–40) is the result of Philip's explaining to him the christological significance of these lines (as presented by Luke) from Isaiah 53:

> [32]Now the passage of the scripture that he was reading was this: "Like a sheep he was led to the slaughter, and like a lamb silent before its shearer, so he does not open his mouth. [33]In his humiliation justice was denied him. Who can describe his generation? For his life is taken away from the earth." (Acts 8:32–33)

What has concerned many interpreters is Luke's omission of the references in Isaiah 53 to the servant's vicarious suffering (e.g., the verse immediately preceding Luke's citation: "But he was wounded for our transgressions, crushed for our iniquities; upon him was the punishment that made us whole, and by his bruises we are healed" [Isa 53:5]). But this concern is misplaced. For one thing, it should be obvious that the eunuch was reading the whole text of Isaiah 53 (or 52:13—53:12), and for Luke (as for Isaiah), this would include the fact of the servant's suffering and his exaltation, plus the various interpretive comments about these events in Isaiah. For another, Luke's overall understanding of Israel's Scripture, particularly Isaiah, is that it is the interpretive framework for the entire story of Jesus (including his suffering and exaltation), on the one hand, and for the related story of God's gracious mission to redeem Israel and save all the nations (and all kinds of people), on the other.[28] In other words, the story of the eunuch's conversion represents the effectiveness of the word about Jesus' suffering and death in extending the mission of God—and thus the covenant people of God—to Ethiopians and to eunuchs, to Gentiles and to the marginalized.[29] This does not require an explanation of how Jesus' death works but only a witness to

27. Thompson, *Acts of the Risen Lord Jesus*, 71–87 Parsons (*Luke: Storyteller*, 104) interprets Jesus' *exodos* as a unified event of suffering and death followed by resurrection and exaltation, not just his death. So also, e.g., Johnson, *Luke*, 153, 162.

28. See Luke 24:25–27, 47–49, and the likely connection between Acts 8 and that text suggested by Parsons (*Luke: Storyteller*, 105–7). On Isaiah as interpretive framework for Luke, see Mallen, *Reading and Transformation of Isaiah*.

29. Johnson (*Acts*, 158) notes that Isaiah's hopes for the future depicted the inclusion of Ethiopians (Isa 11:11) and eunuchs (Isa 56:3–5).

the fact that it does work—and it works with this particular, unexpected result.[30]

Acts 20:28 reads as follows: "Keep watch over yourselves and over all the flock, of which the Holy Spirit has made you overseers, to shepherd the church of God that he obtained with the blood of his own Son."[31] The endless debates about whether this text reflects an understanding of Jesus' death as an atoning sacrifice are understandable and, indeed, significant. But they are sometimes an exercise in confusing the penultimate with the ultimate and thereby missing Luke's main points, which are two—neither of which is about the "mechanics" of atonement. The first point is ecclesial, new-covenantal: in the death of "his own son" God has "obtained" a people, "the church of God." The verb "obtained with the blood" probably alludes to both election and covenant ("obtained"), on the one hand, and to purchase, redemption, and atonement ("with the blood"), on the other.[32] The Lukan Paul's emphasis, in context, is on the *effect* of this death, the creation of the church. God has created something and charged humans with its oversight and care. It is not the duty of church leaders to debate the intricacies of atonement theory, says Paul/Luke, but to protect the church that now belongs to God from "savage wolves" (Acts 20:29). This leads to the second point: church leaders, including Paul, participate in the ongoing work of God's Spirit and, in effect, in the death of God's Son, by offering themselves sacrificially to insure that no "blood" (life) is lost among those who are part of the people obtained by the blood of God's Son (Acts 20:26).[33]

This "church of God" obtained by the Son's blood is multicultural, multinational. The death and resurrection of Jesus that effects the resurrection

30. Similarly, e.g., Parsons, *Luke: Storyteller*, 95–107.

31. A similar text is Rev 1:5, discussed below.

32. There are numerous translational and interpretive difficulties surrounding Acts 20:28. Johnson (*Acts*, 363) points out that the verb "obtain" or "acquire" (*peripoieō*) is associated in the LXX with Israel's election (i.e., covenant). For a recent argument that Acts 20:28 focuses on Jesus' atoning sacrifice and is the functional equivalent of Mark 10:45, see Marshall, "Place of Acts 20.28." Marshall also allows for a *Christus victor* dimension to both texts (165–66) and sees clearly the pastoral co-text of the word about atonement.

33. Says Paul immediately before the words of Acts 20:28: "Therefore I declare to you this day that I am not responsible for the blood of any of you, for I did not shrink from declaring to you the whole purpose of God" (Acts 20:16–27). A few lines later, he speaks of his self-supporting manual labor as an example of caring for the weak and putting into practice Jesus' pronouncement that "It is more blessed to give than to receive" (Acts 20:34–35). In his own letters, Paul identifies his self-support by manual labor as an imitation of Christ's self-gift on the cross (1 Thess 2:5–9; 1 Corinthians 9; cf. 2 Thess 3:7–9).

of Israel means also for Luke the inclusion of the Gentiles, as the Spirit is poured out on people of all nations, creating a restored and unified people that the new-covenant prophets barely imagined.[34] The Spirit enables the apostles and others to live communally and hospitably, welcome Jews and Gentiles alike, preach the good news and prophesy, forgive sins, forgive enemies, heal, suffer faithfully for the good news, and generally continue the activity and mission of Jesus.[35] The founder of the new covenant continues to shape the life of the community of the new covenant, by the Spirit, in order that it might continue that which Jesus "began to do and teach" (*ērxato ho Iēsous poiein te kai didaskein*; Acts 1:1).[36] Although Luke does not relate this activity explicitly to the cross, it is clear that such ecclesial practices as suffering for the gospel (faithfulness to God) and practicing radical self-donation and hospitality (love for others, especially the "weak" [Acts 20:35]) are rooted in Luke's story of Jesus that culminates on the cross in those very practices. And it is those cruciform practices that Luke, in the words of Paul, highlights in the context of Acts 20:28 as the sign of the Spirit's powerful presence ("captive to the Spirit"; Acts 20:22).

CROSS AND NEW COVENANT IN THE GOSPEL OF JOHN

The Gospel of John has a rather full theology of Christ's death. Craig Koester finds four Johannine themes about Jesus' death in the Gospel: an expression of love, a sacrifice for sins, victory over sin, and revelation of divine glory.[37] In a word, paradoxically, God's love in the death of Jesus means his death brings life:

34. There are of course hints about the eschatological inclusion of Gentiles in the prophets. Of particular importance may be Isa 2:2-4, with its language of international reconciliation—a coming covenant of peace.

35. Hays (*Moral Vision*, 123-24) notes that the community of goods (Acts 4:32-35) is in fulfillment of the ideal covenant community described in Deut 15:4-8. By the presence of the Spirit, the community of the new covenant is called to embody that ideal.

36. RSV. The NRSV unfortunately misses this connection with "all that Jesus did and taught from the beginning." See Hays, *Moral Vision*, 112, 120-22, for an affirmation of the RSV sort of translation and of my point here. See also Thompson, *Acts of the Risen Lord Jesus*, though Thompson (curiously) devotes little attention to key aspects of Jesus' ongoing salvific presence in the church described in Acts, such as healing and hospitality.

37. Koester, *Word of Life*, 110-23. The first three of these, interestingly, correspond quite closely to the three traditional models of the atonement.

> The centrality of love holds together the human and the divine, the sacrificial and the militant dimensions of Jesus' death. Love also creates the consummate paradox in John's understanding of the crucifixion: the death of Jesus can be a source of life. It is by dying that Jesus reveals the love of God, and when this love evokes faith, it brings people into the relationship with God that is true life (3:16).[38]

To these eloquent words we might add two corollary points that are particularly significant for our study. First, for John, as John 3 as a whole tells us, the cross is connected to new birth; it is those who embrace Jesus' death (John 3:11–21) who are born again/anew/from above by the Spirit (John 3:1–10), a clear allusion to the rebirth of God's people forecast by Ezekiel 37. Second, although it is clear that individuals—represented by Nicodemus—must enter this "relationship," this "life," one by one, it is equally clear from the echo of Ezekiel's promise that this life will be a life in community, the new-covenant community formed by Jesus' life-giving, resurrection-effecting death. John does not dwell on the "mechanics" of how Jesus' death effects life in this new community, but he does draw careful connections between the crucifixion and the community it creates. The cross is like a magnet, drawing people to Jesus (John 12:32).

Several texts in the so-called "farewell discourse" (or "discourses") of John 13–17 express the themes about Christ's death identified by Koester. However, although speaking of John 13–17 as the farewell discourse tells us something about the form and basic rhetorical function of these chapters, the phrase says very little about their theological content and function.

John 13–17 constitutes more than just a farewell discourse. Rekha Chennattu calls these texts "discipleship discourses." She argues (independently from the present writer) that John 13–17 draws heavily on Old Testament covenant motifs. The discourses constitute Jesus' teaching about his forming a new-covenant community of disciples marked especially by a relationship of intimacy and covenant-keeping vis-à-vis God, and of love for one another. They will share in the divine mission enacted in Jesus, with similar obligations and risks. John 20–21, Chennattu contends, actualizes the promissory teaching given in chapters 13–17.[39]

---

38. Ibid., 123.

39. Chennattu, *Johannine Discipleship*. Chennattu also discusses the handful of other scholars who have dealt similarly with this subject.

Chennattu's observations are insightful and her argument compelling. Although the word "covenant" does not appear in John 13–17, it is clear that Jesus is assembling a community of committed and loyal friends (15:13–15) who will be the core group of a new-covenant community that embodies his divine mission after his death.[40] He is saying to them, in effect, "We (Father, Son, and Spirit) will be your God, and you will be our people." In these chapters we find community and covenant as well as cruciformity (13:1–17, the footwashing scene; 13:34–35; 15:12–13), charismatic revelation and empowerment (14:15–27; 15:26–27; 16:13–15), and mission (15:1–8, 16, 27; chap. 17)—with its attendant consequence of persecution (15:18–21; 16:33; 17:11–16).

Chennattu's work needs to be supplemented, however, by emphasizing more forcefully and consistently the close connection in John 13–17 between covenant discipleship and Jesus' death. These chapters are, in effect, an extended commentary on the synoptic claim that Jesus' death creates the new-covenant community. They contain a description of the community formed precisely by that death.[41] It is a community of forgiven people restored to covenant relationship with God; empowered by the Spirit to live in Christlike, cruciform loyalty to God and love for one another in spite of persecution; and sent out on a Christlike mission. John 13–17 tells us why Christ died or, narratively speaking within the Gospel itself, why Christ will die. In both the promissory discourse (chapters 13–17) and the narrative of fulfillment (chapters 20–21), we encounter a missional community of atonement.

The farewell discourse is given as Jesus' hour to depart, to die and return to his Father, has arrived (13:1). The event narrated in these chapters that gives rise to the entire discourse is Jesus' parabolic action of foot

40. Moloney (*Love in the Gospel of John*, 88–92, 150–52) convincingly argues that Jesus' death effects a "gathering"—we might say an "in-gathering"—of peoples as they are drawn to him and to God via the cross. It includes, but is not limited to, his mother and John as symbols of the new community. This motif of gathering is an element of the new covenant, as we saw in chapter one. For a range of new-covenant themes in John and especially 1 John, see also Peterson, *Transformed by God*, 157–84.

41. In the Synoptics, teaching about the shape of the covenant community is presented primarily before the narrative of Jesus' last meal, whereas in John such teaching comes during and after the meal. The overall narrative effect is the same: the death of Jesus creates the kind of covenant community he calls for in his teaching. The "historicity" of the footwashing episode, especially with the setting at Jesus' last meal, has been debated. For the issues, see Clark-Soles, "John 13: Of Footwashing and History," though I would find more features of the account to be likely historical than she does.

washing. Put the other way around, the farewell discourse is an extended commentary on the foot washing (which is itself a parabolic version of the passion predictions and related texts found in the Synoptics).

The enacted parable of footwashing is given two distinct but inseparable interpretations by Jesus (and thus by John). First, it is a unique act of cleansing that only Jesus can perform and that is mandatory for a relationship with him (13:8b–10); this is the salvific, or atoning (forgiving) dimension of his death. Second, the foot washing is a paradigmatic act of servant-love that is mandatory for his disciples to replicate (13:12–17). Jesus' example (*hypodeigma*; 13:15) is not merely one of general hospitality or service, but of death-like, cruciform self-giving; the example is, in fact, his exemplary death.[42] Both Jesus, who speaks in the narrative, and John,[43] who has constructed the narrative, move seamlessly from one interpretation to the other.[44] The parabolic action is more, however, than a symbol. It is more like a sacrament, an invitation to *participate* in Jesus' death, both as beneficiaries and as imitators.[45] Disciples *benefit* from the servant-Jesus' death as cleansing from sin and *imitate* it as loving care for others. Both Jesus and John see these two aspects of his death as inherently inseparable. The gift is also demand. *There is no cleansing without discipleship, no vertical relationship without horizontal relationships, no atonement without ethics.*[46]

de Silva har pointed out

42. See Culpepper, "Johannine *Hypodeigma*," 143. The common notion that footwashing was a servant's duty has been challenged by Coloe, "Welcome into the Household of God" (408), who argues that servants generally only brought a basin of water to the guest. If her analysis of the data is correct, then Jesus' example and admonition to imitation are all the more radical. (I owe these references and insights to Chris Skinner in his essay "Virtue in the New Testament," 308n31, 309.) Moloney observes that *hypodeigma* occurs nowhere else in the New Testament, and that it is regularly used elsewhere in Jewish literature of exemplary death (*Love in the Gospel of John*, 106–7).

43. By "John" I mean the final narrator of the Gospel.

44. Indeed, while it is not altogether clear what "these things" (*tauta*) refers to in 13:17—"If you know these things, you are blessed if you do them"—the most likely referent of the plural is both being washed and washing

45. For the participatory sense of imitation in John, see below.

46. This covenantal integration of the vertical and the horizontal, and their connection to Jesus' atoning and paradigmatic death, is particularly strong in 1 John in such texts as 1 John 1:5–7; 2:9–11; 3:14–18 (3:16–17: "We know love by this, that he laid down his life for us—and we ought to lay down our lives for one another. How does God's love abide in anyone who has the world's goods and sees a brother or sister in need and yet refuses help?"); 4:7–13, 19–21 (4:20: "Those who say, 'I love God,' and hate their brothers or sisters, are liars; for those who do not love a brother or sister whom they have seen, cannot love God whom they have not seen"). See further in chapter 5.

Moreover, the horizontal dimension of this covenant life is not independently defined and described; it grows organically out of the one act of
Jesus' self-giving death. Accordingly, Jesus explains the second interpretation of his death as a "new commandment" (13:34), not because the *commandment* to love is new, but because its *shape* is new. It is now Christlike,
cruciform love: "As I have loved you" (13:34; 15:12–13).[47] The self-giving
of Jesus in death embodies the love of God (see John 3:16, arguably the
Gospel's interpretive key[48]) that both liberates and binds. It liberates people
from sin and binds them to God in a covenant relationship that similarly
seeks the good of the other. The liberated and bound community, that is, the
cleansed and covenanted community, is in the process of becoming like the
loving God revealed in the loving death of Jesus (see 13:1b). As Chennattu
emphasizes, the *imitatio Dei* (imitation of God) was an integral part of the
covenantal relationship between the people and God: "You shall be holy for
I am holy."[49] *Imitatio Dei* has become *imitatio Christi*, which, because Jesus
is the Word and self-revelation of God (1:1–18), is ultimately *imitatio Dei*.

Two major issues must still be addressed at least briefly. First, is this
love truly Godlike and Christlike if it is only directed toward fellow disciples, toward "one another"? Second, is an ethic of imitation, especially
imitation of self-giving love, simply a "new commandment" that will remain unrealized due to human sin?

To deal first with the second question, Jesus in John does not present
us merely with an ethic of commandment and imitation. It is better described as a spirituality of mutual indwelling that makes possible the fulfilling of the obligation of imitation, not dissimilar from what we will find in
Paul.[50] Already in John 14, when Jesus refers to the requirement of keeping
his commandments as the demonstration of love for him and the Father, he
makes it clear that the disciples can do nothing on their own power but will
have the indwelling presence of Jesus in the person of the Spirit/Advocate
(14:17–20, 26, 28).[51] The nature of this relationship is further disclosed in

---

47. Skinner, "Virtue in the New Testament," finds significant resonances between
John's ethic of self-giving and sacrifice and Paul's ethic of cruciformity, in each case highlighting the centrality of love.

48. For the view that John 3:16 (or 3:16–17) is the interpretive, or hermeneutical, key
to the Fourth Gospel, see Moloney, *Love in the Gospel of John*, esp. 3, 5–10, 33–34.

49. Chennattu, *Johannine Discipleship*, 59–61.

50. Also, not surprisingly, in 1 John. See the discussion in chap. 4.

51. Even the gift of the Spirit may be connected to the death of Jesus, if the end of
John 19:30 is better translated "he gave his Spirit" rather than he "gave up his spirit"

chapter 15, in which Jesus speaks of a reciprocal residency between himself and his disciples: "Abide in me as I abide in you. Just as the branch cannot bear fruit by itself unless it abides in the vine, neither can you unless you abide in me" (15:4). This does not decrease the force of the expectation. It is still a matter of commandments, or covenantal obligations, but it does alter the *manner* in which the obligations are fulfilled. The prophetic language of the new covenant, made effective by the indwelling of the Spirit or the law within, is behind this formulation of covenantal requirements here even as it will be in Paul.[52] *But the prophetic promises of mutual covenant relationship and (one-way) interiority have merged to become mutual indwelling. We are moving beyond imitation toward theosis: becoming like God by participating in the life of God.*

Now to address the first question: Is love for one another sufficient? What about love for outsiders generally and for enemies in particular? Here we must consider two things: the Johannine context of (current or coming) persecution and the missional impetus of John 17. When a community is experiencing or expecting persecution, it is critical that it sustain itself in love. The community of disciples in John is going to be pursued, persecuted (15:18–21; 16:33; 17:11–16). It will die without an ethos of mutual love, support, and unity, as Jesus himself knows (15:16–17; 17:11–16). But equally important is the corollary ethos of mission. The disciples will share in Jesus' fate because they share in his mission, which is in fact God's mission. Following the promises of persecution in chapters 15–17, Jesus does not order his disciples to flee or hide but to join him in his mission of bringing eternal life to the world. He prays to his Father, "As you have sent me into the world, so I have sent them into the world" (17:18) and asks only for their protection (17:15). Their internal love and unity, therefore, is not merely an end in itself but a means to the success of the mission, of the *missio Dei* (17:21–23). The upshot of all this is that the disciples are in fact called to love the world, even the world that hates and persecutes them, because they participate in the world-centered love and mission of God manifested in the Son, *especially in his death* (3:14–17). *To embrace the Son's death is to embrace God's world-mission and thus to embody God's love in the world.* This will include even enemies. "Jesus does not make intense

---

(NRSV), though this proleptic giving of the Spirit is finally completed only in the resurrection narrative (20:22). See, e.g., Brown, *Gospel According to John XIII—XXI*, 931; Moloney, *Love in the Gospel of John*, 30.

52. The Holy Spirit is "John's answer" to Jeremiah's promise (Lundbom, *Jeremiah 21–36*, 478).

communion among disciples an end in itself; it exists *that God might be made known*."[53] By their missional love, the disciples will bear witness to the sort of God revealed in Jesus, above all in his death: a God who loves "the world," that is, all of humanity.[54]

The narrative and christological basis of this kind of love is found also in the narrative setting of the actual farewell/discipleship discourses.[55] Although interpreters have rightly focused their attention on the footwashing scene as the parable of Jesus' love, they have often overlooked the significance of the entire meal. Jesus shares this final meal as a symbol of his love for and commitment to all of his friends, even the one who would soon betray him (Judas) and the one who would soon deny him (Peter). Moreover, the evangelist tells us that Jesus does this fully aware that Judas and Peter would betray and deny him (13:26, 36–38)! In other words, Jesus himself did not limit his love to friends who were true friends. He laid down his life for friends (15:14–15) who were, like Peter and Judas, deniers and betrayers—for enemies, in other words. Thus when Jesus offers himself as the paradigm of loving friendship, his definition of "friends" is so broad that when he extols laying down one's life for one's friends (15:13), it should be heard *inclusively* rather than *exclusively*. Judas the betrayer has left, but Peter the denier is still present. To love friends as God does in Jesus is, in effect, to love enemies. What Paul says explicitly and bluntly in Rom 5:6–10 about the cross as God's act of enemy love, John says implicitly and gently but no less powerfully, even if it is not his primary intent or focus.

To summarize the theological importance of the farewell discourse in relation to the atonement: the death of Jesus will create a community of committed friends of Jesus who indwell him and are indwelt by him/his Spirit. Within this relationship they will participate in his death in four ways: receiving his forgiveness, fulfilling the obligations of a covenant relationship by continuing his self-giving love for others, experiencing hatred and persecution similar to that which caused his death, and extending God's mission to the world. That is, as a community of atonement they are a covenantal, cruciform, charismatic, missional community.

---

53. Moloney, *Love in the Gospel of John*, 131, referring especially to John 17.

54. See especially Moloney's discussion of "What Sort of God" (answer: a God who loves the world, a God who sends) in ibid., 55–68.

55. I am indebted to Moloney (ibid., 107–21) for stimulating the following observations, though Moloney does not use the word "enemy" in his discussion, and he probably reads Jesus' giving of the morsel of bread (13:18–30) to Judas a bit too positively.

When the crucified but resurrected Jesus returns to his disciples, it is these and other new-covenant themes that appear in his words with them, but with particular emphasis on the missional dimension (John 20:19–23). The risen Jesus twice speaks words of peace (vv. 19, 21a). Sandwiched in between these words is the evangelist's narrative of Jesus' self-identification as the crucified-but-risen Lord: he reveals his wounded hands and side (v. 20). This Jesus then sends the disciples out to continue his mission of forgiving sins and furthering that which forgiveness makes possible: new and abundant life because of the cross, because of the crucified. He gives them the promised Spirit to accomplish that task (vv. 21b–23). This "Johannine Pentecost," then, continues the new-covenant motif: Spirit, mission, forgiveness.

CONCLUSION

In this chapter we have considered the links between the cross and the establishment of the new covenant in the four canonical gospels and Acts. Throughout the chapter we have found that these writings express, in various ways, the reality that the death of Jesus effected the promised new covenant and thereby created the community of the new covenant. Those who embrace this life-giving death begin a journey of participation in it that will be marked especially by peaceful practices of faithfulness and love—the two dimensions of the covenant—empowered by the Spirit. When we now turn to the rest of the New Testament, we will find these same sorts of foci and themes, the same kind of music with creative but recognizable improvisations.

– 3 –

Cross and New Covenant in the New Testament

From Paul to Revelation

HAVING EXAMINED THE CONNECTIONS between Jesus' death and the new covenant in the four gospels and Acts, we turn now to other parts of the New Testament: the Pauline letters, Hebrews, and Revelation. Although we could also examine the rest of the New Testament (and we will mention James, 1 Peter, and 1 John in subsequent chapters, on specific topics), these three authors contribute significantly—in distinctive but complementary ways—to the connection between cross and new covenant.

CROSS AND NEW COVENANT IN PAUL

Much could be said, and has been said, regarding Paul's interpretation of the cross, though his explicit references to the new covenant are fewer than one might expect.[1] The burden of this chapter, and indeed the entire book,

---

1. There are but two: 1 Cor 11:25; 2 Cor 3:6. Lundbom (*Jeremiah 21–36*, 475) suggests that Paul would have referred to Jeremiah 31 more often except that he wanted to establish a "more ancient base [the Abrahamic promises] for the new faith in Christ." Nevertheless, Lundbom rightly argues, especially regarding Romans, that Paul's lack

is that "new covenant" as a theological term and reality is far more per-vasive in the New Testament, including Paul, than the occurrences of the term or citations of particular scriptural texts could suggest. We will limit ourselves in examining Paul to a small selection of texts from five different letters, all of which bear, explicitly or implicitly, on the connection between the cross and the new covenant and on the significance of that connection. Before considering those texts, however, we need to mention one impor-tant book that has, unfortunately, received less attention than it deserves: T. J. Deidun's *New Covenant Morality in Paul*, published in 1981.[2]

Deidun argues that the new covenant, promised by Jeremiah and Eze-kiel and fulfilled by God through Christ in the giving of the Spirit, is the center of Paul's theology. Paul's morality, he argues, "was coloured from the very beginning by his interpretation" of Ezek 36:27 and Jer 31:31ff.[3] Deidun

---

of new-covenant *language* should not be confused with lack of new-covenant *theology* (476). I cannot, therefore, agree with Dunn—in an otherwise insightful essay at many points ("Did Paul Have a Covenant Theology?")—that Paul's use of "new covenant" lan-guage is merely his citing tradition (1 Cor 11:25) rather than actually theologizing him-self and is generally of little theological consequence (10). In fact, for Dunn "covenant" and "new covenant" ideas "lay somewhat on the periphery of this [Paul's] thought" (11), even though in one sense Paul, as a Jew, is of course always engaged in covenant theology (4–5). I think Dunn seriously underestimates the place of covenant/new covenant in Paul's theology, especially in his claim that Paul himself does not link Christ's death to the new covenant (11). I do think Dunn is quite correct, however, to stress the continuity in Paul's thinking (such as it is, in his view) about the covenant and the new covenant (11–19). McKnight (*Jesus and His Death*, 300–301) also argues that "a new covenant her-meneutic is not central to Pauline theology" even though it "could have been the cutting edge for the Pauline gospel." The recent "apocalyptic" interpreters of Paul (e.g., J. Louis Martyn) also frequently minimize the covenant/new covenant in the (understandable) interest of preserving the radical newness of the gospel. But the opposition of "covenant" or "new covenant" and "apocalyptic" in Paul is both unnecessary and unwise, as N. T. Wright argues especially in *Paul and the Faithfulness of God*. That is, the apocalyptic event of Jesus and the Spirit means that the new covenant is effected in unexpected ways. See also Shaw, "Apocalyptic and Covenant," who suggests that Paul was a "[t]heologian of the [a]pocalyptic [c]ovenant" (162) and that attending to Paul's new-covenant theology actually preserves appropriate concerns of apocalyptic interpreters. For Paul's implicit new-covenant theology, see also Peterson, *Transformed by God*, 129–55.

2. Another often overlooked but important work, which interprets Romans in terms of the new covenant, is Kaylor, *Paul's Covenant Community*. See also now the important work of Whittle on Romans and Paul's theology more generally (*Covenant Renewal*). Whittle argues that Paul's theology is greatly indebted to Deuteronomy, Ezekiel, and Jer-emiah (and their theologies of covenant renewal/new covenant), that Romans 9–11 is an exposition of covenant-renewal texts, and that Romans 12–15 depicts the reconstituted people of God in which the Law is fulfilled by the power of the Spirit.

3. Deidun, *New Covenant Morality*, 228.

finds strong evidence that Paul uses the language of Jeremiah and Ezekiel, not only in 2 Corinthians 3, but also in his earliest letter (1 Thess 4:8–9). Moreover, he argues compellingly that Paul refers throughout his letters to the content of the new covenant: being God's holy people empowered by the Spirit to forsake idolatry and immorality and to love God and others (especially fellow believers). Although there are a few areas of Deidun's work with which I would quibble, it is overall a persuasive argument. What is absent from the book is a clear and consistent connection between new covenant and Christ's death.[4] That will be our focus now, starting with the letters in which the phrase "new covenant" occurs (1 and 2 Corinthians) and then considering, more briefly, three other Pauline writings.

First Corinthians

The earliest explicit occurrence of the term "new covenant" in Paul's letters is in 1 Cor 11:25:

> [23]For I received from the Lord what I also handed on to you, that the Lord Jesus on the night when he was betrayed took a loaf of bread, [24]and when he had given thanks, he broke it and said, "This is my body that is for you. Do this in remembrance of me." [25]In the same way he took the cup also, after supper, saying, "This cup is the new covenant in my blood. Do this, as often as you drink it, in remembrance of me." (1 Cor 11:23–25)

This is, of course, early Christian tradition that Paul has delivered to the Corinthians, but it is not *merely* early Christian tradition, as if this tradition were insignificant to Paul.[5] Just the opposite is the case, as the similar situation of Paul's quoting tradition about the resurrection in 1 Cor 15:3–7 clearly demonstrates. Paul's fundamental claim in 1 Cor 11:23–25 is that Jesus himself interpreted his own death as the inauguration of the new covenant.[6] His death, and his interpretation of his death, mean that the Cor-

---

4. For Deidun, the cross in Paul functions primarily as Christ's exemplary self-offering, which is also the demonstration of the love of God, and which becomes the ongoing work of the Spirit in believers. While this is all true for Paul, there is more that needs to be said.

5. As suggested by Dunn, "Did Paul Have a Covenant Theology?," 11.

6. If Whittle (*Covenant Renewal*) is right, then the language of "a new covenant in my blood" is also the language of a peace offering, which is not fully exploited here, but (I would suggest) it is in 2 Corinthians and in Romans.

inthians—and all those in Christ—are part of the community of the new covenant. As such, they have certain covenantal obligations, both vertical and horizontal.

Accordingly, one of several concrete manifestations of the significance of this cruciform communal covenant-keeping in Paul is his discussion in 1 Corinthians 10 and 11:17–34 of the meaning of "the Lord's Supper," derived from the tradition about Jesus' "Last Supper" that Paul has just quoted. Elsewhere I have suggested that Paul makes four key theological claims about the Lord's Supper: it is (1) "not a sequence of private meals but an experience of solidarity or fellowship (*koinōnia*)" with both Christ and one another; (2) an "event of memory," meaning not recollection but present appropriation and participation; (3) "an act of proclamation—a parabolic sermon"; and (4) a "foretaste of the future messianic banquet."[7] To these four we may now add the following: the Lord's Supper for Paul is also (5) a microcosm of the new-covenant life effected by the cross.

In 1 Corinthians 10 Paul concludes his discussion of believers' partaking of meat offered to idols by pronouncing the Lord's Supper as a participatory and exclusive meal: "You cannot drink the cup of the Lord and the cup of demons. You cannot partake of the table of the Lord and the table of demons" (10:21). First of all, this is a meal of participation, like meals in other ancient temples: "sharing the life of the divinity in whose temple" one eats.[8] But this Lord (Jesus) is an odd divinity indeed: a crucified Messiah whose cup and table are not ordinary temple elements but the constitutive elements of his sacrificial death, as Paul will make clear in chapter 11. Secondly, then, this is an exclusive meal. One cannot be in relationship/partnership/fellowship with the Lord Christ and also with Lord Serapis or whomever. Participation in one covenantal relationship of absolute loyalty excludes all others. Attempting to participate in the life of multiple deities violates the "vertical" dimension of the new covenant (i.e., faithfully loving the Lord); it is spiritual adultery and idolatry (10:7, 14).

In 1 Cor 11:17–34 Paul, from a very different angle, asserts that the Corinthians are no longer celebrating the Lord's Supper (11:20). That is, he says to them, "Your practice (intentional or not) of separate meals and times, plus the consequent disdain for the lowly, subverts the realities to which the meal points—Christ's past atoning death, Christ's present role as host and communion partner, Christ's future return, Christ as Lord, the

7. Gorman, *Apostle of the Crucified Lord*, 268–69; original emphasis omitted.

8. Wright, *Paul and the Faithfulness of God*, 429.

inherent connection between the cross and the weak (cf. 1 Cor 1:26–31), and the unity of the church." And that's just for starters.

Focusing simply on the first of these, we can say that the Corinthians have failed to be a "community called atonement" (borrowing the title of Scot McKnight's book[9]). Why? They have misunderstood the covenant-renewing, in-gathering character of Jesus' death by their inappropriate exclusion of some in the community (11:21–22), that is, by their failure to fulfill the horizontal demands of the new covenant. This horizontal failure is likely grounded in the vertical failure. The Lord's Supper at Corinth looks like a symposium offered by, to, and with any other first-century deity, performed in a context where inclusivity of deities (Tuesday, Serapis; Wednesday, Asclepius; and so on) and exclusivity of humans (honored peers, yes; their lowly slaves, no) are the norms. That is not the way of the Lord and banquet host who was crucified on a cross.

Ironically, the Corinthians have rendered the Lord's Supper null and void by making its exclusive (i.e. vertical) dimension inclusive, and its inclusive (i.e. horizontal) dimension exclusive. In two distinct but inseparable ways, the Corinthians have failed to understand and practice the ritual that connects them to the atonement and that embodies the atonement in concrete practices. What was intended to be a living remembrance of and participation (*koinōnia*; 10:16) in the Lord's death—that is, his (one) body and blood—is not occurring and cannot occur as long as these incompatible practices continue: "When you come together, it is not really to eat the Lord's supper" (11:20).

The only way this kind of Pauline pronouncement makes any sense is if the new covenant in Jesus' blood creates—or is meant to create—a community in which the vertical and horizontal are seamlessly merged and concretely practiced. Paul assumes the inseparability of orthodoxy and orthopraxy, and he assumes the inseparability of the vertical and the horizontal in the atonement. Some may be tempted to say, "Paul is talking about ethics, not atonement." Therein lies the kind of problem that Paul addresses; ethics is not a separate category! Ethics is atonement in action, not as a supplement, but as constitutive of atonement itself. The horizontal is not the *result* of atonement, it is one of the principal *components* of atonement. Paul was amazingly sophisticated and integrated as a theologian; he saw the inseparable connections among various alleged "sub-disciplines" of theology and Christian existence: liturgy (worship), spirituality, ethics,

9. McKnight, *Community Called Atonement.*

theology in general, and soteriology (doctrine of salvation) in particular, to name just a few.

Theologically, the meaning of this integrated new-covenant existence for Paul is grounded in the cross. The cross was not merely an act of the Lord Jesus, however. It was the work of God (i.e., God the Father), a display, paradoxically, of divine wisdom and power in the form of divine folly and weakness (1 Cor 1:18–25).[10] As such, the cross becomes for Paul the norm for adjudicating the ongoing work of God's Spirit, the presence of whom is the sign of the new covenant. Thus throughout 1 Corinthians Paul reminds the charismatic Corinthians that true spirituality is *cruciform* spirituality.[11] The cross is a self-revelation of God—Father, Son, and Spirit—and therefore also a revelation of the church and of Christian existence—an "eccleisophany."[12] And that leads us directly to 2 Corinthians.

Second Corinthians

As already noted, the term "new covenant" appears in 2 Cor 3:6, the only occurrence in Paul besides the account of the Last Supper in 1 Cor 11:25: "[God] who has made us competent to be ministers of a new covenant, not of letter but of spirit [or the Spirit]; for the letter kills, but the Spirit gives life."[13] Our focus in looking at this text will be the connections Paul implicitly makes in 2 Corinthians 3–4 among the cross, the Spirit, and the new covenant, and then the connections between 2 Corinthians 3–4 and 2 Corinthians 5.

In considering the reference to the new covenant in 2 Corinthians, we need to keep in mind one critical matter of interpretive strategy: *we should assume that Paul assumes that the Corinthians know and remember the tradition he passed on to them orally and then reinforced in writing (1 Cor 11:23–25): that Jesus' death is that which effected the new covenant.* Paul thinks that the phrase "new covenant" will trigger an automatic connection

---

10. See further in chapter 5.

11. See further my chapter on 1 Corinthians in *Apostle of the Crucified Lord* (227–86).

12. See Gorman, "The Cross in Paul: Christophany, Theophany, Ecclesiophany." In fact, Brent Laytham has added the term "anthrophany"—the cross as revelation of true humanity (in a presentation on Pauline theology and practice, St. Mary's Seminary & University, November 9, 2012).

13. The NRSV here curiously fails to recognize that "spirit" ("not of letter but of spirit") is a reference to the "Spirit," i.e., the Spirit of God.

to the cross. Moreover, the language of "new covenant" suggests for Paul an intimate connection to the reality, the earthiness (for lack of a better term), of Jesus' death as an actual suffering human being.[14] Thus 2 Cor 3:6 is part of an extended description of Christian ministry (specifically, of Paul and his colleagues) and, within that, also of Christian existence more generally, that has been generated by the new-covenant-generating cross.[15] Paul describes the Corinthians who *benefit* from the ministry of the new covenant as a community formed by the Spirit of God, who has written on their hearts (3:3), as the prophets promised. This covenant is one that brings about life, righteousness/justification, and glory rather than death and condemnation (3:6–11). Throughout, with Exodus 34 and the original covenant as his base text, the prophets Ezekiel and Jeremiah with their new covenant as his interpretive lens, and the death and resurrection of Jesus as his starting point and definitive context, Paul merges the prophetic new-covenant images of Ezekiel and Jeremiah with the realities of the gospel, in which he finds the prophetic images' fulfillment.[16] The original covenant is not thereby disparaged, but it is (to borrow, once again, a musical image) re-arranged in a dramatically new setting, more magnificent than ever, as the prophets foresaw.[17]

We know implicitly in 2 Corinthians 3–4, and explicitly elsewhere in Paul, that in speaking of these realities he is referring to the effects of preaching the gospel, which is the word of the cross (in addition to 1 Cor 11:25, see Rom 1:16–17 in light of 3:21–26; Rom 5:12–21; 1 Cor 1:18–25; 2 Cor 5:14–21). Those who participate in this new covenant are in the process of being transformed into the image of Christ: "And all of us, with unveiled faces, seeing the glory of the Lord as though reflected in a mirror, are being transformed into the same image from one degree of glory to another; for this comes from the Lord, the Spirit . . . [Unlike others, we see]

---

14. As several commentators have pointed out, there is a very high concentration of references to the name "Jesus" in 2 Cor 4:5–14 (nine occurrences in five different verses), where the reality of Jesus' death and of apostolic participation in it are stressed.

15. In 2 Corinthians 3, "Paul is claiming . . . that by the spirit his own apostolic ministry, and indeed the life of the Corinthian Christians, is a fulfillment of that complex of new-covenant promises . . . The spirit, in other words, enables the Messiah's people to fulfil Torah in new-covenantal fashion" (Wright, *Paul and the Faithfulness of God*, 725).

16. See also Wright's longer discussion of 2 Corinthians 3 in ibid., 980–84.

17. What appears to be a comparatively negative evaluation of Moses and the old covenant can also be read as Paul's pointing to the story of Moses as "a parable of grace . . . a prefiguration of the truth to which the gospel also points" (Hays, *Echoes*, 147).

the light of the gospel of the glory of Christ, who is the image of God" (3:18; 4:4). But this glory has a paradoxical character. It was the death of Christ that brought this new covenant of life and glory, empowered and shaped by the Spirit, into existence. Furthermore, it is paradoxically the death of Christ that continues to define Christian existence as ongoing transformation into glory, and it is the death of Christ that shapes Christian ministry. Such ministry entails "always carrying in the body the death of Jesus, so that the life of Jesus may also be made visible in our bodies" (2 Cor 4:10). Those who minister on behalf of the God of this covenant will embody in daily life the very act that effected the new covenant, and the communities they form will also take on a cruciform shape.[18] The work of the Spirit is to form cruciform communities, as Paul has already told the Corinthians in the first letter.[19]

The following list summarizes the major explicit and implicit affirmations that Paul makes about the cross (shorthand for the death of Jesus) in 2 Corinthians 3–4 inasmuch as it *effects the new covenant and thereby unleashes the Spirit* (cf. Gal 3:1–5).[20] We begin with this critical assumption that Paul connects cross and Spirit, which sets everything else in motion:

- the cross effects the new covenant and inaugurates the age of the Spirit (2 Cor 3:3, 6; cf. 1 Cor 11:25 for "new covenant");

- the death of Jesus effects, not a ministry of death, but of life, glory, the Spirit, and freedom (2 Cor 3:7–9, 17–18);

- the cross effects, and effects a ministry of, justification, not condemnation (2 Cor 3:9; cf. Rom 5:14–19);

- the cross effects a permanent covenant, as promised by the prophets (2 Cor 3:11);

- the cross effects the process of corporate Spirit-empowered transformation into glory, meaning the image of Christ (2 Cor 3:18; cf. Rom 8:29–30);

---

18. See my *Cruciformity*. Hays refers to the Spirit-filled community described by Paul as an "incarnation" and a "breathing instantiation" of the gospel (*Echoes*, 129, 131).

19. See also, e.g., Phil 2:1–4 in light of Phil 2:6–8.

20. Of course none of these would be true without the resurrection. My point here is to stress the generative nature, for Paul, of the cross, but this ultimately means the crucified and resurrected Messiah Jesus. That Paul associates the gift of the Spirit with the cross is evident not only from 2 Corinthians 3 and Gal 3:1–5, but also from Rom 5:1–11.

- the cross of Jesus, which is the focal point of the gospel, reveals the glory of Christ, who reveals the glory of God (2 Cor 4:4, 6);

- the cross is the paradigm for apostolic ministry, which, like the death of Jesus, is paradoxically life-giving both to those who minister and to those receiving that ministry (4:8–12); and

- the cross is followed by resurrection, and both Christian existence and Christian ministry participate in this two-stage pattern of suffering leading to glory (4:13–18).

Despite the rather narrow rhetorical context that generates 2 Corinthians 3–4 (Paul's self-defense), it would be difficult to find a fuller description of the transformative nature of the atonement. Christ's death is covenant-effecting, community-creating, empowering, paradigmatic, and mission-generating. The contrast with the "old covenant" is not a dismissal of the value of the former covenant, but rather a reinterpretation of the prophetic new-covenant motif in light of the reality of a crucified yet glorified Messiah and a life-giving yet cruciform Spirit.[21] The entire passage is laced with paradox, and the primary paradox is precisely the idea that life and glory come out of suffering and death. This glorious life in the Spirit is indeed new, but it is also old—it is what Scripture, not least the prophets of the new covenant, promised.[22]

When we turn to 2 Cor 5:14–21, we see a parallel and equally full description of cross and covenant, but with more explicit references to the cross. The death of Christ narrated in this text is described as his act of love, and that love expressed in death continues to motivate those who minister to others: "For the love of Christ urges us on, because we are convinced that one has died for all; therefore all have died" (5:14). That act of love had human transformation as its purpose, as is evident in Greek purpose clauses (*hina*; "so that"). Paul explains this purpose in two different ways:

21. This way of construing Paul's manner of theologizing derives directly from 2 Corinthians 3–4, but the wording is indebted as well to N. T. Wright, particularly in his *Paul: In Fresh Perspective* and *Paul and the Faithfulness of God*.

22. Cherith Fee Nordling writes of the paradoxical experience of glory in the midst of our own, and the world's, suffering—and its connection to mission. As we participate in Jesus' suffering and resurrection, she says, we "groan with the Spirit, who intercedes for us and empowers us to bear our share of the weight of a fallen world, and of its future glory. We taste this glory only in part, but each foretaste of glory divine reminds us that God is restoring, not forsaking, his beloved world . . . Every time we exchange life for death, justice for oppression, healing for brokenness, joy for mourning, and hope for despair, heaven meets earth in a burst of resurrection" ("Resurrection," 189–90).

> And he died for all, so that (*hina*) those who live might live no longer for themselves, but for him who died and was raised for them. (5:15)

> For our sake he made him to be sin who knew no sin, so that (*hina*) in him we might become the righteousness of God" (5:21).

All of this drives Paul once again to use the word "new," but this time it is "new creation" (5:17) rather than "new covenant." Yet the two are closely related.[23] The prophetic promises that God will bring about a new covenant (and thus a new people), and also bring about a new creation, are both being fulfilled in and through Christ, inaugurated by his death and resurrection. Paul summarizes that covenant-effecting, community-creating act in the word "reconciliation" (5:18–20). It is clear that this reconciliation involves forgiveness ("not counting their trespasses against them"; 5:19), but also much more. As in Matthew's account of the Last Supper, forgiveness is the prerequisite for participation in the new creation/covenant, the start of the transformation into the righteousness of God. But Christ did not die merely to forgive sins, or to create a people who know themselves to be forgiven. Rather, he died to create a covenant-keeping forgiven people, a people that is absolutely devoted to this crucified and resurrected Lord and that embodies the kind of divine righteousness displayed in his self-giving incarnation and death (cf. 2 Cor 8:9). The ministry of the new covenant is a ministry of righteousness/justice (2 Cor 3:9; Greek *dikaiosynēs*; NRSV "justification."). Accordingly, its effect is to create a righteous/just people.

Richard Hays has offered the following important comment on 2 Cor 5:21:

> Notice carefully what Paul actually says here: Not "so that we might know about the righteousness of God." Not "so that we might believe in the righteousness of God." Not "so that we might proclaim the righteousness of God." Not even "so that we might be justified by the righteousness of God." Rather, he says, "so that we might *become* the righteousness of God." Our commission from God is that we as a community are called to embody the righteousness of God in the world—to incarnate it, if you will—in such a way that the message of reconciliation is made visible in our midst. And of course reconciliation made visible is something that can appear only in practices that show unity, love, mercy, forgiveness

23. See, e.g., Martin, *2 Corinthians*, 152–53; Wright, *Paul and the Faithfulness of God*, 503, 1489–90.

and a self-giving grace that the world could not even dream of apart from Christ.[24]

Not only do I concur with Hays, but also, in agreement with Morna Hooker and others, I have argued that 5:21 is about justification understood as transformation; there is nothing about "imputation" here. In fact, what Hooker calls the Pauline patterns of interchange—Christ became what we are so that we might become what he is—constitute the Pauline basis for the early Christian doctrine of theosis.[25] 2 Cor 5:21 in its context is another way of stating the claim of 2 Cor 3:18 and related verses in its context: the cross is the basis for the radical transformation of human beings by God's Spirit; the cross is implicit in 2 Cor 3:18, and the Spirit is implicit in 2 Cor 5:21, but both cross and Spirit are either explicitly or implicitly present in both, as the larger context makes clear. This transformation takes place, not by imitation, but by indwelling, being "in him." For Paul this indwelling is not a one-way relationship but mutual: we in Christ, Christ in us; we in the Spirit, the Spirit in us (see, e.g., Rom 8:1–17). The new-covenant promise of interiority has been fulfilled but also altered, as in John, to become mutual indwelling.[26]

Some may think that the idea of God's reconciling us to himself (5:18) restricts the notion of reconciliation to the vertical realm. But that interpretation flies in the face of the evidence of Second Corinthians as a whole. In this letter Paul is at pains to effect reconciliation between himself and the Corinthians, an effort not only grounded in his gospel of reconciliation

24. From a sermon preached June 1, 2010 and based on his *Moral Vision*, 24; see http://www.faithandleadership.com/sermons/the-word-reconciliation, 2. There has been some debate about the identity of the "we" that becomes the righteousness of God, but Grieb makes a compelling case (against N. T. Wright) that the "we" refers to all those in Christ. See Grieb, "'So That in Him.'" Unless we want to posit a new version of limited atonement—Christ died only for Paul and other ministers—then we must conclude that some of the "we" texts in Second Corinthians clearly and deliberately refer to all believers, and preeminent among them is 5:21.

25. Hooker, *From Adam to Christ*, 13–69; Gorman, *Inhabiting the Cruciform God*. Interest in this aspect of Paul is on the rise. In *Inhabiting*, I define theosis, especially in Paul, as "transformative participation in the kenotic, cruciform character of God through Spirit-enabled conformity to the incarnate, crucified, and resurrected/glorified Christ" (7). For similar interest in Paul and theosis, see Campbell, *Deliverance of God*; Blackwell, *Christosis*; Litwa, "2 Corinthians 3:18" and *We are Being Transformed*; and even (though differentiating justification from theosis) Wright, *Paul and the Faithfulness of God*, 546, 955, 1021–23, 1031. See also my "Paul's Corporate, Cruciform, Missional Theosis in Second Corinthians."

26. See the discussion of John in chapter 2.

but also presented as an essential part of that gospel. How can Paul, or the Corinthians, claim to themselves or others that they are reconciled to God if they are not reconciled to one another? That is the narrative logic and theo-logic of Second Corinthians, especially chapters 1–7, but also of the entire letter.[27]

Moreover, for Paul the *message* of reconciliation and righteousness is also a *mission* of reconciliation and righteousness (5:20—6:2). Though the text may put the primary emphasis on Paul's apostolic mission team as "ambassadors for Christ" (5:20), it is difficult to think that Paul wants the righteous, reconciled community in Christ to be anything less than a community of righteousness/justice and reconciliation in and for the world.[28]

Once again, we see in Paul the transformative nature of the atonement: Christ's death is God the Father's act of faithfulness, love, and reconciliation that, in concert with the work of the Spirit,

- effects our own death (2 Cor 5:14; cf. Gal 2:19–20; Romans 6);

- inaugurates the new creation (2 Cor 5:17);

- redirects, transforms, and empowers both knowledge and existence (2 Cor 5:15–16, 21);

- effects righteousness/justice (2 Cor 5:21);

- produces the new covenant and the new-covenant community marked by love and righteousness/justice (2 Cor 5:14, 21);

- serves as the motive and paradigm of Christian existence and ministry (2 Cor 5:14, 20); and

- generates mission (2 Cor 5:18–20).

All of this is by grace, a free act "for all" (2 Cor 5:14–15), "for our sake" (2 Cor 5:21), indeed even "for me" (Gal 2:20)—which leads us to Galatians.

Galatians

The term "new covenant" does not appear in Galatians, and Paul seems quite occupied with the covenant made with Abraham.[29] Yet the fulfill-

---

27. We return to this topic in chapter 7.

28. See Grieb, "'So That in Him.'" See also my "Justification and Justice in Paul," esp. 37–38.

29. See Gal 3:17; 4:24, and their contexts.

ment of the promises made to Abraham is, for Paul, nothing other than the promised new covenant, so new-covenant theology does exist, implicitly, in Galatians. Three brief but highly significant points need to be made. (Elsewhere I have developed these points at greater length.[30])

First, in his discussion of justification, Paul is in part defining the nature of the (new) covenant community: who is in, why, and how. The "Israel of God" (6:16) is defined, not as the community of the circumcised, but as those Gentiles and Jews, men and women, slaves and free (3:28) who have received the eschatological gift of the Spirit, which is now in and among them, as God had promised through Jeremiah and Ezekiel (and, even earlier, to and through Abraham; see 3:6–18). This Spirit is, of course, the Spirit of God, but also—and this is crucial for Paul—the Spirit of the Son (4:6; cf. Rom 8:9).

Second, the members of this new-covenant community have received this Spirit of the Son, the Messiah, by responding in faith to the proclamation of the gospel of the crucified Messiah (3:1–5). This response of faith is nothing less than participation in the death of Jesus/the Son of God/the Messiah (2:15–21).[31] Paul does not spell out the "mechanics" of this salvific moment, but he makes it clear that there is a close association between expressing faith that leads to justification, being crucified with the Son/Messiah, and receiving the Spirit; the three are essentially one.[32] *In fact, this may well be Paul's most innovative and important contribution to the theology of the new covenant: the "new spirit" that comes to dwell in the people is the Spirit of the crucified Messiah; it is, therefore, the cruciform Spirit, the spirit of cruciformity.*[33]

Third, if we understand the occurrences of the noun *pistis* ("faith," "faithfulness") in Gal 2:15–21 as references to Christ's own faith (i.e., faithfulness), then Paul characterizes Jesus' death as an act of both faithfulness toward God (2:16 [twice], 20) and love for us (2:20).[34] It is thus the quint-

---

30. See Gorman, *Cruciformity*, especially 122–54, 214–67; and *Inhabiting the Cruciform God*, 40–104.

31. For a philosophically oriented treatment of the atonement that relies heavily on the motif of participation found in Paul, see Bayne and Restall, "Participatory Theory of the Atonement."

32. For the broader theological ramifications of this claim, see Macchia, *Justified in the Spirit*.

33. See Gorman, *Cruciformity*, 50–62.

34. See ibid., 95–121; and Gorman, *Inhabiting the Cruciform God*, 40–104. This interpretation is of course debated.

essential act of covenantal faithfulness and fulfillment, the paradigmatic symbiosis of the vertical and the horizontal requirements of the covenant. To live in the Son/Messiah, and to have the Spirit of the faithful and loving Son/Messiah within, means that the covenant community will be people of "faith working through love" (5:6), in whom Torah is fulfilled when they are filled with *this* Spirit.[35] It will be impossible to separate the vertical from the horizontal, or the spiritual from the ethical and missional.

Galatians, to summarize, demonstrates that for Paul participation in the faithful and loving, covenant-fulfilling death of the Messiah—and that alone—is the basis for reception of the Spirit and membership in the new-covenant community. Furthermore, this participation is the reason why the community and all those within in it are both required and able to fulfill the covenantal requirements of faithfulness and love (see 5:14; cf. Rom 8:3–4; 13:8–10[36]).

Ephesians

We turn next to Ephesians. Although the authorship of this document is disputed, its witness within the Pauline corpus to the new-covenant-making death of Jesus is critical.[37] The letter begins with a Christianized Jewish *berakah* (blessing) in which God's lavish grace toward "us" is celebrated (1:3–13). The list of blessings includes elements of the prophetically promised new covenant, including forgiveness, redemption, unity, and the gift of the Spirit. The theme of God's gracious initiative continues in 2:1–10, which focuses on God's resurrecting the (spiritually) dead and making of them a people willing and able to do the "good works . . . God prepared beforehand to be our way of life" (2:10). The final phrase of that verse, better translated "so that we might walk in them (*hina en autois peripatēsōmen*)," alludes to the purposes of the covenant people of God described in Deuteronomy and elsewhere in Scripture:

> Today you have obtained the Lord's agreement: to be your God;
> and for you to walk in his ways, to keep his statutes, his command-
> ments, and his ordinances, and to obey him. (Deut 26:17)

35. See, similarly, Wright, *Paul and the Faithfulness of God*, 512–13.

36. Rom 13:8–10 shows that Paul refers to the second table when speaking of love as fulfilling the Law. We should also note the importance of peace in Galatians. See especially Gabrielson, *Paul's Non-Violent Gospel*, 79–138.

37. I will refer to the letter's author as Paul.

> If you obey the commandments of the Lord your God that I am
> commanding you today, by loving the Lord your God, walking in
> his ways, and observing his commandments, decrees, and ordi-
> nances, then you shall live and become numerous, and the Lord
> your God will bless you in the land that you are entering to pos-
> sess. (Deut 30:16)[38]

In Christ, then, God has graciously created a new people of the covenant who will walk in God's ways. But Paul now makes it clear that the identity of this new-covenant people is in fact also new, consisting of Gentiles
as well as Jews, the "uncircumcision" and the "circumcision" (2:11). Those
who had been "strangers to the covenants of promise" (2:12) are now full
members of the new/renewed covenant.[39] The death of Christ has brought
those who were distant near (2:13), reconciling Gentiles and Jews into one
new people who together have access in Christ to God by the Spirit.[40] The
words of the text bear eloquent witness to this divine act of peacemaking:

> [14]For he [Christ] is our peace; in his flesh he has made both groups
> into one and has broken down the dividing wall, that is, the hostil-
> ity between us. [15]He has abolished the law with its commandments
> and ordinances, that he might create in himself one new human-
> ity in place of the two, thus making peace, [16]and might reconcile
> both groups to God in one body through the cross, thus putting to
> death that hostility through it. [17]So he came and proclaimed peace
> to you who were far off and peace to those who were near; [18]for
> through him both of us have access in one Spirit to the Father. [19]So
> then you are no longer strangers and aliens, but you are citizens
> with the saints and also members of the household of God . . .
> (Eph 2:14–19)

Thus God's action in Christ's death reconciles people to God and to
one another—inseparably. To walk in God's ways, then, will mean not only

38. In Deuteronomy, see also 8:6; 10:12; 11:22; 13:5; 19:9; 28:9.

39. Although Ephesians does not use the term "new covenant" or specify which
"covenants" are being referred to here, it is certainly likely that the phrase "covenants of
promise" would mean all of the covenants God made with or promised to Israel, culminating in the new covenant announced by the prophets and inaugurated in the Messiah.
See also Snodgrass, *Ephesians*, 127. The phrase "covenants of promise" may also be an
echo of "the Holy Spirit of promise" (NRSV, "the promised Holy Spirit") in 1:13, which
would further strengthen the new-covenant reading proposed here. In any event, Gentiles are now included in this covenantal relationship (cf. 3:6).

40. See also Rom 1:16; 10:12; 1 Cor 1:24; 12:13; Gal 3:28; Col 3:11 (all using "Greek"
with "Jew"), as well as Rom 15:7–12.

to bless God for the forgiveness received, but also to embody the forgiving and reconciling love of God, the self-giving love of Christ, in daily life (4:32—5:2).[41]

Romans

We turn, finally for Paul, to Romans, Paul's *magnum opus*.[42] Although Paul does not specifically name the new covenant in Romans, he might summarize his new-covenant theology and spirituality that we have examined in other letters in phrases he penned for the Romans, such as the following:

> [A] person is not a Jew who is one outwardly, nor is true circumcision something external and physical. Rather, a person is a Jew who is one inwardly, and real circumcision is a matter of the heart—it is spiritual and not literal. Such a person receives praise not from others but from God. (Rom 2:28–29)

> God's love has been poured into our hearts through the Holy Spirit that has been given to us. (Rom 5:5b)

> Do you not know that all of us who have been baptized into Christ Jesus were baptized into his death? (Rom 6:3).

> But now that you have been freed from sin and enslaved to God, the advantage you get is sanctification. The end is eternal life. (Rom 6:22)

> There is therefore now no condemnation for those who are in Christ Jesus. For the law of the Spirit of life in Christ Jesus has set you free from the law of sin and of death. For God has done what the law, weakened by the flesh, could not do: by sending his own Son in the likeness of sinful flesh, and to deal with sin, he condemned sin in the flesh, so that the just requirement of the law might be fulfilled in us, who walk not according to the flesh but according to the Spirit. (Rom 8:1–4)

> I appeal to you therefore, brothers and sisters, by the mercies of God, to present your bodies as a living sacrifice, holy and

41. See further my forthcoming chapter on "Becoming the Gospel of Peace" in *Becoming the Gospel*, and chapters 6 and 7 of the present book.

42. See especially Whittle, *Covenant Renewal*.

acceptable to God, which is your spiritual worship. Do not be conformed to this world, but be transformed by the renewing of your minds, so that you may discern what is the will of God—what is good and acceptable and perfect. (Rom 12:1–2)

Owe no one anything, except to love one another; for the one who loves another has fulfilled the law. The commandments, "You shall not commit adultery; You shall not murder; You shall not steal; You shall not covet"; and any other commandment, are summed up in this word, "Love your neighbor as yourself." Love does no wrong to a neighbor; therefore, love is the fulfilling of the law. (Rom 13:8–10)

Welcome one another, therefore, just as Christ has welcomed you, for the glory of God. For I tell you that Christ has become a servant of the circumcised on behalf of the truth of God in order that he might confirm the promises given to the patriarchs, and in order that the Gentiles might glorify God for his mercy. (Rom 15:7–9a)

The quotation from Romans 2 is a rich echo of the Old Testament promises of a circumcised heart for God's people and an internalization of the covenantal relationship—and thus of the new covenant.[43] The gift of the Spirit to those who believe the gospel of the crucified Messiah (see Rom 3:21–31) marks them out as the members of this new-covenant community, justified by faith and infused with the Spirit, as Romans 5:5b (with all of 5:1–11) indicates. But the nature of that justifying faith is captured in the reality of baptism, which for Paul (and we can assume he is not inventing this idea as he writes to the Romans) means dying and rising with the Messiah (Romans 6). That is, to enter the community of Christ-followers through faith and baptism is to enter personally into the story and the reality of the crucified Messiah that has already generated the new-covenant community that walks "in newness of life" (Rom 6:4) and in which "the just requirement of the law" is "fulfilled" by "walk[ing] not according to the flesh but according to the Spirit" (Rom 8:4). It is a new-covenant community with a new life because its participation in the *death* of Jesus was, and is, coupled with participation in the *resurrection* of Jesus (Rom 6:4, 13).[44] The Spirit effects both death and resurrection (Rom 8:11, 13), accomplishing in

---

43. See also Wright, *Paul and the Faithfulness of God*, 512–13, 814, 924.

44. For a perceptive argument for present participation in the resurrection of Jesus in Paul's theology, see Belcher, "In Christ, There is no Opposition."

believers—as a result of Jesus' death—the covenantal obligations that could not be accomplished among those mastered by sin (Rom 8:3–4; cf. 2 Cor 5:21).[45] *The beneficiaries of Christ's death are such only as participants in it.*[46]

Here, then, is the ultimate Pauline paradox: the resurrection-life of the new-covenant, Spirit-filled community retains the shape and substance of its crucified Lord. The real fulfilling of the law is in devoted self-giving to God (Rom 6:22; 12:1–2) and in cruciform love for others (Rom 13:8–10). This takes place—must take place—in a community that unites Gentiles and Jews into one new-covenant people (Rom 15:1–13); that is the burden of the letter to the Romans and a summary of "the entire narrative of God's saving purposes" according to Paul.[47] It might even be called theosis—transformative, communal participation in the life of God as the new-covenant people of God.[48]

Summary of Paul, Jesus' Death, and the New Covenant

In the five portions of the Pauline corpus we have examined—and others could be added to these—we have discovered, despite the objections of some interpreters, that Paul is indeed a theologian and practitioner of the new covenant. This new covenant was inaugurated by the death of God's Son, Jesus the Messiah, and brought to existential reality by the presence of God's Spirit, who is also the Spirit of the Son/Messiah. Those who live in the Spirit embody the faithful and loving death of the Son.

We move now, though more briefly, from Paul to Hebrews and to Revelation.[49]

---

45. Cf. Wright, *Paul and the Faithfulness of God*, 725. It is clear in Rom 8:3–4 that the effect of Jesus' death is transformation and Torah-fulfillment by the Spirit. The "mechanics" of this—substitution? representation? sacrifice or "interchange" more generally?—are less clear. On the parallels between Romans 6 and Gal 2:15–21, see my *Inhabiting the Cruciform God*, 63–85.

46. See Belousek, *Atonement, Justice, and Peace*, 313–327, for a critique of atonement theologies, especially rooted in Paul, that neglect the essentially participationist thrust of Paul and the rest of the New Testament.

47. Wright, *Paul and the Faithfulness of God*, 399.

48. See my "Romans: The First Christian Treatise on Theosis."

49. Many early, and some contemporary, Christians have mistakenly thought that the (unsigned) document called the Letter to the Hebrews is from Paul's hand. This is highly unlikely.

CROSS AND NEW COVENANT IN HEBREWS

The word "covenant" appears seventeen times in Hebrews, associated with the adjective "new" four times. Significant attention has been paid to the theology of covenant and sacrifice in Hebrews, and some serious concerns about that theology have been raised. One common concern is that Hebrews endorses supersessionism, which seems to some to be inherent in the notion of a new and better covenant, and arrogant or even dangerous, especially for Jews.[50] In order to look at the topic of the new covenant and the cross per se, we need to consider the purpose and theme of Hebrews. After examining the purpose and theme, we can attend to cross and new covenant and then, finally, to the question of supersessionism.

Hebrews, like Revelation (see below), is a summons to covenant faithfulness.[51] Those whose "hearts [have been] sprinkled clean from an evil conscience" (10:22; cf. Ezek 36:25–27) must "hold fast to the confession of [their] hope without wavering" (10:23). Hebrews is also a warning that even participation in the blessings of the (new) covenant does not guarantee final salvation. Thus according to Hebrews it is possible to "lose" one's salvation, one's part in the new covenant (6:1–8; 10:19–39). This possibility would seem to call into question the efficacy of Christ's supposedly once-for-all (7:27; 9:12), new-covenant-effecting, sacrificial death, rendering it nothing better than the repeated animal sacrifices it allegedly replaced (see 9:12–22; 10:1–4, 11). But Hebrews does not allow us to draw that conclusion.

Hebrews presents the death of Jesus as his faithful, obedient action toward God, on behalf of God's people (and implicitly all people), in the roles of both high priest and victim/sacrifice. His death is the ultimate and ultimately effective sacrifice for sins, and as such it both terminates the sacrificial system and makes possible a permanent state of forgiveness, cleansing, and holiness for those who come to faith in its efficacy and its efficacious high priest. Although no New Testament writing stresses the self-sacrifice of Jesus as both priest and victim more than Hebrews, which is an extended interpretation of Yom Kippur (the Jewish Day of Atonement),[52]

---

50. Another, more recent, concern is that Hebrews endorses violence by grounding this new and better covenant in blood and sacrifice. See, e.g., Finlan, *Options on Atonement*, 44–53. We will address the issue of atonement and violence in chapter 8.

51. So also Attridge, *Hebrews*, 13, 21–23.

52. It is not our purpose here to explore, much less resolve, all the debates about the atonement in Hebrews, but rather to focus on the connection between atonement and covenant. The phrase "the death of Jesus," however, should be understood as inclusive of

it would be wrong to read Hebrews as portraying the atonement narrowly, as only the forgiveness of sins. Quite the opposite is in fact the case. In Hebrews, the purpose of the death of Jesus is precisely to effect the new covenant promised by Jeremiah. "Not only is it [Jesus' death] an atoning of- fering, it is also a covenant-inaugurating event."[53] Thus the results of Jesus' death are everything that Jeremiah promised, even though Hebrews does not provide a "list" of these results. Nonetheless, it is clear that the effects of the atonement are those realities articulated in Jeremiah 31. Hebrews 10 names several of these:

> [10]And it is by God's will that we have been sanctified through the offering of the body of Jesus Christ once for all . . . [14]For by a single offering he has perfected for all time those who are sanctified. [15]And the Holy Spirit also testifies to us, for after saying, [16]"This is the covenant that I will make with them after those days, says the Lord: I will put my laws in their hearts, and I will write them on their minds," [17]he also adds, "I will remember their sins and their lawless deeds no more." [18]Where there is forgiveness of these, there is no longer any offering for sin. (Heb 10:10, 14–18)

These verses suggest at least the following elements of the new covenant from Jeremiah (1) a renewed covenant relationship with God (v. 16); (2) sanctification (vv. 10, 14); (3) the interiority of God's law or Spirit (v. 16); (4) forgiveness (v. 17); and (5) permanence (v. 18). Hebrews is an extended interpretation of the new covenant in light of the once-for-all death of Je- sus, which therefore highlights the dimension of permanence.

Thus the author of Hebrews makes it clear that the purpose of Christ's death, and the evidence of genuine participation in the new and perma- nent covenant it inaugurated, is—not surprisingly—covenantal perma- nence. Jesus' own permanent high priesthood (e.g., 5:6; 6:20; 7:3, 17–28), including his ongoing intercessory role (2:17–18; cf. 4:14–16) on behalf of those tempted to be faithless, reinforce this reality. The author's repeated

---

both the death itself and the high-priestly act of offering the victim's blood. In the case of Jesus, this means his own blood and may refer to his exaltation into the heavenly Holy of Holies to present his life-giving blood there. For the issues, and arguments for focusing on the resurrection and exaltation, see especially Moffitt, "Blood, Life, and Atonement," and *Atonement and the Logic of Resurrection*.

53. Attridge, *Hebrews*, 253. See also most other interpreters, such as Lincoln, *Hebrews*, 52–53. Lincoln argues from the text that the recipients faced suffering, persecution, social marginalization, and fear of death, resulting in discouragement, eschatological uncertainty, insecurity, and the temptation to turn back from their Christian confession (54–60).

exhortations to faithfulness assume both that faithlessness is nonsensical in a permanent covenant *and*, paradoxically, that faithlessness is a real possibility.[54] The prophecy of Jeremiah, quoted at length in Hebrews 8, is therefore both a promise and a warning that the fate of Israel and Judah not be repeated in the new and different covenant, "for they did not continue in my covenant" (Heb 8:9, referring to Jer 31:32 in the LXX [= 38:32]).[55] The new covenant offers a permanent place, "an eternal inheritance" (9:15). The death of Christ is not just a *one*-time offering but an *all*-time offering (10:14). Moreover, because Christ's death was the ultimate demonstration of his faithfulness despite shame and suffering (12:1–3; cf. 2:17; 3:1–6), associating with his death in faith means sharing in his faithfulness, even in the face of persecution. (We will return to this topic in chapter 4.)

Those who benefit from and participate in Christ's one-time, for-all-time, faithful self-offering must therefore remain permanently faithful to the new covenant it effects. This requirement does not, however, entail a form of Pelagianism, for it is the promissory character of the new covenant and of the God who has established this new covenant that makes permanent covenant faithfulness possible: "Let us hold fast to the confession of our hope without wavering, for he who has promised [i.e., promised permanence in Jeremiah 31] is faithful" (10:23). God's faithfulness, coupled with the paradigmatic example of Jesus' faithfulness to death (12:1–3), creates the possibility of human faithfulness. The human responsibility is to assemble together to promote this covenant faithfulness, as well as "love and good deeds," within the covenant community (10:24–25).

How might this understanding of what the cross has done—that is, to effect the permanent covenant promised by Jeremiah—address the question of "supersessionism"? The first thing to be said is that Hebrews is not about Christianity replacing Judaism, or about Gentiles replacing Jews; either conclusion would be both anachronistic and insensitive to the text. The fundamental claim of Hebrews is that the God of Israel has acted to fulfill the very promises that same God made to and for Israel.[56] The recipients of the letter to the Hebrews, whether then or now, stand in line with the great cloud of witnesses (chap. 11) who were both faith-filled and faithful, culminating in the faith-filled and faithful one par excellence, Je-

---

54. This may seem logically problematic, but it is theologically appropriate, existentially realistic, and rhetorically powerful.

55. Hence the other warnings in Hebrews, culminating in 12:18–29.

56. See also, e.g., Johnson, *Hebrews*, 33–34 *et passim*.

sus, the uniquely obedient Son and faithful high priest. With Jesus and the covenant his death effects, there is great continuity with the past, but there is also of course great discontinuity. God has not changed, but God has effected a change, as promised; the Law of Moses has not been renounced, but it has been rewritten on hearts, as promised; the need for forgiveness by sacrifice and holiness has not ended, but the death of Jesus has offered a new and permanent way into that state of forgiveness and holiness, as promised. These are all theological claims, but they are not theological claims about replacement; they are theological claims about covenantal promises fulfilled that necessarily render previous ways of doing covenantal business—specifically, and in large measure only, the sacrificial system—old.[57]

CROSS AND NEW COVENANT IN REVELATION

In contrast to Hebrews, the word "covenant" appears in the book of Revelation only once, and it is in reference to the ark of the covenant (11:19). Nonetheless, there is a strong emphasis in the book on covenant faithfulness in connection to Jesus' death.

The central figure of the book of Revelation is Jesus as the Lamb; he is referred to as the Lamb 28 times, meaning the slaughtered Lamb (5:6, 9, 12; 13:8). In addition to the possible sacrificial connotations of that image, Jesus' death in Revelation should above all be viewed as an act of faithful witness, the culmination of his loyalty to God. Indeed, Jesus is called "the faithful witness" in the same breath as he is called the one who "loves us and freed us from our sins by his blood" (1:5; cf. 3:19); he is also called "the faithful and true witness" (3:14), and simply "Faithful and True" (19:11). Thus, John can speak of the faith(fulness) of Jesus (14:12) and possibly also of the witness of Jesus (1:9; NRSV "testimony").[58] Accordingly, as in Paul,

57. For an exegesis that develops this line of thinking throughout the letter, see Johnson, *Hebrews*. Johnson argues that Hebrews stands in the prophetic tradition of requiring an obedience from the heart that is not possible by ritual, and Jesus' own faithful obedience is both the example and the source of such obedience (see, e.g., 252–53). On the larger question of supersessionism, see also Hays, "'Here We Have No Lasting City,'" and the excursus on "Old and New Covenants" by Johnson in his *Hebrews*, 210–15. Neither Hebrews itself nor the articles by Hays and Johnson nor this brief discussion can settle all the issues, especially their implications for contemporary Jewish-Christian relations, but these remarks can at least dispel, I hope, some misunderstanding. For a general treatment of new-covenant theology in Hebrews, see also Peterson, *Transformed by God*, 77–103.

58. On this christological theme in Revelation, see especially Hays, "Faithful Witness, Alpha and Omega."

Jesus is portrayed as both faithful to God and loving toward others—the one who fully embodies the basic obligations of the covenant. The emphasis here, however, falls on faithfulness.

Throughout Revelation, disciples are depicted as those who share—or who should share—in the faithfulness, witness, suffering, and possibly even slaughter of Jesus. "Be faithful until death," Jesus tells the church at Smyrna (2:10), while the church at Pergamum is commended for its faithfulness, as is their deceased brother Antipas, the sole named martyr in Revelation: "my witness, my faithful one" (2:13). All the martyrs now in heaven were slaughtered for their witness (NRSV "testimony"; 6:9; cf. 18:24). Faith (*pistis*) as a virtue in Revelation means not assent or even trust, but faithfulness, and it is coupled with endurance (*hypomonē*; 2:19; 13:10; cf. 14:12), the combination suggesting also "resistance." The opposite of faith/*pistis*, therefore, is faithlessness (21:8).

Therefore, the sacrificial, liberating death of Jesus is also the faithful, witness-bearing death of Jesus, and it has created a people who are forgiven and liberated by his death in order to share in that death—whether figuratively or literally—as his faithful witnesses. In other words, Jesus' death has created a new-covenant, faithful, cruciform, and missional multinational (5:9) people, a community of kings and priests (1:6), a new people of God in which *all* members have royal and sacerdotal status.[59]

The role of Christ's death—his "blood"—in this is absolutely critical. It is by his blood that Christ "freed us from our sins" (1:5) and "ransomed saints for God" (5:9), and it is by "washing" in his blood that the saints survive the great ordeal, or tribulation (7:14), and are victorious, or "conquer" (12:11). John seems to ascribe a kind of power to Christ's death. It may well be that John wants us to understand that part of the role of the Spirit who continually speaks (2:7, etc.) to the churches is to make the faithful death of Jesus palpably present to the communities so that they replicate the faithfulness of Jesus exhibited in his death.[60] This is certainly a central aspect of "being in the Spirit" in Revelation (e.g., 1:10; 4:2): participating in the ongoing heavenly worship of the slaughtered Lamb (chap. 5) and thereby preparing for ongoing public witness to that Lamb.

---

59. For an interpretation of Revelation as displaying the transition from broken covenant to new covenant by means of the blood of the Lamb, see Campbell, *Reading Revelation*, esp. chap. 7.

60. The close association of the Spirit with the slaughtered Lamb is evident in Rev 5:6.

With good reason, then, Charles Talbert has characterized Revelation as a summons to first-commandment faithfulness.[61] Yet while the vertical dimension of the covenant—loyalty to God and the faithful, slaughtered Lamb—is clearly the emphasis in Revelation, the book does not lack a summons to the horizontal dimension of the covenant. In fact, both dimensions appear to be combined in several places. One such place is the message to Ephesus that criticizes the church for having abandoned "the love [they] had at first" (2:4). Some interpreters think the lost love is love for God, or for both God and others, but in the message the Ephesians' loyalty to and love for God/Christ is evident; they "are enduring patiently and bearing up for the sake of [Christ's] name" (2:3). The love they need to regain, therefore, is for one another.[62]

Similarly, John combines the vertical and horizontal in describing the faithful as those who "keep the commandments of God and hold the testimony of Jesus" (12:17), which is better translated "maintain the witness to Jesus" or "maintain the witness of Jesus."[63] Further, the saints' "endurance" or "resistance" is defined as "keep[ing] the commandments of God and hold[ing] fast to the faith of Jesus" (14:12). David Aune argues that in Revelation "the commandments of God" serves as a summary of the Law's ethical requirements (i.e., the second table). If he is right, as he probably is, then in these two texts, as well as in chapter 2, John describes covenant faithfulness as the inseparable vertical and horizontal practices of bearing faithful witness to and like Jesus (the vertical) and fulfilling obligations of the Law to others (the horizontal).[64] If the faithful Jesus loves (1:5; 3:19), so must his faithful followers. Gordon Campbell's interpretation of the messages in chapters 2 and 3 as "mini-covenants" therefore seems apt.[65]

One last point needs to be made about Revelation. Despite its images of a slaughtered Lamb whose blood effects ransom, liberation, and victory (not to mention its graphic images of divine judgment), Revelation does not—or at least does not intend to—produce a violent people. In fact, just the opposite is the case; the faithful are called to accept suffering and death

61. See Talbert, *Apocalypse*, 11.

62. Commentators are divided on this issue, but they frequently fail to see the connection between love for God and loyalty to God that makes the charge of the Ephesians' lacking love for God unlikely.

63. See Aune, "Following the Lamb," 282.

64. For further treatment of these themes in Revelation, see Gorman, *Reading Revelation Responsibly*.

65. Campbell, *Reading Revelation*, chap. 7.

if necessary, but not to inflict it (13:9–10). The new-covenant people is a community of peace, and specifically of nonviolence.[66]

CONCLUSION TO CHAPTERS 2 AND 3

Our primary goal in the preceding two chapters has been to rediscover the features of a new-covenant model of the atonement in various parts of the New Testament. The basic claim has been that the New Testament writers we have considered view the several aspects of the promised new covenant as having been effected by the death of Jesus. This is not to assert that any or all of these writers had, or could articulate if asked, a systematic doctrine of the atonement that they would label "the new-covenant model of the atonement." Rather, we have found that these writers, in various ways— sometimes deliberately, sometimes perhaps not—interpreted the death of Jesus in senses that correspond to those aspects of the new covenant found especially in Jeremiah and Ezekiel. The prophets expected a new-covenant people who would be liberated, restored, forgiven, sanctified, covenantally faithful, empowered, missional, peaceful, and permanent. The New Testament writers are convinced that Jesus' death created that people.

At the risk of neglecting the differences and distinctives among these writers, we may now summarize our findings, and thus the new-covenant model of the atonement in the New Testament. *Christ's death effected the new covenant, meaning specifically the creation of a covenant community of forgiven and reconciled disciples, inhabited and empowered by the Spirit to embody a new-covenant spirituality of cruciform loyalty to God and love for others, thereby peaceably participating in the life of God and in God's forgiving, reconciling, and covenanting mission to the world.*

I am proposing that this kind of holistic, communal, participatory, missional model of the atonement—incorporating various metaphors for its "mechanics"[67]—reflects the heart and soul of the New Testament and is

---

66. Hays insightfully comments on this issue: "A work that places the Lamb that was slaughtered at the center of its praise and worship can hardly be used to validate violence and coercion . . . As a paradigm for the action of the faithful community, Jesus stands as the faithful witness who conquers through suffering . . . Those who read the battle [or, we might add, sacrificial] imagery of Revelation with a literalist bent fail to grasp the way in which the symbolic logic of the work as a whole dismantles the symbolism of violence" (*Moral Vision*, 185). See further discussion in my *Reading Revelation Responsibly*, especially chap. 8; my "*Shalom* in the Book of Revelation"; and the brief remarks in chapter 7.

67. In the conclusion of the book (chapter 8) we will consider some of these models

precisely what the church needs to appropriate, articulate, and actualize today. At the same time, it is imperative that we be clear that participation in Christ (or in his death) is not a vague, purely "spiritual" term. New-covenantal, participatory love for God and neighbor manifests itself in concrete practices, some of which we have already considered in general terms.[68] It is also worth remembering at this point the poignant words of Augustine: "Anyone who thinks they have understood the divine Scriptures, or any part of them [such as texts about atonement], but cannot with this understanding increase in the twofold love of God and neighbor has not yet understood them."[69]

In the next four chapters, we explore practices of new-covenant faithfulness, love, and peace found in the teaching and example of Jesus and Paul, as well as other New Testament witnesses. That is, we explore more fully the meaning of the Messiah's death and his people's participation in it.

---

in connection with the new-covenant model.

68. On this more generally, see my article "This-Worldliness."

69. Augustine, *On Christian Teaching* 27 (MJG trans.).

—4—

Baptized into the Messiah's Death

New-Covenant Practices
of Cruciform Faithfulness

IN THE PREVIOUS TWO chapters we discovered that there is within the New Testament a widespread presentation of the death of Jesus as that which effects the promised new covenant. The prophets had indicated that the new covenant would be one in which the law of God would be inscribed within the people so that they could and would do God's will. Thus we also first noted at the end of chapter 1 that there is a close relationship in the New Testament between the death of Jesus and the life of the people of the new covenant, particularly the fulfillment of the law's twin covenantal requirements of faith (faithfulness to God) and love, a love that is closely related to *shalom*. That is, the cross is not only the *source*, but also the *shape*, of salvation. Life within the new covenant is participatory, a participation in the event that brought about the new covenant and created the new-covenant people.

But participation can be a vague word. In this chapter and the following three chapters, therefore, we consider some of the concrete practices of the new covenant's participatory discipleship, or cruciform existence, found in the New Testament. In this chapter and the next, we will focus our attention on the Gospel of Mark (on which Matthew and Luke depend)—specifically on the three passion predictions and their corollary calls to discipleship—and on Paul, with some consideration as well of the Fourth Gospel and of other New Testament writings. In this chapter, we explore some introductory issues before examining new-covenant faithfulness: cruciform witness to the gospel, even to the point of suffering.

BAPTISM AND OTHER IMAGES OF PARTICIPATION IN JESUS' DEATH

Why should we speak at all about "participation" in Jesus' death? Wouldn't a word like "imitation" (of his death) suffice? One main reason is the language we find in some parts, at least, of the New Testament. First of all, the metaphor of *baptism* into Jesus' death vividly captures the reality of new-covenant participation, the relationship between cross and covenant, between death and discipleship:

> [35]James and John, the sons of Zebedee, came forward to him and said to him, "Teacher, we want you to do for us whatever we ask of you." [36]And he said to them, "What is it you want me to do for you?" [37]And they said to him, "Grant us to sit, one at your right hand and one at your left, in your glory." [38]But Jesus said to them, "You do not know what you are asking. Are you able to drink the cup that I drink, or be baptized with the baptism that I am baptized with?" [39]They replied, "We are able." Then Jesus said to them, "The cup that I drink you will drink; and with the baptism with which I am baptized, you will be baptized; [40]but to sit at my right hand or at my left is not mine to grant, but it is for those for whom it has been prepared." (Mark 10:35–40)

> [1]What then are we to say? Should we continue in sin in order that grace may abound? [2]By no means! How can we who died to sin go on living in it? [3]Do you not know that all of us who have been baptized into Christ Jesus were baptized into his death? [4]Therefore we have been buried with him by baptism into death, so that, just as Christ was raised from the dead by the glory of the Father, so we too might walk in newness of life. [5]For if we have been united with him in a death like his, we will certainly be united with him in a resurrection like his. [6]We know that our old self was crucified with him so that the body of sin might be destroyed, and we might no longer be enslaved to sin. [7]For whoever has died is freed from sin. [8]But if we have died with Christ, we believe that we will also

live with him. [9]We know that Christ, being raised from the dead, will never die again; death no longer has dominion over him. [10]The death he died, he died to sin, once for all; but the life he lives, he lives to God. [11]So you also must consider yourselves dead to sin and alive to God in Christ Jesus. (Rom 6:1–11)

The Romans passage reminds us that another metaphor for baptism into Jesus' death, at least for Paul, is dying with Christ, specifically being crucified with him (Rom 6:5, 6, 8), which we find also in Gal 2:19–20:

[19]For through the law I died to the law, so that I might live to God. [20]I have been crucified with Christ; and it is no longer I who live, but it is Christ who lives in me. And the life I now live in the flesh I live by faith in the Son of God, who loved me and gave himself for me.

The image of co-crucifixion, in turn, brings us back to the synoptic accounts of Jesus summoning his disciples to take up their cross:

[34]He called the crowd with his disciples, and said to them, "If any want to become my followers, let them deny themselves and take up their cross and follow me. [35]For those who want to save their life will lose it, and those who lose their life for my sake, and for the sake of the gospel, will save it. (Mark 8:34–35; cf. Matt 16:24–25; Luke 9:23–24)

Although these images, or metaphors, of participation—baptism, co-crucifixion, taking up one's cross—are not pervasive in the New Testament, I would suggest that they powerfully and accurately capture the overall spirit of the diverse New Testament witnesses. Moreover, the images are themselves quite open-ended and even generative, useful for theological reflection beyond the significance they bore in their original contexts (though even there, they are already rather open and generative). The kinds of death suggested by the metaphors are quite wide-ranging, from literal suffering and death to more metaphorical deaths like the death of the self, referring to the termination of certain practices or desires. They also imply a willingness to suffer and die, rather than kill.[1] In addition, such metaphors are not as moribund as they might at first sound. In each of the texts cited above, participation in the death of Jesus is linked in some way (metaphorical or literal) to participation in his resurrection or glory, which may take place in the present and/or in the future.

---

1. For a contemporary exploration of the gospel's inherent rejection of killing and embrace of faithful dying, see York and Barringer, *A Faith not Worth Fighting For.*

The terms "cruciform" and "cruciformity" are often, and rightly, associated with Paul.[2] In chapter 2, however, we noted that, according to the Synoptic Gospels, Jesus calls his disciples to a life of "taking up their cross" (Mark 8:34, cited above, and parallels) that is analogous to his own death, a passion-shaped vocation that can therefore also be termed "cruciform existence" or "cruciformity." We also noted that this cruciform existence, as stated by Jesus in connection with the three predictions of his suffering and death, consists of three fundamental types of practices: (1) self-denial—losing oneself as the path to finding oneself—in witness to the gospel (Mark 8:31–34 and parallels); (2) hospitality to the weak and marginalized, represented by children (Mark 9:31–37 and parallels); and (3) service to others rather than domination (10:32–45 and parallels), all with the possibility of suffering (Mark 13:9–13 and parallels). These practices represent the two tables of the Law, now re-imagined through the lens of the Messiah's death, with (1) corresponding especially to faithfulness to God, and (2) and (3) corresponding especially to love for others.[3] At many levels the nature of this cruciform existence is paradoxical, not least in the very notion that the life of the living should take the form of dying, which is life-giving.

In the remainder of this chapter and in the next, we will explore each of these three types of practices enjoined by Jesus in the gospels (basing our work primarily on Mark) and their counterparts in Paul and elsewhere in the New Testament. As for Jesus in the gospels, so also especially for Paul, whose constant participation in the death of Jesus paradoxically means life for himself and especially others (e.g., 2 Cor 4:8–12). Paul's spirituality of Spirit-enabled conformity to Christ crucified includes the summons to embody Jesus' threefold call: (1) bearing faithful witness even to the point of suffering; (2) identifying with the weak as an expression of God's cruciform wisdom and power; and (3) lovingly, as a servant, seeking the benefit of others rather than self. In sum, Paul's spirituality of participation in the death of Christ is congruent with—indeed fundamentally the same as—Jesus' call to cross-shaped discipleship. In addition to considering the connections between Jesus in the gospels and Paul, we will also note the same or similar themes in other New Testament witnesses.

---

2. See especially Gorman, *Cruciformity.*

3. At the same time we must stress again that these vertical and horizontal dimensions of life in the new covenant are inseparable from each other, and that together they are inseparable from peace and nonviolence.

By following the three passion predictions, I do not mean to suggest that the three themes contained in their corollary summonses exhaust the meaning of participatory discipleship in the New Testament. Quite the contrary, in fact: these themes refer to central and non-negotiable practices for the community formed by Jesus' death, but like the generative metaphors with which they are associated, these themes—and the texts in which they are on display—should be the beginning, rather than the end, of serious grappling with the practical connections between cross and new covenant.

Before beginning our consideration of these three practices and the various texts, we should pause for a brief consideration of some aspects of the relationships among the gospels, Jesus, Paul, and the other New Testament writers.

JESUS, THE GOSPELS, AND THE REST OF THE NEW TESTAMENT

Jesus versus Paul?

Frank Matera's important book on ethics in the New Testament bears a subtitle that is a fitting summary of the New Testament: "The Legacies of Jesus and Paul."[4] A natural question arising from this characterization is whether and how these two figures and their legacies are in sympathy or in conflict. Interest in the connection between Jesus and Paul, and between the gospels and Paul—two related but not synonymous topics—has been experiencing something of a revival recently. This may be partly driven by concern in certain quarters that while Jesus preached and practiced a radical and inclusive reign of God, Paul altered and restricted that message.[5] The difficulty, of course, is that our access to Jesus is more indirect than it is for Paul, since we only have writings *about* Jesus, not *by* him. We will return to this problem below.

One significant area of interest in the discussion about Jesus and Paul is the topic of the freedoms and demands associated with the offer of salvation—that is, ethics and, specifically, ethical behaviors, or practices. In the Bible behaviors or practices are never discussed or demanded in a vacuum.

4. Matera, *New Testament Ethics*.

5. See Kirk, *Jesus Have I Loved, but Paul?* For the scholarly discussion, see, for example, Still, *Jesus and Paul Reconnected*; Dunn, *Jesus, Paul, and the Gospels*; Bird and Willitts, *Paul and the Gospels*.

They are always part of a relational, or covenantal, framework. As the initiator of the covenant, God makes both promises and demands within that covenant, as we have seen in previous chapters. The people with whom God covenants make promises in return, particularly promises to fulfill the demands of the covenant. These promises, especially within the framework of the *new* covenant, can be fulfilled (and can only be fulfilled) by the power of God's Spirit. We therefore should refer to the practices the people of God promise to fulfill as covenantal practices, or new-covenantal practices.

Cruciformity as a Potential Key Connection between Jesus and Paul

Despite its potential significance, the cruciform connection between Jesus and Paul has received insufficient attention (especially among scholars[6]), normally only mentioned briefly in discussing this or that text rather than viewed as a fundamental link. We begin, therefore, with a brief review of two scholarly hints at the significance of this connection.

A recent helpful contribution to the Jesus–Paul question comes from James Dunn.[7] He posits three major continuities between (the historical) Jesus and Paul: (1) the openness of God's grace, (2) eschatological tension and the Spirit, and (3) the love command, specifically in relation to the Law.[8] While each of these has ethical implications, only the last is specifically ethical in focus. Dunn concludes that "*Paul drew his attitude to the Law from Jesus,*" that "*nowhere is the line of continuity and influence from Jesus to Paul clearer than in the love command,*" and that both Paul and Jesus "summed up the whole law" in the love command and used it "to discern the commandments that really mattered."[9]

Dunn is certainly on to something important here, but he does not tell us much about the nature, or content, of this love command. Nor, curiously, does Dunn connect this ethical theme materially to Jesus' death.[10] In the

---

6. Non-scholars tend to intuit these connections between Jesus and Paul in ways that scholars often, somehow, fail to perceive.

7. Dunn, *Jesus, Paul, and the Gospels.*

8. Ibid., 95–115.

9. Ibid., 114–15; emphasis original.

10. Dunn does note that for Paul (Rom 8:4) the purpose of Christ's death was so that the Law might be fulfilled in believers (ibid., 113). He also briefly links Jesus' death to the first two continuities, but only in discussing Paul (103–4, 108)—not Jesus. Elsewhere, however, Dunn makes it clear that Jesus expected his disciples to be marked, as he himself was, by service and suffering (*Jesus Remembered*, 560–62), and that Jesus could

conclusion to his book on New Testament ethics, however, Frank Matera begins to make the connection that Dunn, at least here, fails to note.[11] Matera offers seven themes as a synthesis of the enduring ethical legacy of Jesus and Paul, their common "soteriological ethic."[12] The fourth theme is this: "The personal example of Jesus and Paul instructs and sustains believers in the moral life."[13] At the core of this theme is not merely the *form* of imitation but its *substance*: as Jesus called the disciples to follow him, which includes following him in his manner of dying, Paul called believers to follow Jesus by "entering into the mystery of his death and resurrection,"[14] as Paul himself had done. In other words, an essential component of the material continuity between Jesus and Paul is cruciformity (my term, not Matera's)—conformity to the pattern of the Christ-story told in both the gospels and the Pauline letters.[15]

Matera's sixth theme connecting Jesus and Paul is "love"—for God, neighbor, and enemy, meaning Godlike mercy and compassion (for Jesus), and Christlike self-sacrifice as manifested on the cross (for Paul).[16] A bit surprisingly, Matera does not posit here a connection between cruciformity and love in Jesus, though the overall argument of the book suggests that he does actually make that connection.[17]

In this book I suggest not only that there is a cruciform thread connecting Jesus to Paul, but that the same kind of thread connects Jesus to much of the rest of the New Testament.

The Nature, Purpose, and Authenticity of the "Passion Predictions"

The three "passion predictions" in Mark's gospel (with parallels in Matthew and Luke), as they are usually called, are followed by misunderstanding on

have expressed the language of suffering, at least, in the image of crucifixion (561n86). Once again, however, although Dunn believes that for Jesus love is "the motivating force for disciples' relations with others" (589), he does not explicitly connect love with either service or suffering.

11. Matera, *New Testament Ethics*, 248–55.

12. Ibid., 249.

13. Ibid., 252.

14. Ibid., 252.

15. Ibid., 252.

16. Ibid., 254–55.

17. For example, Matera interprets Jesus' self-giving service and ransom in Mark (Mark 10:45) as the supreme example of Jesus' compassion (ibid., 34).

the part of the disciples and then corrective teaching by Jesus about discipleship in light of his own fate.[18] This combination of passion prediction and summons to passion-shaped discipleship is so consistent (especially in Mark), and so indicative of the inseparability of Christology and discipleship for the synoptic evangelists, that two conclusions seem to follow.

The first conclusion is that each of these texts should be referred to not merely as a "passion prediction" but as a "passion prediction-summons," meaning a call to passion-shaped discipleship, or, in a word, cruciformity.[19] The key point here is the substantive correlation between the form of Jesus' death and the shape of the disciples' life, with each being paradoxical.[20]

The second conclusion, perhaps a bit more controversial in some scholarly circles, is that Mark—no matter how creative or insightful a storyteller-theologian he was—is probably portraying something inherent to the message of Jesus himself. The following summary of a line of argument for this claim (which cannot be justified at any length here) may be helpful:

1. Diverse authors and expressions of early Christianity associated Jesus' death with the demands of discipleship (e.g., apart from the gospels, Heb 12:1–2; 1 Pet 2:18–25; 3:17–18; 1 John 3:16; Rev 2:10, 13 [with 1:5]; and of course Paul).

2. Mark bears witness to the early Christian conviction that this association between Jesus' death and discipleship goes back to Jesus himself.

3. Matthew and Luke, who each (probably independently) took up Mark's death-and-discipleship theme, confirm the appropriateness of Mark's attributing its origin to Jesus.

4. The putative Q source may also have preserved an independent death-and-discipleship saying of Jesus in Luke 14:27//Matt 10:38.[21]

18. There are also passion predictions in John's gospel, but they are linked primarily to soteriology (drawing all people to Jesus) rather than to discipleship (e.g., John 3:14; 8:28; 12:32–33) The connections of Jesus' death to discipleship are made in the discourse(s) in John 13–17, as noted in chapter 2.

19. Although the verb "crucify" appears in Mark only in the passion narrative, it is clear from 8:34 that the means of Jesus' predicted death will be crucifixion, and this almost certainly goes back to Jesus himself (see below).

20. See especially Santos, *Slave of All*, with a detailed discussion of our texts (145–212). Matera rightly notes that in Mark the "key to unlocking this paradoxical reasoning" about discipleship lies in adopting God's point of view about Jesus as suffering Messiah (*New Testament Ethics*, 22).

21. So Marcus, *Mark 8–16*, 616, and many interpreters, though the texts may be just restatements of Markan material or a distinct oral tradition.

5. John also preserves the connection, linking it specifically to love (13:1, 34–35; 15:12–13).

6. By virtue of the criterion of multiple attestation, then, the origin of this connection in Jesus is quite plausible. *The remembered Jesus, or better, the remembered-and-narrated Jesus—who is the only Jesus about whom we have direct knowledge—is consistently the Jesus who connects his cross to that of his disciples.*

7. Moreover, it is historically quite plausible that Jesus expected his own death by crucifixion as the consequence of his own mission to redeem Israel, his being perceived by the Jewish authorities as a religious and political threat, and his being perceived by the Roman authorities as a political threat.[22]

8. It is also quite plausible that once Jesus came to this realization, he began to summon his followers to participate in this aspect of his vocation, just as he had earlier summoned them to participate in his mission of preaching, healing, and exorcising.

9. By the time of Jesus, "taking up one's cross" was possibly already an idiom for self-consecration to the point of death.[23]

Jesus and New Testament Theology

Our working assumption, therefore, is that Jesus himself most likely expected his own death and called his disciples to follow him in a kind of death-like life. I have devoted space to this issue because of the significance of the topic before us. It is certainly possible that I am wrong and that someone in the early church first made the connection between Jesus' death and discipleship, and if so, so be it. The connection would have then made its way into the Jesus tradition and into the gospels, with one or the other (or perhaps both) influencing and/or being influenced by Paul and perhaps other New Testament writers. (Reconstructing that maze of interrelationships, however, would probably be impossible.) From the perspective of

22. See, e.g., Evans, "Did Jesus Predict His Death and Resurrection?" Evans stresses Jesus' own self-understanding as a martyr. He believes that the call to cross-like discipleship came early in Jesus' ministry, after the death of John the Baptist, but the prediction of his own death only after he arrived in Jerusalem to die. That Jesus separated these two, predicting his own death only at the very end, seems highly unlikely.

23. Marcus, *Mark 8–16*, 617.

New Testament *theology*, what ultimately matters is the contribution (and, in some sense at least, the coherence) of the New Testament *writings*. Nonetheless, if one is proposing a new model of the atonement, one would hope—and would probably argue!—that it is consistent with the teachings of Jesus.[24]

The line of argument about the passion predictions offered above still allows for the possibility that the early church shaped the teachings of Jesus they remembered (e.g., the addition of precise details from the passion narrative, as in Mark 10:33–34, or of interpretive glosses, such as "daily" in Luke 9:23). It also allows for the possibility that Mark creatively brought together, for his theological narrative, Jesus' passion predictions and Jesus' summonses to cross-shaped discipleship. If Mark did so, however, I suggest that he was almost certainly constructing a literary narrative that was faithful to the intentions of Jesus. Similarly, this argument also allows for the possibility that Paul or other figures had some effect on the content and structure of Mark.[25]

In the discussion that follows I will refer to "Jesus" rather than "Mark" or even "the Markan Jesus," meaning the Jesus remembered and narrated by Mark (and similarly for the other evangelists as they are discussed). I do this in part because of the argument I have just outlined, in part out of respect for the evangelist himself, who clearly wants us to think/know that Jesus is the source of the summons to discipleship in the way of the cross. At the very least, as we will see, there is significant similarity between Mark (as well as Matthew and Luke, to the degree they use Mark) and Paul, in particular,[26] but also between Mark and other parts of the New Testament,

24. In considering the sayings attributed to Jesus, I have chosen to focus on the passion predictions rather than the theme of the new covenant because the amount of relevant text to examine is slightly larger. But of course one could also attempt to make an argument for the authenticity of Jesus' references to the covenant/new covenant.

25. There was undoubtedly movement in both directions, a reciprocity of influence, so to speak. If others think the flow is largely in reverse (i.e., Paul to Mark to the remembered/narrated Jesus), there will obviously be significant differences in historical reconstruction, but we will be able, theoretically, to agree on the congruity. (We must also keep in mind, of course, that the remembered Jesus who speaks in the New Testament is also the *translated* Jesus.) For a balanced treatment of the influence of the Jesus tradition on Paul, see Thompson, *Clothed with Christ*.

26. Although Joel Marcus lists numerous important parallels between Mark and Paul (*Mark 1–8*, 73–75), including their common stress on "Jesus' crucifixion as the apocalyptic turning point of the ages" (74), surprisingly he does not mention cruciform existence. Bøe, on the other hand, concludes that cross-bearing in Luke resonates loudly and clearly with the Pauline theme of cruciformity (*Cross-Bearing in Luke*, 223–26).

with respect to the three themes we will consider. Of particular interest, later in the chapter, will be the way Jesus is remembered and represented in the Gospel of John.

THE FIRST PASSION PREDICTION–SUMMONS: CRUCIFORM WITNESS TO THE GOSPEL

Jesus (as Remembered and Narrated by Mark)

The dialogue that prompts Jesus' first passion prediction in Mark and its corollary summons to discipleship (Mark 8:31—9:1) concerns his identity and, implicitly, the identity and character of the Messiah (8:27–30).[27] Peter's confession of Jesus as the Messiah (v. 29) leads Jesus to order the disciples to keep silence concerning his messianic identity before teaching them about the character of his messiahship (v. 30). Although Jesus does not explicitly accept the title "Messiah," it is clear from the context that he is both accepting and redefining that role. His messiahship will be one of suffering and death before resurrection, shame before honor; in fact, the command to silence probably gives voice to his refusal to pursue honor.[28] The power of exorcisms, healings, and other works narrated in the first half of the Gospel will be largely transformed into the powerlessness of shame, suffering, and death anticipated and finally narrated in its second half.

It is clear, too, that the disciples' acknowledging Jesus as the Messiah will require a dramatic intellectual and personal conversion. The narrative in 8:31—9:1 moves (as also in the subsequent passion prediction-summonses) from (1) passion prediction to (2) misunderstanding to (3) corrective teaching and call to discipleship. The intellectual transformation the disciples need is a conversion of their imagination[29] about what messiahship entails for *Jesus*, while the personal transformation they need is a conversion of their imagination about what Jesus' messiahship entails for *them*: a conversion of their very lives. Believing in this Messiah—in this *sort* of Messiah—is no mere academic exercise but one with serious, inseparable, and unexpected existential consequences. Indeed, the narrative of this Messiah's mission will become the pattern for theirs; in a very real sense, his story will become their story. As Richard Hays has remarked,

---

27. See also Matt 16:13–28; Luke 9:18–27.

28. See Watson, *Honor among Christians*.

29. I borrow the term from Hays, *Conversion of the Imagination*.

"When we embrace Mark's answer to the question, 'Who do you say that I am?' we are not just making a theological affirmation about Jesus' identity; we are choosing our own identity as well."[30]

The disciples, in other words, are called to "take up their cross and follow" Jesus in a deliberate act, or better, an intentional practice, of re-living his story in new ways in their own situations. The two occurrences of the verb *follow* ("If any want to become my followers, let them . . . follow me") suggest that Jesus is referring to both one's initial decision and one's ongoing life.[31] The specific form of cross-shaped discipleship required in this first prediction-summons is self-denial, even self-abandonment, in witness to Jesus and the gospel, with the possibility of suffering and yet also the hope of salvation for those who embrace the shame of the Messiah's cross:

> [34]He called the crowd with his disciples, and said to them, "If any want to become my followers, let them deny themselves and take up their cross and follow me. [35]For those who want to save their life will lose it, and those who lose their life for my sake, and for the sake of the gospel, will save it. [36]For what will it profit them to gain the whole world and forfeit their life? [37]Indeed, what can they give in return for their life? [38]Those who are ashamed of me and of my words in this adulterous and sinful generation, of them the Son of Man will also be ashamed when he comes in the glory of his Father with the holy angels." (Mark 8:34–38)

The summons is not "'a counsel of perfection' addressed to a spiritual elite but the apocalyptically realistic advice that, for *everyone*, life is *only* to be found in treading the pathway of death."[32]

This call to self-denial and self–abandonment—"a living death"[33]—is offered as the antithesis of attempts at self-preservation and self-advancement that, ironically, yield just the opposite. The parallel phrases "for my sake" and "for the sake of the gospel" (v. 36), together with the mention of shame vis-à-vis the words of Jesus (v. 38), suggest a context of public testimony (of word or deed or both), that either bears glad and faithful witness to, or else denies, the teaching, ministry, and messiahship of Jesus that constitute the "good news." This denial, in the interest of self-preservation,

---

30. Hays, *Moral Vision*, 79. We might substitute the words "Jesus' and Mark's answer" for Hays's "Mark's answer."

31. Donahue and Harrington, *Mark*, 263.

32. Marcus, *Mark 8–16*, 624.

33. Ibid., 625.

may refer to active denunciation or to more passive accommodations to social pressures and norms.

The "mutual rebuking contest"[34] between Peter and Jesus (vv. 32–33) suggests that a non-negotiable dimension of faithful witness is embracing the notion, with all attendant consequences, of Jesus as *suffering* Messiah. At the same time, because there is an inseparable connection between Christology and discipleship, this portrayal of discipleship as faithful witness implies that Jesus too was a faithful witness, exemplified above all in his willingness to suffer and die.

Thus we may identify six key elements of cruciformity in the first passion prediction-summons: it has a *christological, narrative* shape with *faithfulness* and *suffering* (rather than *shame*) as its specific ethical content, and a *paradoxical* character of gaining *life through death*. All of these elements are also found in Paul's letters.

Paul

Throughout Paul's letters, faithful witness to Jesus and the gospel, even to the point of suffering, is a prominent theme connected both to Paul himself (and other ministers of the gospel) and to Pauline communities as a whole.[35]

Paul is well known for his references to his own suffering, whether in the form of brief, even cryptic, passing references (1 Cor 15:30–32; 2 Cor 1:8–10), so-called catalogues, or short interpretive narratives. In 2 Cor 4:7–11, for instance, we find a catalogue of sorts merged with an interpretive narrative that describes for the Corinthians the life of Paul and his companions. Paul uses a passive form of the verb *paradidōmi* ("hand over, deliver up") to characterize their ministry: "we are always being given up [*paradidometha*] to death for Jesus' sake" (4:11). Not only is this verb, especially in the passive voice, commonly used in the New Testament of Jesus' deliverance to death, but it appears precisely in the passive voice in two of the three passion predictions.[36] That is, Paul characterizes the apos-

---

34. Hays, *Moral Vision*, 79.

35. In each section of this chapter and the next about Paul, I will begin with, and concentrate on, the undisputed Pauline letters before noting parallels in the disputed letters.

36. Mark 9:31: *paradidotai*, NRSV "is betrayed" (similarly Matt 17:22; Luke 9:44); Mark 10:33: *paradothēsetai*, NRSV "will be handed over" (similarly Matt 20:18; Luke 18:32). Cf. also *paradōsousin*, NRSV "they will hand him over," in Mark 10:33 (similarly,

tolic life of suffering in the same language of deliverance to death that Jesus uses in Mark to describe his passion. The point, for the moment, is not the question of influence but simply of linguistic similarity and substantive congruence.[37]

In a brief reference to his suffering for the gospel as he writes to the Thessalonians, Paul also characterizes his team's missional witness in language with notable similarities to Mark 8: "though we had already suffered (*propathontes*) and been shamefully mistreated at Philippi, as you know, we had courage (*eparrēsiasametha*) in our God to declare to you the gospel (*euangelion*) of God in spite of great opposition" (1 Thess 2:2). Though the three Greek terms highlighted here are not unexpected in their context, it is worth noting that forms of the same words or words with shared roots also appear in Mark 8: suffer (*pathein*, 8:31), courage/boldness (*parrēsia*, 8:32; only here in Mark), and gospel (*euangeliou*, 8:35). That these parallels are more significant than one might initially think will become evident below in the discussion of Philippians.

If 1 Thessalonians is any indication, although Paul worries about his communities when they suffer, he does not find their suffering surprising. Indeed, such suffering is both an emblem of faithfulness to the gospel and an experience of conformity—involuntary imitation, so to speak—to the fate of Jesus, Paul, and other believers (1 Thess 1:6; 2:14–16; 3:3–4).

Matt 20:19).

37. Two additional points need to be made here. First, the absence of this passive verb from the passion prediction-summons in Mark 8, which is more specifically about the disciples' suffering than either Mark 9 or Mark 10, is not of great significance. For one thing, there are passive forms of other, related verbs in Mark 8 (be rejected, be killed in v. 31) to show that this fate is inflicted upon Jesus. For another, and more importantly, Mark 8 is the only prediction-summons that specifically mentions Jesus' suffering (*polla pathein*; v. 31), which becomes the focus of the summons as well as the prediction. If Paul is drawing on the Jesus tradition, he is echoing the tradition's close association of three elements (being handed over/*paradidōmi*, suffering, and death), though perhaps not the precise words that will become the text of Mark 8.

Second, it is possible that Paul's use of *paradidōmi* derives, not from the traditions of Jesus' teaching behind Mark 8–10, but from more generic early Christian traditions of describing Jesus' death with this verb. Paul seems to quote such traditions in Rom 4:25 (passive voice) and 8:32 (active voice, with God the Father as subject/actor), as well as Gal 2:20 (active voice plus reflexive pronoun, with Jesus as the subject/actor and object/recipient; cf. Eph 5:2 and Gal 1:4, which uses *didōmi*). This possibility still raises the question of the genesis of this way of describing Jesus' death. Did Jesus' teaching influence the traditions, or did the tradition shape the way Jesus' words were remembered and/or conveyed?

Paul's expectation that his communities will suffer comes to sharpest expression in Philippians.[38] Writing while in prison (1:7, 13–14), in the first chapter he weaves together his own suffering for Christ/the gospel, its effects both on the advance of the gospel and on his own spiritual condition, and the role of the Philippians as coparticipants both in spreading and in suffering for the gospel.[39]

We have already seen that several key words of Paul's vocabulary for his own suffering echo Jesus' description of his suffering and death in Mark. Similarly, in Philippians (especially in chapter 1, but also later), there are several words and themes that appear also in passion prediction-summons texts in Mark, especially Mark 8. These words and themes refer both to Paul's suffering and to that of the Philippians. The following table illustrates these connections:[40]

Suffering in Mark and Philippians

Word/phrase/theme	*Mark*	*Philippians*
Christ/Messiah	"You are the Messiah (*christos*)" (8:29)	"Christ" (*christos*) 37x in Philippians, 18x in chapter 1 (the highest concentration of occurrences of "Christ/Messiah" in any letter and in any chapter of the Pauline corpus)
Suffering	the Son of Man must undergo great suffering (*polla pathein*) (8:31)	my suffering (*thlipsin*) (1:17) the privilege . . . of suffering (*paschein*) for him as well (1:29) the sharing (*koinōnian*) of his sufferings (*pathēmatōn*) (3:10)[A]
Openness/boldness[B]	He [Jesus] said all this quite openly (*parrēsia*). (8:32)	dare to speak the word with greater boldness and without fear (*tolman aphobōs*) (1:14)[c] my speaking with all boldness (*en pasē parrēsia*) (1:20)

38. 2 Tim 3:12 ("Indeed, all who want to live a godly life in Christ Jesus will be persecuted") also undoubtedly summarizes Paul's perspective; cf. the discussion below.

39. Paul uses both the noun (Phil 1:7; *synkoinōnous*) and the verb (Phil 4:14; *synkoinōnēsantes*) forms of participation/"in common" (the root *koin-*) with the prefix "co-" (Greek *syn*). The same idea appears without the compound word in 1:5 and 4:15; financial participation is the focus of the latter.

40. Superscript letters refer to notes at the end of the table.

Word/phrase/theme	Mark	Philippians
Self-denial[D] Taking up the cross	"If any want to become my followers, let them deny themselves and take up their cross and follow me." (8:34)	Do nothing from selfish ambition or conceit, but in humility regard others as better than yourselves. Let each of you look not to your own interests, but to the interests of others. (2:3–4) he humbled himself and became obedient to the point of death—even death on a cross. (2:8) enemies of the cross of Christ (3:18) by becoming like him in his death (3:10)
Save/gain—lose/forfeit Life Salvation For my [Christ's] sake For the gospel	"For those who want to save their life will lose it, and those who lose their life for my sake, and for the sake of the gospel, will save it. For what will it profit them to gain (*kerdēsai*) the whole world and forfeit (*zēmiōthēnai*) their life? Indeed, what can they give in return for their life?" (8:35–37)	It is my eager expectation and hope that . . . Christ will be exalted now as always in my body, whether by life or by death. For to me, living is Christ and dying is gain (*kerdos*). (1:20–21) my imprisonment is for Christ (1:13) proclaim Christ . . . proclaim Christ . . . Christ is proclaimed (1:16–18) your sharing in the gospel from the first day until now. (1:5) you share in . . . the defense and confirmation of the gospel (1:7) what has happened to me has actually helped to spread the gospel (1:12) I have been put here for the defense of the gospel (1:16) Only, live your life in a manner worthy of the gospel of Christ . . . striving side by side with one mind for the faith of the gospel, and are in no way intimidated by your opponents. For them this is evidence of their destruction, but of your salvation. (1:27–28) Yet whatever gains (*kerdē*) I had, these I have come to regard as loss (*zēmian*) because of Christ. More than that, I regard everything as loss (*zēmian*) because of the surpassing value of knowing Christ Jesus my Lord. For his sake I have suffered the loss (*ezēmiōthēn*) of all things, and I regard them as rubbish, in order that I may gain (*kerdēsō*) Christ (3:7–8)

Word/phrase/theme	Mark	Philippians
Shame[E] Coming	"Those who are ashamed of me and of my words in this adulterous and sinful generation, of them the Son of Man will also be ashamed when he comes in the glory of his Father with the holy angels." (8:38)	It is my eager expectation and hope that I will not be ashamed in any way (1:20)[F] the one who began a good work among you will bring it to completion by the day of Jesus Christ. (1:6) so that in the day of Christ you may be pure and blameless (1:10)

A. Or, more accurately, "the participation in his sufferings."

B. The precise nuance of *parrēsia* in the two texts is debated, but the significance for our purposes is merely the presence of the same Greek word in connection with similar words in both contexts.

C. That which is signified by the phrase *tolman aphobōs* is semantically similar to *parrēsia*.

D. The content of Phil 2:1–4 is more closely linked to the third passion prediction-summons, about non-domination and service, but the notion of self-denial is present in the first prediction-summons, too.

E. Whatever its origin in Christian circles, the theme of "no shame" echoes Isa 52:14; 53:3, 8, as Marcus rightly notes (*Mark 8–16*, 629). Keener suggests that Paul's mention of shame in Rom 1:16 and elsewhere may derive from texts about eschatological shame in Isa 28:16 LXX as well as Isa 45:17; 54:4; 65:13; 66:5 (*Romans*, 26n37). Jesus may have been indebted to the same texts.

F. I have altered the NRSV ("will not be put to shame"), following Ware, *Paul and the Mission of the Church*, 204–5.

What are we to make of all this? It seems highly probable that these two texts (Mark 8 and the letter to the Philippians) are related in some way. At the very least, we must conclude that in multiple ways Paul describes his own life and that of the Philippians in language that is remarkably reminiscent of the words attributed to Jesus in Mark 8. All six of the key elements of cruciformity in Jesus' first passion prediction-summons identified above are emphatically present in Philippians as well. That is, Paul's narrative of both apostolic and ordinary existence in Christ (that is, the community of the new covenant) focuses on the vocation of faithful, bold witness that leads to suffering with and for a suffering Messiah, without shame (cf. Rom 1:16–17; cf. 2 Tim 1:8–12). Such faithfulness to the point of suffering will guarantee the salvation of those who practice it, even if it costs them their life; it is the ultimate gain in spite of being the greatest apparent loss.

We find the theme of suffering for Christ and the gospel also in the disputed letters of Paul. In Colossians and Ephesians, there is a similar emphasis on the benefits of Paul's sufferings to the church (Col 1:24; Eph 3:13). In addition, the Colossians text highlights the participatory nature of Paul's sufferings—"I am completing what is lacking in Christ's afflictions (*thlipseōn*)" (1:24) This does not mean that Christ's sufferings were somehow soteriologically deficient, but that they are not over; Paul's suffering continues Christ's afflictions, as the apostle suffers on behalf of "his [Christ's] body, that is, the church" in his mission work.[41] Second Timothy picks up a theme found in both the gospels and the undisputed Pauline letters—the choice of suffering instead of shame vis-à-vis the gospel: "Do not be ashamed, then, of the testimony about our Lord or of me his prisoner, but join with me in suffering for the gospel" (2 Tim 1:8; cf. v. 12). In 2 Timothy, suffering is not only a regular feature of Paul's own life (1:8, 12; 2:8–13; 3:11; 4:6–7, 16–18), it is a non-negotiable aspect of ministry (2:3; 4:5) and, in fact, of all faithful existence: "Indeed, all who want to live a godly life in Christ Jesus will be persecuted" (3:12). *To be in Christ is to participate in his suffering.*

CRUCIFORM WITNESS ACCORDING TO JESUS AS REMEMBERED AND NARRATED IN THE GOSPEL OF JOHN

In addition to Mark 8 and parallels, which we considered above, there are other texts in the Synoptic Gospels that speak of faithful witness even to the point of suffering, particularly in Mark 13 and parallel passages in various parts of Matthew and Luke (see table below). There are also such texts in the Gospel of John, some of which, as we will see, are quite similar to the synoptic tradition, especially Mark 13 and parallels.[42]

In chapter 2 we briefly noted the theme of persecution in the farewell, or discipleship, discourses in the Gospel of John (John 13–17), in which the

41. Lincoln ("Colossians," 614) says that sharing in Christ's sufferings is "not redemptive but missionary in character." Such suffering will always be part and parcel of faithful witness to the gospel in a hostile world.

42. In the discussion below, we will focus on John 13–17. But John also has additional parallels with the synoptics on the subject of suffering in discipleship, most importantly John 12:25–26 on the subject of loss of life as gain: "Very truly, I tell you, unless a grain of wheat falls into the earth and dies, it remains just a single grain; but if it dies, it bears much fruit. Those who love their life lose it, and those who hate their life in this world will keep it for eternal life." See Mark 8:35 and parallels, plus Matt 10:38–39.

community of the new covenant is being formed. A key text about faithful witness to the point of suffering is found in John 15:

> [18]If the world hates you, be aware that it hated me before it hated you. [19]If you belonged to the world, the world would love you as its own. Because you do not belong to the world, but I have chosen you out of the world—therefore the world hates you. [20]Remember the word that I said to you, "Servants are not greater than their master." If they persecuted me, they will persecute you; if they kept my word, they will keep yours also. [21]But they will do all these things to you on account of my name, because they do not know him who sent me. [22]If I had not come and spoken to them, they would not have sin; but now they have no excuse for their sin. [23]Whoever hates me hates my Father also. [24]If I had not done among them the works that no one else did, they would not have sin. But now they have seen and hated both me and my Father. [25]It was to fulfill the word that is written in their law, "They hated me without a cause." [26]When the Advocate comes, whom I will send to you from the Father, the Spirit of truth who comes from the Father, he will testify on my behalf. [27]You also are to testify because you have been with me from the beginning. (John 15:18–27)

Several features of this text are noteworthy, some echoing themes found in the Synoptics (and elsewhere in the New Testament) but with a unique twist, and some distinctively Johannine. First, the Johannine idiom of suffering includes both "hatred" and "persecution"; this persecution may lead to death (see 16:2). Second, this hatred and persecution come from "the world" (15:18–19; cf. 16:33), which, ironically, is the object of divine love (3:16) and the focus of the mission of both Jesus and the disciples (e.g., 17:18, 23). Third, the world's hatred of Jesus' followers is a logical continuation of its hatred of Jesus and of the Father.[43] There is, in fact, a line of continuity in the dispensing and receiving of rejection, a "chain" of hatred dispensed by the world that moves from the Father to the Son to the disciples. This corresponds, appropriately, to the chain of mission that also extends from the Father to the Son to the disciples, as Jesus prayed to his Father—"As you have sent me into the world, so I have sent them into the world" (17:18)—and then, after his resurrection, said directly to his disciples: "As the Father has sent me, so I send you" (20:21b). Thus the persecution the disciples will experience is a direct result of their missional activity, which is actually not their mission but God's, in which they

43. Cf. John 1:11; 17:14.

participate. It appears, in fact, that Jesus' disciples may be persecuted by the world simply for bearing the name of Christ/the Messiah (15:21).[44] For this reason, in the prayer that concludes the discipleship discourses, Jesus prays, not for his disciples to escape the hostile world, but for them to be protected from "the evil one" as they are in mission to that world (17:11–16). Fourth and finally, the disciples will be gifted with the Advocate, the Spirit of truth, to assist them in their testimony (15:26–27; 16:7).

These major elements, and others, of faithful witness in John may be usefully compared to the Synoptics as follows[45]:

Faithful Witness in John and the Synoptics

Element	John	Synoptics
Hatred/persecution	If the world hates you, be aware that it hated me before it hated you. If you belonged to the world, the world would love you as its own. Because you do not belong to the world, but I have chosen you out of the world—therefore the world hates you. (15:18–19)	and you will be hated by all because of my name (Mark 13:13a; cf. Matt 10:22a; 24:9; Luke 21:12, 17)
Deliverance to and/ or action by authorities, with fate of death	His parents said this because they were afraid of the Jews; for the Jews had already agreed that anyone who confessed Jesus to be the Messiah would be put out of the synagogue. (9:22) Nevertheless many, even of the authorities, believed in him. But because of the Pharisees they did not confess it, for fear that they would be put out of the synagogue. (12:42) They will put you out of the synagogues. Indeed, an hour is coming when those who kill you will think that by doing so they are offering worship to God. (16:2)	As for yourselves, beware; for they will hand you over (*paradōsousin*) to councils; and you will be beaten in synagogues; and you will stand before governors and kings because of me, as a testimony to them . . . When they bring you to trial and hand you over (*paradidontes*) . . . Brother will betray brother to death, and a father his child, and children will rise against parents and have them put to death. (Mark 13:9, 11a, 12; cf. Matt 10:17–18, 21–22; Luke 21:12, 16)

44. In addition to the synoptic parallels listed in the table, see also 1 Pet 4:16, noted below.

45. This table is intended to be illustrative, not necessarily exhaustive.

Element	John	Synoptics
Missional context	I am not asking you to take them out of the world, but I ask you to protect them from the evil one . . . As you have sent me into the world, so I have sent them into the world. (17:15, 18; cf. 15:26–27)	And the good news must first be proclaimed to all nations. (Mark 13:10; cf. Matt 24:14)
For the name of Jesus/the Messiah	But they will do all these things to you on account of my name, because they do not know him who sent me. (15:21)	and you will be hated by all because of my name (Mark 13:13a; cf. Matt 10:22a; 24:9b; Luke 21:12, 17)
Continuity with the treatment of Jesus	If the world hates you, be aware that it hated me before it hated you . . . Remember the word that I said to you, "Servants are not greater than their master." If they persecuted me, they will persecute you . . . (15:18, 20; cf. 12:26a) [T]he world has hated them because they do not belong to the world, just as I do not belong to the world. (17:14)	A disciple is not above the teacher, nor a slave above the master; it is enough for the disciple to be like the teacher, and the slave like the master. If they have called the master of the house Beelzebul, how much more will they malign those of his household! (Matt 10:24–25)
Public testimony	When the Advocate comes, whom I will send to you from the Father, the Spirit of truth who comes from the Father, he will testify on my behalf. You also are to testify because you have been with me from the beginning. (15:26–27)	and you will stand before governors and kings because of me, as a testimony to them (Mark 13:9b; Matt 10:18b, 32–33; 24:14; Luke 21:13)
Endurance and ultimate vindication/salvation	In the world you face persecution. But take courage; I have conquered the world! (16:33b)	But the one who endures to the end will be saved. (Mark 13:13b; cf. Matt 10:22b, 32–23; 24:13; Luke 12:8–9; 21:19)

Element	John	Synoptics
Assistance of Spirit, divine protection, no need for fear	Peace I leave with you; my peace I give to you. I do not give to you as the world gives. Do not let your hearts be troubled, and do not let them be afraid. (14:27) When the Advocate comes . . . he will testify on my behalf. (15:26) I have said this to you, so that in me you may have peace. (16:33a) [Holy Father,] I am not asking you to take them out of the world, but I ask you to protect them from the evil one. (17:15; cf. 17:11b–12)	do not worry beforehand about what you are to say; but say whatever is given you at that time, for it is not you who speak, but the Holy Spirit (Mark 13:11; cf. Matt 10:19–20; 24:19–20; Luke 21:14–15; see also Matt 10:26, 28, 31; Luke 12:4, 7b)

It is beyond the scope of this chapter to try to explain the relationships among these various texts, though I suspect that all of the evangelists are drawing on common traditions passed down from Jesus in the earliest churches.[46] The point of the table is simply to demonstrate the general coherence among all four Gospels concerning the possible, and perhaps even inevitable, fate of those who follow Jesus faithfully. Perhaps the key to these traditions is the significance of bearing "the name," which means sharing in the identity of the one whose name is borne. *Because Jesus' disciples' identity is a participation in his identity, represented in the bearing of his name, they will also participate in his fate—his rejection, suffering, and death. Or, to put it in narrative terms, his story will become their story.* It is sharing Jesus' cup (Mark 10:39; 14:23 and parallels), participating in his sufferings (Phil 3:10; cf. 2 Cor 1:5, 7). The only remembered-and-narrated Jesus in the canonical Gospels is the Jesus who invites participation in his faithful fate.

CRUCIFORM WITNESS TO THE GOSPEL ELSEWHERE IN THE NEW TESTAMENT: 1 PETER, HEBREWS, REVELATION

Suffering for the gospel also figures prominently in three other New Testament documents, 1 Peter, Hebrews, and Revelation, each of which we will consider briefly.

46. New Testament scholars are beginning once again to take oral tradition seriously for our understanding of early Christian life and the emergence of the earliest Christian documents. See, e.g., Dunn, *The Oral Gospel Tradition.*

Cruciform Faithfulness in 1 Peter

The theme of suffering pervades 1 Peter.[47] The letter's recipients have "suffer[ed] various trials" (1:6), which are clearly the result of their Christian witness, perhaps simply for bearing the name "Christian" (4:16), i.e., having their identity defined by Jesus the Christ. The writer (we will call him "Peter") starts the letter with a double interpretation of this experience: that it is a test of their faith(fulness), and that it will end with the (second) coming of Christ, when they receive their reward, the fullness of salvation (1:6–10). According to 1 Peter, Udo Schnelle writes, faith is "faith-under-attack . . . faith that remains steadfast in trouble and consequently receives salvation."[48]

But Peter cannot and does not leave it there. Instead, he introduces a thick christological interpretation of their suffering with two major elements: Christ is the exemplar of suffering unjustly, and Christ's suffering was followed by glory. In other words, the story of Christ offers both the *paradigm* for the manner in which his people should suffer and the *promise* concerning suffering's consequences. The letter's recipients, who bear the name of the Messiah, are inscribed into the Messiah's story—in its entirety of both suffering and glory.

The narratival ethic is presented at some length in 2:18–24 and in 3:8–20.[49] Most importantly, Peter presents Christ as the exemplary recipient of suffering and as the exemplary respondent to suffering (2:21; *hypogrammon*; NRSV, "example"; cf. 4:1). Proper, or righteous, suffering is that which is unmerited and thus unjust (2:19–20, 22; 3:14, 17–18), and the proper response to such suffering is non-retaliation and even blessing toward the perpetrators (2:23; 3:9), as well as trust in God (2:23).

The narratival promise is stated implicitly in 1:11—the prophets had "testified in advance to the sufferings destined for Christ and the subsequent glory"—and explicitly in 4:13: "But rejoice insofar as you are sharing (*koinōneite*) Christ's sufferings,[50] so that you may also be glad and shout for joy when his glory is revealed" (cf. 5:10). The latter text reminds us that

47. See also, e.g., Green, *1 Peter*, 225–28, and Schnelle, *Theology of the New Testament*, 603–17, on 1 Peter's theology of suffering.

48. Schnelle, *Theology of the New Testament*, 610.

49. Space does not permit an exegetical or theological discussion of the difficulties surrounding the connections between unjust suffering and slavery in 1 Peter 2, or abuse more generally. The key point for 1 Peter is that the suffering addressed here is suffering for one's Christian identity and witness.

50. See also Phil 3:10, noted above.

for Peter, as for Paul and for Jesus (at least in Mark), faithful suffering for Christ is not merely imitation, it is participation, "an inner link with the suffering Christ."[51] This faithful participation in, or obedience to, Christ is made possible by the Spirit (1:2).

For these reasons—sharing in his sufferings now and sharing in his glory in the future—those who suffer for bearing the name of Christ should feel honor rather than shame at this privilege (4:16). In addition, they should recognize that suffering is a normal part of Christian existence, experienced by apostles like Peter (5:1) as well as by everyday Christians elsewhere (5:9).

Cruciform Faithfulness in Hebrews

The letter (or letter-homily) to the Hebrews was almost certainly written to a community of Jewish believers who were being harassed and otherwise mistreated, and therefore being tempted to revert back to their previous, non-Messianic confession and way of life in order to alleviate the suffering. The sufferings seem to have been especially intense in the early days of the community:

> [32]But recall those earlier days when, after you had been enlightened, you endured a hard struggle with sufferings, [33]sometimes being publicly exposed to abuse and persecution, and sometimes being partners with those so treated. [34]For you had compassion for those who were in prison, and you cheerfully accepted the plundering of your possessions, knowing that you yourselves possessed something better and more lasting. (Heb 10:32–34)

Although the recipients of Hebrews are told, "you have not yet resisted to the point of shedding your blood" (12:4), there is serious danger from their perspective, and there is a serious crisis of faith from the writer's perspective. He urges them not to give up, for the day of salvation is coming soon (10:37). To further encourage them, the writer recalls Moses and others who suffered for their faithfulness (11:26, 36). But such pastoral encouragement is insufficient for the occasion, and the writer therefore makes a prolonged argument about the superiority of Christ, the new covenant he inaugurated, and his faithfulness, as we noted in chapter 3.

With respect to the suffering itself, the theological substance of the writer's response is twofold. First, with respect to Christology, he makes

---

51. Schnelle, *Theology of the New Testament*, 617.

several claims. Although Jesus was God's son, he was tested by, and learned obedience through, suffering (2:10; 5:8). His death was the means of salvation for human beings (2:9), and because of his faithful suffering to death he has now been "crowned with glory and honor" (2:9). Moreover, he can now empathize with and assist those who suffer (2:17–18; cf. 4:14–16). In addition, not only did Jesus die a sacrificial death for humanity, but his pattern of glory following death is God's gift to all who have become part of the new-covenant community inaugurated by his death and exaltation (2:10; 12:2). Thus Hebrews has much in common especially with 1 Peter, as well as with Paul.

Hebrews 12:5–11 interprets the believers' suffering in terms of divine discipline. This does not mean that the suffering is punishment but, rather, a means of moral formation, specifically formation into the likeness of the Son, who also suffered in the process of perfection/attaining God's ultimate will for him (Heb 5:7–10). What Hebrews calls, variously, "obedience," "perfection," and "holiness" means covenant faithfulness, specifically fidelity in spite of strong opposition and persecution, even if not (yet) to the point of counting martyrs. Furthermore, Hebrews depicts Jesus, within this context of suffering, as the faithful priest who offered himself in atonement (2:17; cf. 7:27; 9:12, 26; 10:10–14), as the faithful son/servant (3:1–6); he is therefore "the pioneer and perfecter" of faith (12:2), even faith under fire ("hostility"; 12:3).

Second, with respect to salvation, the writer of Hebrews says there can be no turning back from the new (and better) covenant to the old. Suffering, rather than something to avoid at all costs, can be a formative tool of testing, instruction, and perfecting in God's hands, as it was for Jesus (2:18; 4:15; 5:7–9; 12:4–11).[52] The example of Jesus (12:1–3), preceded by many other faithful witnesses (chap. 11), can encourage the suffering to ignore the cultural "shame" and "hostility" they are experiencing and still remain faithful:

> [1]Therefore, since we are surrounded by so great a cloud of witnesses, let us also lay aside every weight and the sin that clings so closely, and let us run with perseverance the race that is set before us, [2]looking to Jesus the pioneer and perfecter of our faith, who for the sake of the joy that was set before him endured the cross, disregarding its shame, and has taken his seat at the right hand

52. Indeed, their suffering may be a form of divine discipline for their own good (12:5–10). Cf. James 1:2–4.

of the throne of God. ³Consider him who endured such hostility against himself from sinners, so that you may not grow weary or lose heart. (Heb 12:1–3)

Faithfulness in Hebrews, argues Matthew Marohl, means a "shared life story." This sharing takes place among three parties: Jesus as the prototype of faithfulness, the audience of Hebrews, and others who have been faithful.[53]

The writer of Hebrews is not afraid to raise the threat of divine anger and disastrous consequences for faithlessness, including the possible permanent loss of salvation (6:1–8; 10:19–39). But he also knows that telling the story of Jesus, and inviting participation in it, has at least equal rhetorical power.

Cruciform Faithfulness in Revelation

The book of Revelation is often associated with suffering and persecution. The older scholarly consensus that Revelation was written for a group of churches under siege by the emperor Domitian has been replaced, for the most part, by a different view of the socio-historical situation. Many scholars today argue that Revelation was written to churches who had experienced some persecution, mostly local, and who were being tempted (perhaps even urged by certain leaders) to accommodate to their local culture in order to avoid persecution.[54] This accommodation seems to have included especially participation in local cultic activity, including (though not limited to) participation in the imperial cult.[55] "The overall message of the seven letters [Rev. 2–3] is to call for sharper boundaries between the church and the world."[56]

We have already considered, in chapter 3, the primary message of Revelation. It is, as with 1 Peter and Hebrews, primarily a christological message in the service of a call to discipleship. The specific angle of Revelation is particularly appropriate to the subject of the first passion

---

53. Marohl, *Faithfulness and the Purpose of Hebrews*, 125–48.

54. This does not mean there was no persecution of the churches addressed in Revelation. In all likelihood John had been sent into exile as a political consequence of his Christian activity (1:9), and Antipas of Pergamum was killed during a time of persecution there (2:13). Moreover, John characterizes the time as a period of persecution (1:9).

55. For further elaboration on this perspective, see my *Reading Revelation Responsibly* and the bibliography referred to there.

56. Hays, *Moral Vision*, 171.

prediction-summons: Jesus the Faithful Witness (1:5; 3:14; 19:11) is the example of faithful witness.[57] He has been rewarded with glory in the presence of God. And, as with Hebrews, there is a host of faithful witnesses who have died rather than renounce their faith. The visions of Jesus in his glory in the heavenly throne room (1:12–20; chap. 5), and of the faithful martyrs and saints also in God's presence (5:8–14; chap. 7; 14:1–5), function, in part, to assure those on earth that they too must and can remain faithful. If they do, they will be similarly rewarded and will have a share in the coming new creation. Practically speaking, this faithfulness will mean avoiding the daily cultural practices (only some of which are normally labeled "religious") that are incompatible with the gospel of the Lamb who was slain.

Revelation is filled, therefore, with the common New Testament conviction that Jesus' faithful witness (specifically to and against imperial power, including imperial violence), and his own path from suffering to glory, constitute the new-covenant paradigm of faithfulness to God. The cross, once again, is both the source and the shape of salvation, as John tells us in the opening of the book: "[Grace and peace from] Jesus Christ, the faithful witness, the firstborn of the dead, and the ruler of the kings of the earth. To him who loves us and freed us from our sins by his blood, and made us to be a kingdom, priests serving his God and Father, to him be glory and dominion forever and ever" (Rev 1:5–6). Those liberated from sin by Jesus' death (the cross as the *source* of salvation) are now shaped into faithful witnesses, even to the point of suffering and death (the cross as the *shape* of salvation). Moreover, John describes the situation that he and his churches find themselves in with the language of participation: "I, John, your brother and fellow participant (*synkoinōnos*) in the tribulation and the kingdom and the resistance that we have in Jesus . . ." (1:9).[58]

Thus Revelation is actually focused less on persecution per se (and *much* less on the alleged events of the imminent last days) than it is on a christologically grounded response to the temptation to accommodate in order to avoid persecution. The key word, then, is witness.[59] The most significant characteristic of the church as the people of God in Revelation is its calling to be a faithful witness (e.g., 2:10; 17:14). This call must be heed-

57. See especially Hays, "Faithful Witness, Alpha and Omega."

58. My translation. Cf. the NRSV: "I, John, your brother who share with you in Jesus the persecution and the kingdom and the patient endurance . . ." The Greek noun *synkoinōnos* is related to the words for co-participation used by Paul in Phil 1:7 and 4:14, and noted above.

59. The next three paragraphs are based on my *Reading Revelation Responsibly*, 131–32.

ed even despite the interrelated pressures of opposition and temptation. Rooted in Jesus the faithful witness, it is exemplified in John the faithful witness now on Patmos (1:9), the martyred Antipas of Pergamum (2:13), and all the faithful witnesses/martyrs now in heaven (6:9–11; 7:13–17; 12:11; 17:6). The call is also highlighted by the parabolic vision of the two witnesses (11:1–13).[60] John's commission to be a Christlike, prophetic, faithful witness is reaffirmed in his vision of eating the bittersweet scroll (10:8–11; cf. Ezek 3:3), but the exiled John then recognizes that God has called others as witnesses, too. Their faithful, prophetic testimony to and among the nations (symbolized by the temple's court of the Gentiles in 11:2) caused them to share the fate of their faithful Lord—both death and resurrection.

The task of a witness is to speak courageously in word and deed, testifying to the truth of God and prophesying against all falsehood that distorts and parodies divine truth. Witnesses offer testimony to the vision of God given them in the hope that others will repent from error and turn to the truth, but their success is measured, not by the quantity of their converts, but by the steadfastness of their testimony. This suggests that the community of the new covenant (i.e., the new faithfulness) should be missional and prophetic, a martyrological community, a gathering of witnesses.[61]

Such a calling is difficult and dangerous, but it carries with it the promise of God's protection in the present and God's reward in the future. The protection, symbolized in Revelation by the ancient practice of sealing (7:3–8; 9:4; contrast the antithetical marks/seals of the beast in 13:16–17; 14:9, 11; 16:2; 19:20; 20:4), does *not* mean that the church avoids temptation and tribulation, but that it is protected from defeat by these inevitable realities. That is, it is and will be victorious—another major motif in Revelation (e.g., 2:7, 11, 26, 28; 3:5, 12, 21; 5:5; 12:11; 21:7).

Those who bear witness to the victory of God and the Lamb will not be able to separate their "vertical" faithfulness from horizontal action. As Richard Hays has eloquently said, "No one can enter imaginatively into the world narrated by this book [Revelation] and remain complacent about things as they are in an unjust world."[62]

---

60. See the succinct but insightful discussion in Bauckham, *Theology*, 80–88.

61. The Greek word *martys* (whence "martyr") means "witness." The entire church, then, is called to be martyrological, and some martyrs will be asked to give up their lives to death.

62. Hays, *Moral Vision*, 183.

CONCLUSION

The main concern of this chapter has been to explore the meaning of Jesus' first passion prediction-summons and its echoes throughout much of the rest of the New Testament. We have discovered a rather consistent message about the nature of giving, and even losing, oneself for Christ and the gospel. This should not surprise us if there is any truth to the claim that the New Testament is a "martyrs' canon"—a collection of writings that functions to sustain the Christian church's faithful witness in times of persecution, and to assure it of the hope of eternal reward for that faithfulness.[63]

Five principal conclusions have emerged, from the variety of witnesses we have considered, concerning the shape of the new-covenant community inaugurated by Jesus' death and baptized into it:

1. Faithful witness to Christ and the gospel is the fulfillment of the covenantal requirement of love, faithfulness, and loyalty toward God.

2. This faithfulness will often result in some form of rejection and suffering.

3. One of the primary roles of the Spirit who was promised by the prophets and given after Christ's resurrection is to enable members of the new-covenant community to bear faithful witness to Christ and the gospel, and to endure suffering—and even death—for that witness.

4. Such faithful witness is inseparable from loving concern for others; indeed faithful witness, and its potential consequences, are often related to such loving concern.

5. Those who participate in the Messiah's faithful suffering and death will also share in his glory.

Thus in this chapter we have looked primarily at the "vertical" component of the new covenant (though, again, it is inseparable from the "horizontal"), which has been clearly and dramatically reconfigured by the faithful death of Jesus the Messiah. Yet it maintains great continuity with the new covenant promised by the prophets, especially faithfulness to the true God and turning from all other possible loyalties, thanks to the empowerment of the Spirit.

We turn in the next chapter to the second and third passion prediction-summonses and in doing so to the more specifically "horizontal" component of the new covenant: cruciform love.

63. Farmer and Farkasfalvy, *Formation of the New Testament Canon*, 42.

$$-5-$$

Baptized into the Messiah's Death

New-Covenant Practices of Cruciform Love

IN THE PREVIOUS CHAPTER we examined certain introductory matters related to the topic of baptism into the Messiah's death and new-covenant practices of cruciformity. We then looked at the first practice, derived from the first passion prediction-summons: cruciform witness to the gospel, or faithfulness—the (primarily) "vertical" aspect of the covenant. In this chapter we continue the examination of these cruciform practices by looking at the second and third passion prediction-summonses, and thus the (primarily) "horizontal" practices of cruciform hospitality to the weak and cruciform servanthood. In a word, we consider cruciform love.

THE SECOND PASSION PREDICTION-SUMMONS: CRUCIFORM HOSPITALITY TO THE WEAK

Jesus (as Remembered and Narrated by Mark and Luke)

The second passion prediction–summons in Mark (Mark 9:30–37[1]) again has the pattern of prediction—misunderstanding—corrective teaching and call to discipleship. The prediction itself is the shortest of the three (v. 31).

1. Cf. Matt 17:22–23; 18:1–5; Luke 9:43b–48.

The narrative intimates that Jesus' prediction of his betrayal, death, and resurrection provokes a dispute among the disciples as to their relative "greatness" (9:33–34). This sequence suggests that the disciples were fixating on Jesus' resurrection and the glory that it would mean for him and them, in a way similar to the narrative in 10:35–37. Embarrassed, when confronted they are silent about their own argumentative quest for power (9:34), so Jesus, somehow aware of the subject of their arguing, sits down to teach them the true meaning of greatness:

> [35]He sat down, called the twelve, and said to them, "Whoever wants to be first must be last of all and servant of all." [36]Then he took a little child and put it among them; and taking it in his arms, he said to them, [37]"Whoever welcomes one such child in my name welcomes me, and whoever welcomes me welcomes not me but the one who sent me." (Mark 9:35–37).

Jesus' embrace of a child is an "enacted parable,"[2] a *mashal vivant*. The child is not an example to be imitated (as in 10:13–16) but a person to be taken care of. "Jesus is not teaching a lesson about being childlike, but speaking to the issue of status."[3] Children in antiquity had little status and significance, especially outside the Jewish world.[4] Although Jews valued children as real human beings who should be cared for, in Greco-Roman culture and law children were not persons but possessions, without legal rights, and were often victims of abortion, infanticide, exposure, and other forms of mistreatment that Jews, and then Christians, condemned. Even Jews, however, did not equate children with adults but ascribed to them a subordinate status and significance. Throughout the ancient Mediterranean world children were most often seen as immature, intellectually weak, and of far less significance and status than adults.[5]

The child in Jesus' enacted parable both represents children as a group ("one such child") and serves as an icon of all the lowly: those who are weak, needy, less honored, marginalized ("Whoever wants to be first must be last of all and servant of all"—9:35b). Since the parable is Jesus' response to

---

2. Marcus, *Mark 8–16*, 681.

3. Boring, *Mark*, 281.

4. On children in antiquity, see Francis, "Children and Childhood in the New Testament"; Bakke, *When Children Became People*.

5. This is not to say that parents had no emotional bonds to their own children, but that children's overall status and significance were largely deferred and utilitarian (e.g., economic promise) rather than present and inherent.

the argument about achieving greatness, which would mean also achieving honor and power, his "upside-down logic"[6] means that greatness, honor, and power are achieved by service to those without honor and power. In a claim that is nothing short of a theological revolution, Jesus proclaims that such hospitality to the powerless is in fact hospitality to him and, ultimately, to God the Father (9:37).[7]

The Gospel of Luke draws particular attention to this aspect of Jesus' ministry and of discipleship. Throughout Luke, not only the child (Luke 9:43–48) but all the weak, all the marginalized become the center of Jesus' ministry, as Jesus takes on the Spirit-empowered mission of God's servant described in Isaiah 61: "'The Spirit of the Lord is upon me, because he has anointed me to bring good news to the poor. He has sent me to proclaim release to the captives and recovery of sight to the blind, to let the oppressed go free, to proclaim the year of the Lord's favor'" (4:18–19). Jesus' disciples are privileged to share in Jesus' ministry (9:1–6; 10:1–20), and they are charged to express this preferential option for the poor in the most mundane activities like feasting (e.g., 14:13, 21)—itself a parable of God's surprising love for the status-impoverished.

This ministry of mercy—compassionate, cruciform hospitality to the most needy—receives no greater expression than the so-called "Parable of the Good Samaritan" (10:25–37). The Samaritan pours himself, his compassion, his time, and his resources into the man left half-dead. For this reason the church fathers were correct to interpret the story christologically and soteriologically as a parable of Christ's loving death on our behalf, for the ministry of the "good Samaritan" is, in fact, a participation in the Spirit-empowered ministry of Jesus.[8] It is a ministry of the new covenant; to "go and do likewise" (10:37) is first of all an imperative to participate in the saving, counterintuitive death of Jesus on behalf of weak and half-dead humanity. As such, it is also an imperative to share, by the Spirit's power, in the merciful character of the heavenly Father (6:36), the one who lifts up the lowly and exalts the humble (e.g., 1:52; 14:11; 18:14). Those who do the same share in the mission of the Father and the Son (e.g., 7:22; 14:13, 21) and thereby become both Christlike and Godlike. The Samaritan is an ap-

6. Marcus, *Mark 8–16*, 681.

7. A similar perspective appears in the parable of the sheep and the goats in Matt 25:31–45. It is predicated on the cultural assumption that receiving the sent one equates to receiving the sender.

8. On the patristic interpretation of the parable, see Roukema, "The Good Samaritan."

propriate dramatic representation of Jesus and God the Father because he, unlike the religious officials, rejects the temptation to *define* the neighbor (10:29) and embraces the occasion to *be* a neighbor (10:36)—to act with divine mercy.

So what does all of this mean for Jesus' disciples? Cross-shaped discipleship has a christological, counterintuitive, and countercultural character that is marked especially by hospitality and service to those without status, which implies a decisive predisposition toward the weak rather than toward the powerful. The normal path to greatness—to power and honor—is replaced by a path to "lastness," a path of downward mobility that takes one, paradoxically, both to greatness and to God.

Paul

If for Jesus the little child both represents children as a group and serves as an icon of all the weak, vulnerable, and marginalized, for Paul the "weak" are both less defined and yet more closely tied to the concrete situations that Paul addresses. For him, "weakness" (*astheneia*) is a polyvalent term, yet he clearly affirms the predisposition toward the weak and low-in-status found in Jesus, grounding this predisposition in the salvific act of God in Jesus, who displayed God's love by dying for the "weak"—the ungodly, the sinner, the enemy (Rom 5:6–10).

This perspective appears already in Paul's earliest letter: "help the weak" (1 Thess 5:14). But we see it most fully developed in 1 Corinthians and Romans. Debate about the precise constitution of groups and/or house churches in Corinth and Rome continues, and cannot be rehearsed here. Resolving the debate, however, is not necessary to highlight Paul's fundamental, Jesus-like conviction: communities of those who are in Christ must attend to, and even give preference to, the weak.

In 1 Corinthians, the exhortation is grounded in the gospel itself, indeed in the self-revealing action of God on the cross; in the Corinthian community; and in the ministry of Paul (1:18—2:5). God is revealed as the one who operates through and among the weak—the weakness of the Messiah's shameful death on a Roman cross, which is indeed "the weakness of God" (1:25); the weakness of the status-poor "nobodies" who make up the majority of the Corinthian community, who are the weak chosen by God (1:27b); and the weakness of Paul's own persona and preaching, an apostle beset by illness, unimpressive oratorical skills, and indeed an overall weakness (2:3; cf. 4:10; 2 Cor 10:10). Both weakness itself and a voluntary predisposition toward the weak are characteristic of God, Christ, and Paul. (On Paul's *choosing* weakness, see 9:22; 2 Cor 11:29). In fact, weakness was, paradoxically, both Paul's source of pride and his source of strength in Christ (2 Cor 11:30; 12:5, 9–10), for God's weakness (according to human estimation) is in fact power (1 Cor 1:18–25).

This taking on of weakness and its corollary preference for the weak must find expression in the Corinthian community, as Paul makes abundantly clear. He applies his practical theology of hospitable, divine, Christ-like weakness to the Corinthians in three major places: (1) his exhortation to the community about caring for the weak in conscience, in response to the controversy about eating meat offered to idols in the temple precincts (8:1—11:1);[9] (2) his excoriation of the community for its neglect of those who are without means and come late to the supper they celebrate (11:17–34); and (3) his discourse on the church's need to give greater attention to the weaker members of the body—those of lesser means, status, or gifts (chap. 12, especially v. 22).

This Jesus-like attitude in Paul is summarized well by Rachel McRae in commenting on the apostle's response to the situation regarding the Lord's supper at Corinth:

> In this community, the new code [of honor] embedded in the banquet reflects Jesus' ethics of service, sacrifice, and substitutionary atonement: "do not seek your own advantage, but that of the other" (1 Cor 10:24). The ritual of the Lord's Supper calls the participants to behavior based on values such as equality, rather than hierarchy; mutual servitude, rather than competition; and humility rather than the upward mobility enshrined in the power structures of the Greco-Roman world.[10]

McRae is apparently alluding to all of the calls to discipleship in the Gospels that are associated with Jesus' death (especially Mark 10), but the application of these principles to the treatment of the weak (those without status), not only in 1 Cor 11:17–34 but also in 8:1—11:1 and chapter 12, is especially reminiscent of the second passion prediction-summons.

Similarly, in Romans appropriate treatment of the weak forms the subject of the lengthiest, and arguably the central, exhortation in the letter, which focuses on the mutual treatment of the weak and the strong (Rom

---

9. 1 Cor 8:7–12 mentions the weak four times.

10. McRae, "Eating with Honor," 180.

14:1—15:13). In that text, Paul assigns the lion's share of responsibility to the strong, who are charged with taking care of the weak (the "weak in faith" [14:1], referring to something like scrupulousness about diet and calendar), grounding his exhortation explicitly in the example of Jesus the servant (15:1-3, 8 [*diakonon*]) and implicitly in the teaching of Jesus about love (13:8-10). The text contains echoes of Phil 2:6-11, which suggests that Paul's ethic of embracing the weak is ultimately grounded not only in Jesus' teaching but also in his actions, culminating at the cross, as we will see again in considering the third passion prediction-summons.

Paul, then, contends that the triune God—God the Father (1 Cor 1:18—2:5), Christ (Rom 5:6; 15:1-3, 8), and the Spirit (Rom 8:26)—has a predisposition toward the weak, a preferential option for the poor in status. The apostle constantly seeks to inculcate the same divine mindset, with its corresponding human practices, in the communities of those "in Christ."

Other New Testament Witnesses: Hebrews, James, 1 John

Somewhat surprisingly, the letter to the Hebrews, which devotes almost no space to "ethics" or concrete practices in its main argument, contains in its final chapter a call to mutual love, hospitality to the stranger, remembrance of the imprisoned and tortured, and sharing of worldly goods (Heb 13:1-3, 16). This suggests a generic concern for the weak, with specific examples of who constitutes the weak: those who could be shunned, forgotten, or neglected.

Not surprisingly, on the other hand, the letter of James—which may have been written by the brother of Jesus[11]—resonates in a major way with Jesus' call to welcome the poor and marginalized, and to honor them, rather than the elite. James begins with echoes of the prophets and Psalms, defining "pure and undefiled" spirituality as that which "care[s] for orphans and widows in their distress" (James 1:27). James then counsels against "acts of favoritism" in the assembly, rejecting preferential treatment for the wealthy in favor of preferential treatment for the poor (2:1-7).[12] Likewise, he urges his readers/hearers to supply the needs of their naked or hungry brothers and sisters (2:14-26). Those who practice such hospitality and generosity "fulfill the royal law" of neighbor-love (2:8) and thereby demonstrate the

11. See, e.g., Johnson, *Letter of James*, 108-23.

12. James also excoriates the rich, in the style of the Old Testament prophets (James 5:1-6).

validity—the "aliveness"—of their faith (2:26). The justified—that is, the members of the new-covenant community—are identified as such by their love for the weak and vulnerable. As for Jesus (and thus the gospel-writers) and for Paul, so also for James: faith and love are inseparable. And that is the case, I suggest, because each of them speaks (though in different idioms) the biblical language of covenant, of the twofold covenantal requirement of love for God and for neighbor.

A similar new-covenant symbiosis of belief in / love for God and love for neighbor, especially the one in need, appears in 1 John: "And this is his commandment, that we should believe in the name of his Son Jesus Christ and love one another, just as he has commanded us" (1 John 3:23; cf. 4:15–16; 5:1–2). The entire document operates from two basic and insepa-rable theological claims: that God is light and that God is love (1:5; 4:8). Loving others is therefore one of the chief "proofs" of living in the light and love that God is, and of being a child of God (2:10; 3:10–16; 4:7–13, 17–21; 5:1). Truthfulness, therefore, involves not merely truthful belief and confes-sion (4:2–3, 15; 5:5, 10) and general obedience (2:5; 5:2), but also truthful practices (3:18–19). These truthful practices embody the self-giving love that God and God's Son expressed on the cross. As in the Gospels (not least the Gospel of John) and Paul, the cross is the motivation and the model of love, and particularly for generosity to those who lack:

> We know love by this, that he laid down his life for us—and we ought to lay down our lives for one another. How does God's love abide in anyone who has the world's goods and sees a brother or sister in need and yet refuses help? (1 John 3:16–17).

> God's love was revealed among us in this way: God sent his only Son into the world so that we might live through him. In this is love, not that we loved God but that he loved us and sent his Son to be the atoning sacrifice for our sins. (1 John 3:9–10; cf. 4:19)

As in the Gospel of John (not to mention Paul), the spirituality of 1 John that makes this hospitality and love for the needy possible is a *par-ticipatory* spirituality, a spirituality of mutual indwelling or abiding (3:24; 4:16).[13] This is captured poignantly in two sentences in particular:

> [W]hoever says, "I abide in him," ought to walk just as he walked. (1 John 2:6)

---

13. See also 2:5–6, 15, 24, 27–28; 3:6, 9; 4:4, 12, 15

> So we have known and believe the love that God has for us. God
> is love, and those who abide in love abide in God, and God abides
> in them. (1 John 4:16)

Francis Moloney and others have pointed out that the author of 1 John,
in comparison to the evangelist in the Gospel of John, actually intensifies
the call for cross-shaped love and gives it a rather sharp, polemical edge.
(Polemic can sometimes be the stimulus for insightful theology; witness
Galatians, too.) This intensification is due, Moloney argues, to the situation of community fragmentation that prompted the writing of 1 John.[14]
This interpretation is probably correct; the circumstances of each New
Testament writing do of course determine the specific form of the teaching
about new-covenant love for God and neighbor. For our purposes, what
matters most is the presence of the theme in 1 John—where it is indeed
both intense and pervasive, with special attention to those in material need.

Conclusion to the Second Passion Prediction-Summons

Jesus' call to participate in his death by welcoming the weak and needy, the
poor, those of low status, is the second distinguishing mark of the new-
covenant, cruciform community. We heard echoes of his call, preserved in
the gospels, Paul, James, and 1 John. In all cases, there is an inseparable link
between love of God and love of the (weak, needy, poor, low-status) other.
To be part of the new-covenant community formed by Jesus' death is to
welcome the lowly into the community.[15]

14. See Moloney, *Love in the Gospel of John*, 192–202.

15. The emphasis in some of the New Testament writings seems to be on welcoming
the needy brother or sister, rather than the outsider. It is probably the case, however, as
implied in Paul's references to "all" (e.g., Rom 12:17–18; Gal 6:10; 1 Thess 5:15), that the
focus on insiders is the non-negotiable starting point, not the end point, of cruciform
hospitality. In some writings, in fact (e.g., Luke–Acts), the outsider is prominent.

THE THIRD PASSION PREDICTION-SUMMONS: CRUCIFORM POWER AS LOVING SERVICE

Jesus (as Remembered and Narrated by Mark and Luke)

The third passion prediction-summons (Mark 10:32–45[16]) contains the most detailed prediction of Jesus' death, corresponding "to a T"[17] to the passion narrative in Mark's Gospel and bearing a certain resemblance to the catalogues of suffering in Paul's letters. The summons includes elements of the first two calls (in Mark 8 and 9) but also has a distinct focus of its own: greatness, or power, as service to others—not only to the weak, but to all. In Mark's narrative, this prediction-summons concludes a series of pericopae on the nature of discipleship, with Peter initiating a sort of preface to the prediction-summons by reminding Jesus that he and his companions have left everything to follow him (v. 28). Jesus in turn promises present "rewards" that ironically include persecutions, prior to the ultimate reward of eternal life in the age to come (vv. 29–30). He then promises a general reward, introducing the theme of paradoxical reversal—"the last will be first"—that is the heart of the third summons itself, in vv. 35–45:

> [35]James and John, the sons of Zebedee, came forward to him and said to him, "Teacher, we want you to do for us whatever we ask of you." [36]And he said to them, "What is it you want me to do for you?" [37]And they said to him, "Grant us to sit, one at your right hand and one at your left, in your glory." [38]But Jesus said to them, "You do not know what you are asking. Are you able to drink the cup that I drink, or be baptized with the baptism that I am baptized with?" [39]They replied, "We are able." Then Jesus said to them, "The cup that I drink you will drink; and with the baptism with which I am baptized, you will be baptized; [40]but to sit at my right hand or at my left is not mine to grant, but it is for those for whom it has been prepared." [41]When the ten heard this, they began to be angry with James and John. [42]So Jesus called them and said to them, "You know that among the Gentiles those whom they recognize as their rulers lord it over them, and their great ones are tyrants over them. [43]But it is not so among you; but whoever wishes to become great among you must be your servant, [44]and whoever wishes to be first among you must be slave of all. [45]For the Son of Man came not

---

16. Cf. Matt 20:17–28; Luke 12:50; 18:31–34; 22:24–27.

17. Marcus, *Mark 8–16*, 743.

to be served but to serve, and to give his life (*dounai tēn psychēn autou*) a ransom for many." (Mark 10:35–45)

There are four key aspects of this prediction-summons to note: (1) Jesus' rejection of the disciples' pursuit of glory for a practical theology of the cross; (2) the participatory nature of this practical theology; (3) the countercultural and paradoxical character of power as service rather than domination; and (4) the triple role of Jesus as the summoner, sacrifice, and exemplary servant.

1. Following the promise of eschatological reward (v. 30), James and John approach Jesus with a request that is "the equivalent of asking Jesus for a 'blank check.'"[18] When Jesus asks them to be specific, their absurd open-ended request becomes restricted to one that reflects both Jewish interest in one's place in the age to come and a broader cultural concern for honor and status (vv. 36–37). Jesus eventually says that he does not have the authority to grant such a request (v. 40), but in the meantime he raises questions that imply a different and prerequisite appointment for his disciples, a sharing in his baptism and cup, that is, his suffering and death (vv. 38–39). Here, as Eugene Boring observes, "'Theology of glory' confronts 'theology of the cross,' and not only as Christology but, as always in Mark, inseparably linked to discipleship."[19]

2. This discipleship, more specifically, is participatory in nature, a sharing so intense that it can only be expressed in the language of liquids (vv. 38–39): that which overtakes from without (baptismal waters) and that which fills from within (the contents of the cup); one that consumes like a flood, one that is consumed. Both images combine a sense of overwhelming power with a sense of profound intimacy. Such is the nature of discipleship with the crucified one.

One of the most significant aspects of this passage, and a point of similarity between Jesus and Paul that has received insufficient attention, is this participatory dimension of passion-shaped existence. In the context of Mark 10, this participation would seem to refer, first of all, to the disciples' literal suffering for Jesus at some unspecified future point (cf. the prediction-summons in Mark 8:34–38). But that does not exhaust the meaning of participation in Jesus' passion; Jesus' words about participation are prompted by, and inseparably connected to, James's and John's pursuit of glory and greatness (vv. 35–40). When Jesus surprises them by saying

18. Donahue and Harrington, *Mark*, 310.

19. Boring, *Mark*, 300.

that he does not have the authority to grant the eschatological glory they desire (v. 40b), he redefines greatness in terms of servanthood (vv. 42–45). What he offers them, in other words, is not a seat of glory but a vocation of service. This constitutes another aspect of participating in Jesus' cup and baptism: sharing in the mindset of greatness as service that will even suffer for others rather than "lord it over [*katakyrieuousin*] them."

Jesus' reference to his baptism and his cup are first of all metaphors, but for Mark's audience and all subsequent audiences, there is clearly an allusion to Christian baptism and Eucharist in these words. Therefore, although the primary referents of baptism and cup are not these practices/sacraments, the images do remind Mark's readers—and us—that both entry into Christ and ongoing life in Christ mean participation in Christ's death.[20] As we will see below, this is precisely Paul's understanding of these practices/sacraments.

3. A cluster of "power" words appears in v. 42, indicating the subject at hand: *archein, katakyrieuousin, megaloi, katexousiazousin* ("to rule," "lord it over," "great ones," and "exercise authority," respectively). To pursue honor at the expense of others, or in any way to dominate them in a quest for personal power, is to act like the Gentiles who do not know God, to borrow Paul's phrase (1 Thess 4:5). It is, so to speak, to "Romanize."[21] The disciples are called to share in Jesus' lordship not by acts of "lording" but by acts of self-giving serving. This, paradoxically, is the path to greatness and "firstness," as Jesus has already said (9:35; cf. 10:31).[22] Whereas in Mark 9 Jesus had made it clear that cruciform service to "all" embraces those of low and no status, even so-called non-persons, here he makes clear that it includes absolutely everyone.

The phrase "it is not so among you" (10:43; i.e., in contrast to the Romans)—is an indicative with imperatival force. It means that discipleship is both generally countercultural and specifically counterimperial. Better put, discipleship forms an alternative way of life to the quest for power and position, the domination and defeat of others, that characterizes "normal" human life, particularly existence in imperial mode.[23]

20. See also, e.g., Donahue and Harrington, *Mark*, 311; Boring, *Mark*, 301.

21. I mean this to echo the verb "to Judaize," associated with Galatians.

22. The form of 10:43b–44 is synonymous parallelism, as in 9:35.

23. Many interpreters have drawn attention to this aspect of Jesus' teaching. Commenting on the Lukan version, which appears in the context of the Last Supper in Luke, Carroll says that "Jesus is grooming the Twelve for leadership of a peculiar, countercultural kind . . . [u]nlike [that of] Rome's emperors and their client rulers" (*Luke*, 438–39).

4. Jesus' words preserved in Mark 10:45—"For the Son of Man came not to be served but to serve, and to give his life (*dounai tēn psychēn autou*) a ransom for many"—summarize all three predictions and interpret them in the two images of sacrifice (ransom; Greek *lytron*) and servant. We will not attempt to settle the complex issues regarding the meaning of "ransom" or the background of the "servant" image.[24] What is absolutely clear, however, is that Jesus sees himself as a self-giving servant and as "the best example of his own ideal of servant leadership."[25] It is likely that Mark intends us to interpret Jesus' servanthood not only as one act, his death, but as his entire ministry, culminating in his self-giving death.[26] Jesus' self-donation is expressed in the language of the giving of his own soul or life (his *psychē*)—the total self-gift.

It is clear both that this self-donation is a unique act, since no one else dies for others' sins, and a paradigmatic act, since self-giving servanthood is expected of Jesus' disciples. To summarize the third prediction-summons in Mark: it consists of both the call to countercultural cruciform service rather than domination, and the grounding of that call in the uniquely salvific, but also paradigmatic, death of Jesus.

Luke's handling of the third passion prediction-summons differs significantly from Mark and from Matthew, who follows Mark in keeping the prediction and the summons together while Jesus is on the way to Jerusalem. Luke, on the other hand, splits the summons off from the third prediction and relocates it at the Last Supper; it becomes part of a miniature farewell discourse (Luke 22:21–38) following the sharing of the bread and cup and the announcement of his new-covenant-forming death.[27] In that discourse, Jesus speaks about his betrayal (a kind of fourth passion prediction, with parallels in Mark and Matthew before the sharing of bread and cup), which leads first to a discussion among the disciples about who will betray Jesus (22:23) and immediately (22:24) into the dispute among them about who is greatest. Following his response to that dispute (22:25–28), Jesus predicts Peter's denial and restoration (22:31–34) and instructs his disciples about preparations for what is about to happen (22:35–38).

24. I should note, however, that I side with those who find Isaiah 53 in the background, including Marcus (see below).

25. Donahue and Harrington, *Mark*, 313.

26. Boring, *Mark*, 302.

27. This is what Luke seems to have done, though of course it is possible that his reason for so doing was his use of an otherwise unknown source narrating what Jesus said and did at the Last Supper.

In this rather surprising editorial move, Luke actually keeps much of Jesus' teaching from Mark intact, even if he famously removes the reference to Jesus' death as a ransom (Mark 10:45). Greatness is countercultural service rather than domination, with Jesus as the paradigm—one might almost say the incarnation (22:27)—of service. There are, nonetheless, several differences, but we need to focus only on two: the location at the Supper and the introduction of the noun "benefactors" to describe Gentile rulers (22:25; *euergetai*)

With this call to discipleship at the Supper, Jesus as remembered and narrated by Luke makes it emphatically clear that this summons to countercultural service is connected to his death; Jesus' "service" on the cross is the paradigm for all of his disciples for all time. Moreover, *not* to embody this kind of service would be a betrayal and denial no less significant than the actions of Judas and Peter. In addition, the phrase "those in authority over them are called benefactors" to explain and amplify the phrase "The kings of the Gentiles lord it over them" (22:25) strengthens the counter-imperial character of Jesus' call to participate in practices that reflect his death rather than in the sorts of practices characteristic of those who are about to put him to death. This is because Hellenistic and then Roman rulers were acknowledged throughout the ancient world, especially within the cult of the rulers (such as various forms of the imperial cult of the first century), as the people's benefactors. Jesus is both challenging and redefining benefaction in light of his own imminent beneficent death. As Peter will say in Acts 10, Jesus is in fact the world's true benefactor (Acts 10:38; *euergetōn* [NRSV "doing good"]), enabled by God's Spirit and power to fulfill that role.[28]

Paul

In considering Paul, we are also struck by both the mandate to cruciform service itself and its basis in Jesus. As with Jesus, we find Paul rejecting the "normal" human pursuit of glory and replacing it with a practical, participatory theology of the cross in which power is exercised—counterculturally, paradoxically, and lovingly—as service rather than domination, with Jesus as exemplary servant.

Joel Marcus has constructed a helpful table of similarities between Mark 10 and Phil 2:6–11, suggesting with good reason that the similarities

28. See further Danker, *Benefactor*. I am grateful to Drew Strait for insights about Luke-Acts and benefaction.

"reflect their common background in Isa 52:13—53:12."[29] Marcus focuses on the common elements of slavery/service, death, and subsequent exaltation. In addition, we should note the similar linguistic phenomena that Mark and Paul use: first, the noun "slave" (*doulos*), and second, parallel verbal constructions that convey self-giving, either "giving one's life/soul" (Mark) or "emptying and humbling oneself" (Paul). The reflexive construction in Paul substitutes for the more Semitic expression used by Mark. Closer analysis of these two phenomena is merited.

We have seen in Mark that Jesus implicitly refers to himself as *diakonos* and *doulos* ("servant," "slave"; 10:43–44). As noted above, Paul calls Jesus *diakonos* (servant) in Rom 15:8, and in Phil 2:7 he characterizes Jesus as *doulos* (slave). Furthermore, although Paul does not use the precise verbal phrase about the nature of Jesus' service (*diakonēsai*; Mark 10:45) that Mark attributes to Jesus—*dounai tēn psychēn autou* ("to give his life")—in Phil 2:7 Paul uses similar, semantically equivalent language when he expresses Jesus' self-giving "incarnation" with a reflexive construction, "he emptied himself" (Phil 2:7; *heauton ekenōsen*). The verb "emptied" is best understood not literally but metaphorically, referring to Jesus' total self-donation, his self-abandonment.[30] Similar in substance and grammatically parallel, but referring directly to Christ's death, is the clause in Phil 2:8: "he humbled himself by becoming obedient to the point of death, specifically death on a cross" (my translation of *etapeinōsen heauton genomenos hypēkoos mechri thanatou, thanatou de staurou*). Together these two reflexive clauses echo the words of Mark 10:45, but with Paul seeing Jesus' self-humbling death as the natural sequel to his self-emptying incarnation.

The full meaning of these reflexive phrases for Paul cannot be ascertained without noting their role in the rhetorical structure of Phil 2:6–8. Here Paul uses a pattern that I have elsewhere described as "although [x] not [y] but [z]," meaning "although [status] not [selfish exploitation] but [self-giving]."[31] Paul is depicting the true meaning of Jesus' lordship as service, and in the larger context of Philippians, he is portraying Christ as the

29. Marcus, *Mark 8–16*, 756. Marcus does not, however, note the shared contrast, explicit in Mark and implicit in Philippians, with Roman imperial power. This sort of contrast with oppressive political power may also be implicit in the historical context of the author of Isaiah 53. Neither does Marcus note the similarities between John 13 and Mark 10 / Phil 2:6–11 (see below).

30. So also most recent commentators.

31. See Gorman, *Cruciformity*, 91, 165–74, 186–88, 192, 197, 230–36, 243, 252, 261, 330.

"lordly example."[32] Though not explicit, the contrast to Roman lords and others who seek to dominate or exploit others could not be more sharply drawn for an audience in a Roman colony like Philippi. Here is a lord who freely but obediently—such is the paradox expressed in the use of the reflexive constructions in combination with the word *obedient*—refuses to lord it over others. As a result, he is vindicated and exalted by God as Lord (Phil 2:9–11)—he is made great.

These parallels among Isaiah 53 (following Marcus), Mark 10, and Philippians 2 have not only christological but also ethical import. As in Mark, also in Philippians Jesus' death as the slave/servant is both soteriologically *unique* and ethically *paradigmatic*. In interpreting Isaiah 53, both Jesus in Mark and Paul in Philippians contend that the Servant-Messiah as well as his disciples will be exalted by God after their voluntary-but-obedient humiliation, which Paul expresses with the reflexive constructions noted above.[33]

On two other occasions, Paul does use a form of the verb *didōmi* ("give") found in Mark 10:45 with a reflexive pronoun to express Christ's self-giving death: (1) "who gave himself for our sins" (Gal 1:4; *tou dontos heauton hyper tōn hamartiōn hēmōn*) and (2) "who loved me by giving himself for me" (my translation of Gal 2:20; *tou agapēsantos me kai paradontos heauton hyper emou*). Like Mark 10:45, each of these clauses from Galatians has two principal semantic parts, one communicating the act of self-giving itself and the other conveying the purpose of the self-giving ("for our sins"; "for me"). These texts should be considered examples of synonymous parallelism, first with each other and then, together, with Mark 10:45.

That all four of these reflexive texts in Paul (Phil 2:7; 2:8; Gal 1:4; 2:20) are often considered to represent pre-Pauline traditions does not diminish their theological significance for Paul. It does strongly suggest, however, that Paul is the recipient, rather than the creator, of the interpretation of Jesus' death as his utter self-donation as a servant/slave. Before the time of Paul, during his ministry, and beyond the time of the apostle, the early Christians perceived Jesus' death this way.

But does Paul see this self-giving service even to death also as an act of love? The answer would appear to be yes. Although Gal 1:4 does not mention love, Gal 2:20 does. In Philippians 2, Paul does not explicitly name Christ's death on the cross as an act of love, but the immediate context

32. Hurtado, "Jesus as Lordly Example."
33. On future exaltation/glory, see Mark 10:40; Phil 3:10, 21.

ensures that Paul understands it this way, for he exhorts the Philippians to adopt the same "mind" and practices as an expression of love (2:1). Here and elsewhere, then (e.g., throughout 1 Corinthians), Paul will transfer this understanding of love to himself and to all who are in Christ. When he does so, he will transfer with it the "although [x] not [y] but [z]" pattern seen in Philippians 2.

Paul's letters indicate that he, like Jesus, saw himself as a servant/slave of others, even to the point of suffering for their salvation and edification. Moreover, in that role, Paul—again like Jesus—understood himself also as a model of servanthood for others. At the same time, Paul clearly perceived his paradigmatic servant role to be derivative: "Become imitators of me as I am an imitator of the Messiah" (1 Cor 11:1; my translation).[34]

For our purposes, perhaps the most significant text about Paul's apostolic cruciformity is 1 Thess 2:5–9. Paul's description of the ministry that he and his colleagues offered the Thessalonians includes a clause with a form of *didōmi* ("give") and of *psychē* ("soul, life"), as well as a form of the reflexive pronoun: "we are determined [or, "we determined"[35]] to share with you not only the gospel of God but also our own selves" (1 Thess 2:8; *eudokoumen metadounai hymin ou monon to euaggelion tou theou alla kai tas heautōn psychas*). The vocabulary suggests a blending of Mark 10:45 and the reflexive *(para)didonai* ("to give [over]") texts in Galatians. In addition, Paul and his co-laborers' renunciation of the pursuit of glory (*doxan*; 1 Thess 2:6) echoes, and contrasts with, the desire for eschatological glory sought by Jesus' disciples (Mark 10:37; *tē doxē sou*). Paul has emphatically abandoned the pursuit of such vainglory (*kenodoxian*, Phil 2:3 NAB; NRSV "conceit").

Two additional aspects of this text are significant. First, Paul makes absolutely clear that this apostolic mode of service was a deliberate renunciation of power, or (better said) an exercise of power *for* others rather than

---

34. For a recent argument that Paul's call to imitation is not an exercise of power but a summons to cruciform service—or "christic embodiment"—see Kim, *Theological Introduction to Paul's Letters*, 109–30. He perceptively describes Paul's understanding of imitation as corporate participation in the love of God demonstrated in Christ's death and, therefore, as a form of "heteronomy" or "rule by others," rather than autonomy (120–21).

35. The context makes it likely that the verb refers to a past, not a present, decision. See the table below.

power *over* them. This is expressed within a form of the "although [x] not [y] but [z]" pattern:[36]

although [x]	though we might have made demands [or "thrown our weight around"] as apostles of Christ (v. 6b) ^
not [y]	we never came with words of flattery or with a pretext for greed; nor did we seek praise [*doxan*] from mortals, whether from you or from others (vv. 5–6a)
but [z]	But we were gentle among you, like a nurse tenderly caring for her own children. So deeply do we care for you that we are determined [or "we determined"] to share [*metadounai*] with you not only the gospel of God but also our own selves [*tas heautōn psychas*], because you have [had] become very dear [*agapētoi*] to us. You remember our labor and toil, brothers and sisters; we worked night and day, so that we might not burden any of you while we proclaimed to you the gospel of God. (vv. 7–9)
A. Brackets with English text indicate preferred alternatives to the NRSV.	

Second, Paul sees this apostolic cruciformity as an act of love. This is clear from the metaphor of the nurse caring for *her own* (*ta heautēs*) children and from the actual language of love that is somewhat masked by the NRSV's "very dear to us" (v. 8; Greek *agapētoi*, "beloved"). It is clear in the context that this self-giving love includes, but is not limited to, the Pauline team's voluntary renunciation of financial support from the Thessalonians and thus their engaging in manual labor (2:9).

Similar in substance is Paul's renunciation of apostolic privilege, especially the right to support, in 1 Corinthians 9, where he once again uses the "although [x] not [y] but [z]" pattern.[37] He also specifically identifies himself as a *doulos* (slave), not by using the noun but by using the verb "to enslave" (*douloō*) with a reflexive pronoun, again transferring the reflexive-pronoun christological pattern we see in the texts in Galatians and Philippians:

36. See also my *Cruciformity*, 192–95. I have constructed the table to reflect the sequence of the pattern, which means that v. 6b is displayed before vv. 5–6a.

37. See also ibid., 181–87.

although [x]	Do we not have the right to our food and drink? Do we not have the right to be accompanied by a believing wife, as do the other apostles and the brothers of the Lord and Cephas? (vv. 4–5)
	For though I am free with respect to all (v. 19a)
not [y]	Nevertheless, we have not made use of this right (v. 12b)
	But I have made no use of any of these rights (v. 15a)
but [z]	but we endure anything rather than put an obstacle in the way of the gospel of Christ. (v. 12c)
	I have made myself a slave to all (*pasin emauton edoulōsa*; "I have enslaved myself to all" [MJG]), so that I might win more of them. (v. 19b)

It also appears that Paul has once again blended the "although . . ." and the reflexive patterns with an allusion to Jesus' passion prediction-summons by indicating that his slavery is "to all" (*pasin*; cf. "slave of all," *pantōn doulos*, in Mark 10:44).

As we noted above, one of the most significant points of similarity between Jesus and Paul, but one that has generally been neglected, is the participatory dimension of the call to suffering and servanthood. It is commonly acknowledged that participation is at the heart of Pauline theology and spirituality, indicated by such central terms and phrases as "in Christ," *koinōnia* with/in Christ and the Spirit (e.g., 1 Cor 10:16; Phil 2:1), and words beginning with the prefix *syn-* ("co-").[38]

Especially important for our purposes is Paul's notion of co-crucifixion (Rom 6:6; Gal 2:19), which appears to refer both to initiation into Christ through faith as manifested in baptism and to ongoing existence in Christ. Paul's theology of baptism and its consequences may very well be not only similar to, but actually indebted to, the tradition of Jesus referring to his death as a baptism. As James Dunn puts it, "Paul could speak of a *baptism* into *Christ's death*, only because he was aware of the tradition that Jesus had spoken of his *death* as a *baptism*."[39] As we noted above, it is in Mark's third passion prediction–summons that Jesus speaks of his suffering and death as his baptism, as something that his disciples will share:

38. In addition to my own work on Paul, see (inter alia) the classic work of Tannehill, *Dying and Rising with Christ*, as well as his "Participation in Christ"; Powers, *Salvation through Participation*; and Schnelle, *Apostle Paul*.

39. Dunn, *Jesus Remembered*, 809; emphasis original.

> Are you able to drink the cup that I drink, or be baptized with the baptism that I am baptized with?" They replied, "We are able." Then Jesus said to them, "The cup that I drink you will drink; and with the baptism with which I am baptized, you will be baptized . . ."
> (Mark 10:38b–39)

Here, we might suggest, is the ultimate origin and source of all Christian language about participation in the death of the Messiah. To pick up one's cross and follow Jesus in suffering, generosity, and love (the essence of the three passion prediction-summonses) is not to *imitate* as much as it is to *participate.*

For Paul, as for Jesus, participation in the Messiah's suffering and death has two dimensions: literal suffering and self-giving service to God and others. We see the former in texts like Rom 8:17 (*sympaschomen*; "co-suffer with Christ" [MJG]) and Phil 3:10 (*koinōnian* [*tōn*] *pathēmatōn autou*; "participation in his sufferings" [MJG]), in which suffering is presented as a normal part of participation in Christ, and as the prerequisite to glory.[40] The latter is rooted in the baptismal reality of dying with Christ as the death of the old self that makes possible (and necessary) a life of self-presentation to God that yields, in turn, self-sacrificial service to others (Romans 6; 12). Such service renounces the use of power over others, seeking their welfare rather than one's own (cf. also Rom 12:10; Phil 3:3).

At several points Paul refers to this cruciform existence implicitly or explicitly as servanthood/slavery. The parallels between Phil 2:3–4 and 2:6–8 suggest that those in Christ are to be Christlike slaves to others, while Gal 5:13 explicitly uses the verb *douleuō* ("serve, be a slave to"): "through love become slaves to one another." Moreover, Paul's example of himself as a slave (1 Cor 9:19; 11:1) is offered in the context of the admonition to the "strong" at Corinth to adopt Paul-like slavery—forgoing rights for the good of others—in their treatment of the weak. This understanding of servanthood is consonant with the understanding of the servant practices described by Jesus in Mark 10. And Paul is exemplary to others only as an imitator of—or better, participant in—Christ the servant.

Some of the disputed Pauline writings continue the connection between the cross and servant-love. Colossians urges Christlike love in conjunction with "compassion, kindness, humility, meekness, and patience" (3:12) as well as forgiveness ("just as the Lord has forgiven you";

---

40. See the discussion of the first passion prediction-summons in the previous chapter.

3:13)—certainly all in the spirit of non-domination and servanthood found in the third passion prediction-summons.

Prominent in this regard is Ephesians. Its exhortations to love (4:2, 15–16) are grounded in God's love (2:4) and Christ's love (3:16–19); the church is called to imitate God's love that was manifested in Christ's self-giving death:[41]

> [32][B]e kind to one another, tenderhearted, forgiving one another, as God in Christ has forgiven you. [1]Therefore be imitators of God, as beloved children, [2]and live [lit. "walk"] in love, as Christ loved us and gave himself up for us (*ēgapēsen hēmas kai paredōken heauton hyper hēmōn*), a fragrant offering and sacrifice to God. (4:32—5:2)

> [21]Be subject (*hypotassomenoi*) to one another out of reverence for Christ . . . [25]Husbands, love your wives, just as Christ loved the church and gave himself up for her (*ēgapēsen tēn ekklēsian kai he-auton paredōken hyper autēs*) . . . (Eph 5:21, 25)

This is not the place to present an extensive discussion of this controversial text (Eph 5:21–33),[42] but whatever else one makes of it, it is clear that mutual submission in Christlike love is the norm for the entire community, including husbands in relation to their wives. The verb "be subject" suggests a re-ordering of desires and goals such that domination in any form is excluded and others' needs take precedence over one's own—precisely what we have seen in the gospels and the undisputed letters of Paul. This applies even to slave-owners: "And, masters, do the same [i.e., good—6:7] to them. Stop threatening them [slaves], for you know that both of you have the same Master in heaven, and with him there is no partiality" (6:9).

In both Colossians and Ephesians, furthermore, the exhortations to this kind of love are coupled with an ongoing call to faith. As we have come to expect, faith and love are inseparable, the twin demands and gifts (Col 1:4; Eph 1:15; 6:23) of God to his new-covenant people.[43]

---

41. Texts like these reinforce the claim that faithfulness to God and love for others are inseparable. By loving others in Christlike, Godlike ways, believers are faithful to God.

42. See Gorman, *Cruciformity*, 261–66.

43. Cf. 1 Tim 1:14; 2 Tim 1:13; 3:10.

Paul, Jesus, and Love

Before considering one final New Testament witness, we need to pause for a moment to consider one question about the servanthood enjoined by Jesus in the third passion prediction-summons. As we have seen, when Paul speaks of self-giving service/slavery he sometimes specifically calls it love, connecting, for example, Gal 5:13 to the fulfillment of the neighbor-love command (Gal 5:14). Moreover, in other letters the immediate (e.g., Phil 2:1–11) or wider (e.g., 1 Corinthians) context makes the same connection implicitly. But what about Jesus, according to our primary witness to him in this chapter—Mark?

Richard Hays contrasts Mark's ethic of "simple external obedience," whose norm is the cross, with both Matthew's focus on "the intention of the heart" and Paul's focus on the Spirit as the source of moral power and on the way of the cross as the way of love.[44] Discipleship, the way of the cross, is not about love in Mark; it is "simply the way of obedience."[45] Hays grants that Jesus in Mark affirms the Law's double love command (12:28–34), but only as an answer to a scribe's question, not as an instruction to his disciples.[46]

This distinction seems a bit like splitting hairs; surely hearers/readers of Mark should heed all of Jesus' teaching, whatever its prompt or form. If, for Jesus, rightly understanding the essence of the Law to be love of God and neighbor means being close to the kingdom of God (Mark 12:34), as Hays notes,[47] and if, as Hays rightly claims, in Mark "the secret of the kingdom of God is that Jesus must die as the crucified Messiah,"[48] then does not Mark imply a connection between the way of the cross and the way of love?

Indeed, could one not make the case that for Mark (and possibly therefore for Jesus), it is *precisely the cross that fulfills the double love command, meaning faithful obedience to God and self-giving love for others*? What else could love mean in Mark, or in the teaching of Jesus generally? Even if love of neighbor is mentioned only once in Mark, and the content is not specified there (other than the affirmation that it is something different from offering temple sacrifices), it must have *some* content. And what

44. *Moral Vision*, 83–85, esp. 83.
45. Ibid., 84–85.
46. Ibid., 84.
47. Ibid.
48. Ibid., 76.

better understanding of love does the Gospel of Mark offer, even if only implicitly, than self-giving servanthood after the example of Jesus?[49]

For Paul, cruciform power as service is clearly a critical dimension of his understanding of love, and he seems to think this derives from both the teaching and the example of Jesus.[50] But even Paul may have had to make explicit (in Phil 2:1–4) that which was only implicit in certain christological affirmations (Phil 2:6–11). Similarly, perhaps certain affirmations in Jesus' teaching, as preserved in Mark's Gospel, require connecting the dots to make the implicit explicit. At the same time, it is noteworthy that Jesus' words about the nature of service have a "not this but that" structure to them: not *kyrieuein* or *douleuesthai* but *douleuein* (not to dominate or be served, but to serve; Mark 10:42–43). When taken together, Paul's descriptions of love have a similar structure: not *zētein ta heautou* but *zētein ta heterōn* and *oikodomein heterous* (not to seek one's own interest but to seek the interest of the other and to edify others; see 1 Cor 8:1; 10:23; 13:5; 14:4; Phil 2:1–4).

In summary, then, although the connection between cross and love is much clearer in Paul, it is not absent from, but rather implicit in, the teachings of Jesus preserved in Mark. Perhaps it was left to Paul (and John too—especially in chapter 13), as well as Mark's audiences, to make the connection between servanthood and love explicit. But doing so only makes clearer what Jesus seems to have intended.

Another New Testament Witness: John

There is considerable overlap between the implications of the cross for the new-covenant community in the second and third occurrences of Jesus' passion prediction-summons. Much of what has been said above concerning Hebrews, James, and 1 John could carry over into this section of the

49. Similarly, Burridge, *Imitating Jesus*: Jesus is "the one who rightly interprets the law precisely because of his commitment to the love of God which seeks loving self-giving in response" (172), and Jesus' teaching about power and leadership are related in Mark to his "radicalizing principles of love and the priority of the sovereign rule of God" (185). Burridge may go too far, however, in claiming that Mark puts "the double love command at the centre of Jesus' teaching" (185).

50. See further Gorman, *Cruciformity*, 268–303. McRae ("Eating with Honor," 166) argues that Paul "propose[s] radical changes to the Corinthian meal ritual in order to establish new social and behavioral patterns that reflect the values of humility, mutual upbuilding, and love that Jesus taught."

chapter. We do, however, need to look once again at the Gospel of John, for cruciform service is at the very heart of the Gospel, both theologically and structurally: the footwashing scene in chapter 13 is located at the center of the Gospel, introducing the second half of the narrative and governing our reading of all that follows. We have already explored John's treatment of this scene in chapter 2, but it is important to revisit it for a moment in this context. Two main points remain to be made.

First, the narrative of, and the theology in, John 13 are remarkably similar to what we have seen in Mark 10 and in Paul, especially Philippians 2. Jesus is the self-giving *doulos* who serves in love (13:1). He stoops—descends, condescends even—in an act of self-humbling: the footwashing itself (13:3–5). His story of self-chosen descent is in contrast to the exaltation he will soon experience on and beyond the cross.[51] His single act of footwashing—and the death to which it points—is both soteriologically unique, the means to forgiveness, the washing away of sin, and ethically paradigmatic, the ultimate exemplary act. At the same time, however, both salvifically and morally, this death is an act requiring not mere assent or compliance with a command, but participation, a powerful but intimate involvement with Jesus. This is a baptism into Jesus' death, *koinōnia* with the crucified. It is countercultural, counter-imperial, and implicitly missional:

> It takes very little reflection to see that Jesus turned Caesar's world upside down when he washed his disciples' feet. Savior Lords don't wash the feet of slaves in Caesar's world, but things are different— they must be different, and must be shown to be different—in the eschatological empire that Jesus built on the wrack of Rome . . . [Here] there are no thrones, only footstools, and masters find themselves in the place of slaves, washing the filthy feet of the people over whom they have authority.[52]

Second, as we suggested in chapter 2, the footwashing scene generates the entire farewell discourse and, therefore, the farewell discourse is an extended commentary on Jesus' parabolic action of footwashing. It is rather remarkable that John dedicates five chapters to Jesus' last meal, which

---

51. Although John is more explicit about the cross as Jesus' exaltation/enthronement/glorification, these elements are present also in Mark and Paul. For all three writers, the very notion of glory is reconstructed by the cross. What Koester (*Word of Life*, 122) says regarding John is true, at least in large measure, also for Mark and Paul: "If glory defines what the crucifixion is, the crucifixion defines what glory is. The crucifixion manifests the scope of divine power by disclosing the depth of divine love."

52. Thatcher, *Greater than Caesar*, 138.

means to this parabolic act and its interpretation. As Francis Moloney has said, "If so much space is given to the account of this final evening, it meant a great deal to the final author of the Gospel."[53] The Gospel has been moving toward this evening, when Jesus' "hour" finally arrives (13:1). After the farewell discourse, everything will flow inexorably and quickly from this setting to the culmination of the hour in Jesus' death/exaltation. In between is the extended meditation on the radical servanthood of Jesus.

This radical servanthood is also radical love—love "to the end" (13:1), love that is both qualitatively and quantitatively beyond measure.[54] John may not refer to this love explicitly as power, but it is clear from the narrative that Jesus the king (see 18:33–39; 19:3, 12–22) rules by love, not by domination. The narrative setting of footwashing leading to crucifixion provides the occasion for Jesus' wide-ranging instructions on life in the new-covenant community, especially life after his imminent departure. This combination of setting and teaching suggests that the entire life of the new-covenant community, a life lived in Jesus and with Jesus/the Spirit within ("mutual indwelling"; 15:1–10), is an ongoing participation in the self-giving, loving death of Jesus. The very act of having one's feet washed is an event of participation, a baptism into the loving, serving death of Jesus.[55] Participation in this death is how disciples love their friends and their enemies; how they receive forgiveness and forgive others; how they do mission and evangelize; how they produce the fruit of good works; how they bear witness and survive persecution; how they pray; in a word, how they live. If Jesus' "friends," as he calls them (15:13–15), are to remain in his friendship, his paradigmatic act of radical servanthood must be the structure of their individual and corporate lives.

The paradox in all this, however, is that such a mode of cruciform servanthood is possible only after the resurrection and only in the power of the resurrection, only in the Spirit whose coming the resurrection made possible (20:22). This is also the conviction of the New Testament writers as a whole.[56]

---

53. Moloney, *Love in the Gospel of John*, 101–2.

54. So also ibid., 105: "he [Jesus] loves in a way that is unimaginable."

55. There may be echoes here of the practice and theology of baptism implied in Romans 6. The footwashing "recalls the baptismal practices by means of which the new Christian is drawn into the suffering, death, and resurrection of Jesus" (ibid., 106). The echo of Mark 10:38–39 is perhaps clearer.

56. For a thorough treatment of this topic, see Feldmeier, *Power, Service, Humility*.

CONCLUSION TO CHAPTERS 4 AND 5

We have seen that Jesus, Paul, and many of the other New Testament witnesses agree that passion-shaped discipleship, or participatory cruciformity, consists of cross-shaped (1) witness to the gospel, (2) hospitality to the weak, and (3) power as loving service.[57] We have also suggested that the first of these represents especially faithfulness to God, while the second and third represent especially love for others, though we have also repeatedly found that the "vertical" and the "horizontal" dimensions of covenant fulfillment are inseparable.

Did Jesus offer these three interconnected dimensions of discipleship as something like a three-point homily or sermon on the way of the cross while he and his disciples were on the road to Jerusalem? The situation is likely more complicated than that, though Mark arranges Jesus' teaching, in some sense, as precisely that. And what about Paul? Did he think of cruciformity as having precisely these three dimensions? Again, the situation is perhaps more complex, but at the very least Paul agrees with Mark and with Jesus that these three types of practices are in fact the most crucial aspects of life for those who know Jesus as the Messiah. So too with other New Testament witnesses.

Indeed, I would suggest that the entire body of Paul's letters may be viewed as an interpretation of Jesus' passion prediction-summonses in a new idiom, the idiom of Spirit-enabled participation in Jesus' death and resurrection, an idiom with its roots in one of those passion prediction-summonses (the third). Paul may very well have even had a name for this reality, at least the "horizontal" aspect of it: "the law of Christ" (Gal 6:2; cf. 1 Cor 9:21). At the same time, paradoxically, the Gospel of Mark, the earliest bearer of those words of Jesus in written form, "provides a profound understanding of God as the one who manifests power in the weakness and folly of the cross" and calls every community of disciples to live "after the model of the one who came to serve and give his life a ransom for many."[58] We could write similarly about the Gospel of John, or even of Luke. Similarly, we find throughout the New Testament numerous pieces of evidence that one or more of these new-covenant practices of cruciformity expressed in

57. Thompson (*Clothed with Christ*) finds all of these themes in Romans 12–15; see his summary (237–41).

58. Matera, *New Testament Theology*, 21, appropriately connecting 1 Cor 1:18–25 and Mark 10:45.

the passion prediction-summonses has made their way to center stage in many of the New Testament's writings.

One final dimension of the passion prediction-summonses needs to be mentioned as a segue into the next chapter. As we have examined the practices of faithfulness and love that the predictions of Jesus' death generate, and that are the essence of participation in that death, we have seen that these practices are all counterintuitive and countercultural. They are also inherently political, if we define that word as referring to the public life of a community. Moreover, these practices also clearly represent a politics of nonviolence, of suffering and of suffering love. This politics would support neither a theology of Roman, imperial domination nor a theology of messianic hatred and violent overthrow, since the "Lord" and the "Messiah" of the passion predictions, and of the New Testament writings more generally, is the Lord who willingly dies at the hands of the imperial authorities after subverting their theology and practices in his life and teaching. A strange sort of Lord and Messiah indeed.

All of this means that Jesus' three-dimensional way of the cross outlined by Mark and reinforced throughout the New Testament is a way of *peace*—a Spirit-empowered way of overcoming sin and evil and death, of engaging powerful enemies, that has the shape of Jesus' cross.[59] This is because the new covenant the prophets promised is also the covenant of peace they promised. We turn to this aspect of the new covenant in the next two chapters.

59. Swartley (*Covenant of Peace*, 107–12) has an insightful analysis of the Markan passion prediction-summonses as "the crux of Mark's peace theology."

–6–

The (New) Covenant of Peace

WE CONCLUDED THE PREVIOUS chapter with a suggestion that the practices of cruciform faithfulness and love that flow from participation in the death of Jesus are inherently a form of nonviolent resistance and peacemaking. The practices of faithfulness and love we have examined challenge ideologies of both imperial and messianic violence. Theologically, the three theological virtues of faith, love, and hope, as we noted in the book's introduction, all have specific practices inherent to them in light of the death of Jesus. The practice of hope, grounded in the death of Jesus and with a vision of God's future perfect peace, is the practice of peace. The new covenant, as we will now see, is the covenant of peace.

In chapter 1 we had noted that one of the several features of the new covenant, and thus of the new-covenant community, would be its peaceable character. In that chapter we quoted this text from Ezekiel 37:

> I will make a covenant of peace with them; it shall be an everlasting covenant with them; and I will bless them and multiply them, and will set my sanctuary among them forevermore. (Ezek 37:26)

Similar is a line slightly earlier in the book:

> I will make with them a covenant of peace and banish wild animals from the land, so that they may live in the wild and sleep in the woods securely. (Ezek 34:25)

And the book of Isaiah promises the following:

> For the mountains may depart and the hills be removed, but my
> steadfast love shall not depart from you, and my covenant of peace
> shall not be removed, says the Lord, who has compassion on you.
> (Isa 54:10)

These three occurrences of the phrase "covenant of peace" point us to
a fundamental dimension of the new covenant, and of the New Testament
writings, that is generally under-appreciated and under-explored. Moreover, the Christian tradition, even when it has focused on participation in
Jesus' death, has too often failed to make the connection between a spirituality of participation in that death and a spirituality of peace. Nonetheless,
although the precise phrase "covenant of peace" does not appear in the New
Testament, we will see that two of the New Testament's principal authors,
Paul and Luke, make the covenant of peace and the corollary "way of peace"
(which phrase they *do* use) central to their theological project.[1] And they
connect peace to Jesus' death.

Paul and Luke make peace central, and cross-related, in various ways.
In this chapter, we will establish that Paul and Luke see the ministry and/
or death of Jesus as that which inaugurates God's covenant of *shalom*, especially as promised by the books of the prophets Isaiah and Ezekiel. In the
next chapter, we will explore more specifically the connection of the cross
to peace in both Paul and Luke, before considering the corollary ecclesial
practices of peace that constitute the "way of peace" in which the community of the (new) covenant of peace is to walk, once again especially
according to Paul and Luke.

ONCE MORE, THE ABSENCE OF THE OBVIOUS

In chapter 1 we noted how odd it is that there is no "new-covenant" model
of the atonement. It is perhaps equally odd how relatively little attention
is paid by most people, including many scholars, to the theme of peace
in the Bible, whether Old Testament or New, whether the Gospels or the
letters of Paul. In his important book *Covenant of Peace*, Mennonite New
Testament scholar Willard Swartley includes a lengthy appendix in which
he shows the scarce notice of peace themes in New Testament studies
generally. Among the works Swartley indicts, and attempts to supplement
and correct in his own work, are Rudolf Bultmann's highly influential New

---

1. This is not to imply that peace and peacemaking are insignificant to other New
Testament writers.

Testament theology and James Dunn's more recent, but already standard, theology of Paul.[2] There are, of course, exceptions, according to Swartley, especially in certain treatments of New Testament ethics and occasionally even in theologies of Paul.

There are naturally some scholars who have in fact paid attention to the peace theme in Scripture, including especially Swartley and certain other Anabaptist scholars.[3] Not all biblical scholars interested in peace are Anabaptists, but it is certainly safe to say that peace and peacemaking are not central to many accounts of New Testament theology. An entire account of peace in the New Testament, even simply in its connection to covenant and/or the death of the Messiah, could occupy an entire book. For our purposes, all we need to establish is that there is a sufficient New Testament witness to support the claim that the covenant of peace promised by the prophets has arrived in Jesus and in the community of the new covenant birthed by his death. As already noted, we will appeal primarily to Paul, and then to Luke, to make this case. Together their writings constitute more than 50 percent of the text of the New Testament.[4] We devote much attention to Paul in part because the role of peace in his writings is perhaps less obvious than it might be for Luke, who has a reputation for being one of the New Testament's main "social activists." We will see, however, that peace, for both Paul and Luke, is much more than social activism, and much more central to their theology than that sort of term might imply.

2. Swartley, *Covenant of Peace*, 6–8, 431–71. See Bultmann, *Theology of the New Testament*, vol. 1, part 2; Dunn, *Theology of Paul*.

3. For the Bible generally, with articles on both Testaments, see, e.g., Brueggemann, *Peace*; Yoder, *Shalom*; Schertz and Friesen, *Beautiful upon the Mountains*; and Brenneman and Schantz, *Struggles for Shalom*. For the New Testament generally, in addition to Swartley, see Mauser, *Gospel of Peace*. (Pieter de Villiers has indicated to me that he is preparing a major work on peace and the New Testament.) For Paul, see Gorman, "The Lord of Peace"; Swartley, *Covenant of Peace*, 189–253; Zerbe, *Citizenship: Paul on Peace and Politics*, a collection of essays; Campbell, *Unity and Diversity in Christ*, 127–45 (on Ephesians) and 169–86 (on Romans); de Villiers, "Peace in the Pauline Letters"; Mauser, *Gospel of Peace*, 104–65; Gabrielson, *Paul's Non-Violent Gospel*; and Keazirian, *Peace and Peacemaking in Paul*. My forthcoming book, *Becoming the Gospel*, will have two chapters on peace in Paul. For Luke and Acts, see de Villiers, "Peace in Luke and Acts"; Swartley, *Covenant of Peace*, 121–76; Kilgallen, "'Peace'"; Borgman, *The Way According to Luke*.

4. According to Felix Just, the Greek New Testament contains about 138,000 words, with almost 38,000 of them in Luke-Acts and more than 32,000 in the Pauline corpus, totaling more than 70,000 (approximately 51 percent). See http://catholic-resources.org/Bible/NT-Statistics-Greek.htm, accessed September 20, 2013.

Peace in Recent Scholarship on Paul

Recent scholarship on Paul is something of a mixed bag on the topic of peace.[5] Two significant Pauline theologies pay almost no attention to the theme, while one is much more promising. Udo Schnelle's *Apostle Paul: His Life and Theology* and Frank Matera's *God's Saving Grace* are both insightful and helpful treatments of Pauline theology.[6] They of course treat Christ's death as God's act of peacemaking and reconciliation with humanity. But neither attends to peace in Paul in relationship to the prophetic expectation of an eschatological or messianic age of peace, or a promised covenant of peace, and neither discusses in any detail peace as an ecclesial practice— the "horizontal" dimension of human relationships that is essential to the prophetic vision. In other words, peace in Paul is seen primarily as a "vertical" reality without being rooted in prophetic expectation or embodied in a serious way in Christian life. This is not to say that Schnelle and Matera would completely *deny* these realities if probed, but they do not figure prominently in their work. Schnelle, in fact, refers to the Pauline admonitions to peace as "conventional paraenesis."[7]

Schnelle represents what seems to be the implicit attitude among some (many? most?) interpreters of Paul: for Paul peace is a minor theme that (1) appears primarily in the context of liturgical excerpts at the beginning and end of his letters—liturgical and epistolary flourishes, if you will, but nothing of great theological substance; and (2) elsewhere expresses a "vertical" theology of reconciliation with God that is supplemented with a "conventional" ethic that has little if any specifically messianic/christological import. Matera is more neutral but clearly does not advance the conversation.

N. T. Wright, on the other hand, in his *magnum opus, Paul and the Faithfulness of God*, sees in Paul both peace and justice, on the one hand, and reconciliation, on the other, as central to Pauline theology. Because Wright believes that for Paul Jesus is first of all the Jewish messiah, Wright repeatedly refers to the prophetic hope for an age of peace and justice,

---

5. For a fuller treatment of this situation, see my article "The Lord of Peace."

6. Matera distinguishes between his "Pauline" theology, which treats all of the Pauline corpus, and a theology "of Paul," which considers only the undisputed letters, which is what Schnelle does. N. T. Wright (discussed below) falls somewhere in the middle but closer to Schnelle in what he analyzes, even though Wright holds to Paul's authorship of most, if not all, of the disputed letters.

7. Schnelle, *Apostle Paul*, 187.

claiming that Paul believed that it had arrived—at least in some sense, though clearly not exactly as the prophets had hoped and equally clearly not in its fullness—through the death and resurrection of Jesus. Moreover, Wright argues that reconciliation is at the heart of Paul's own ministry and a cardinal mark of the church.[8] With Klaus Wengst, Neil Elliott, and others, Wright believes that Paul's gospel of peace and justice challenges the Roman gospel of so-called peace and justice, but he insists that the origin of Paul's belief in this peace and justice is christological, or messianic: the prophetically promised peace and justice of the messianic age have arrived in Jesus. In what follows, we will show that Wright is much closer to an adequate interpretation of Paul on this subject than either Schnelle or Matera.

Peace in Recent Scholarship on Luke

One would expect that peace would fare somewhat better in scholarship on Luke, but that is actually not generally the case. François Bovon's *Luke the Theologian* illustrates the situation well. The book is in large measure a collection of articles on the history of research into various topics in Luke, concluding with a lengthy general survey of Lukan research from 1980 to 2005. From time to time Bovon briefly notes that peace is part of Luke's soteriology, but it receives no sustained attention, it does not appear in the index, and it is only mentioned one time in the final chapter's broad survey of research.[9] To Bovon's credit, however, he rightly insists that, though they are eschatological realities, "peace and kingdom in Luke never lose their earthly and political connotations," and peace is a present reality, both in the Gospel and in Acts.[10]

Darrell Bock's recent theology of Luke considers peace as one of the six "benefits of salvation" in Luke's theology, but it receives only a brief paragraph of discussion and is defined solely as "a reconciled relationship between God and humanity."[11] This latter assessment is clearly in conflict

---

8. The first chapter of Wright's book is a brilliant exposition of Philemon as a letter about reconciliation. For further examination and modest critique of Wright's views, see my article "The Lord of Peace."

9. Neville (*A Peaceable Hope*, 91n1) independently notes the same phenomenon.

10. Bovon, *Luke the Theologian*, 223; cf. ibid., 302.

11. Bock, *A Theology of Luke and Acts*, 271, within the larger discussion of benefits (268–72).

h mm

with Bovon's "earthly and political" interpretation and seems to reflect a theological bias more than the actual theology of Luke.

We turn next to a different sort of work, Peter Mallen's very fine technical study of Luke's use of Isaiah for his overall interpretive framework.[12] In his superb analysis of the plot of Luke-Acts as a whole, as well as in his study of Luke's use of seven major Isaianic themes, the word "peace" scarcely emerges; its programmatic occurrences in Luke 1 and 2 are mentioned in passing but do not figure prominently. Mallen is rightly concerned about other obvious themes in Luke, and in Luke's use of Isaiah, such as salvation for the poor, Jesus as God's servant, and mission to the Gentiles. But Mallen goes too far in arguing that Luke portrays Jesus as *not* ushering in the expected age of peace, contrasting it with what he refers to as Jesus' actual prophetic ministry of teaching and healing.[13] However, as we will see below—and this is why we note Mallen's important and otherwise insightful work here—Luke and Isaiah agree about the importance of peace.[14]

Much more promising, finally, is the work of Paul Borgman, *The Way According to Luke: Hearing the Whole Story of Luke-Acts*. Borgman posits "the Way" as that which unites Luke and Acts both structurally and thematically. The "Way of God" (Luke 20:21) is a summary phrase for Luke's reinterpretation of Scripture in light of Jesus, and this way of God is "synonymous with the Way of salvation, the kingdom of God, and the Way of peace."[15] For Luke, argues Borgman, the purpose of God is to bring about a universal *shalom* that fulfills the promise made to Abraham. Not surprisingly, then, the words "peace" and "*shalom*" recur throughout the book—approximately 125 times all together.

SOME QUESTIONS AND A PROPOSAL

From this very brief but revealing survey, it should be evident—despite an occasional ray of hope—that peace is not front and center in some of the most influential work on both Paul and Luke. There may be good reasons

12. Mallen, *Reading and Transformation of Isaiah*.

13. Ibid., 201–2.

14. There have been and are, of course, readings of Luke that focus on the social and political dimensions of his writings, and in these we do find more references to peace. But the main point here is that such readings, as exceptions, prove the rule.

15. Borgman, *The Way according to Luke*, x. Tellingly, perhaps, Borgman is not a professional New Testament scholar but a professor of English.

for this, particularly if one only looks at the actual occurrences of *eirēnē* (peace) and cognates in the two authors. Forty-three occurrences of the noun, and four of related verbs, in the Pauline correspondence, and only twenty-one occurrences of the noun in Luke-Acts, might not seem, and might not be, significant.[16] However, importance is determined not only by the quantity of texts, but also by such semantic indicators as their location, their connection to related words and themes in the author's corpus, their relationship to scriptural texts and motifs, and so on. Any or all of these could either reinforce or challenge an initial impression based solely on quantity.

Schnelle's approach to Paul and peace, as representative of a general approach to the peace theme in the New Testament writings, is therefore highly problematic. Even if it were true that Paul speaks of peace primarily, or only, in specific kinds of epistolary and liturgical contexts, we could not thereby dismiss the references as insignificant, since Paul often speaks of grace in the same breath—and who would want to minimize the place of grace in Paul's theology?[17] Moreover, as many commentators have noted, Paul's epistolary and liturgical excerpts do give voice to his conviction that in Christ God's *shalom* has arrived. But the apparent rote, formulaic repetition of "grace and peace" language, together with the apparent lack of theological development of the notion, often means that interpreters note the presence of peace/*shalom* and then move on to what are (supposedly) Paul's real concerns, outlined in the thanksgiving and developed in the body of the letter.

But what if "grace and peace" is more essential, more central to what Paul is about? Not merely, as in the popular imagination, meaning inner calm,[18] or as in the work of Schnelle and Matera, as a relatively minor aspect of salvation. What if every letter is an exercise in reminding followers of Jesus that the gracious gift of the Messiah is the promised *shalom* of God? In addition to the liturgical formulae, we have from Paul an initial sign that this is in fact the case, as he summarizes, in Rom 5:1–2, the fruit

16. The noun *eirēnē* occurs forty-three times in the thirteen Pauline letters; the verb *eirēneuō* (be/live in peace) three times (Rom 12:18; 2 Cor 13:11; 1 Thess 5:13); and the verb *eirēnopoieō* (make peace) once (Col 1:20). The noun *eirēnē* appears fourteen times in Luke and seven times in Acts.

17. In chapter 8, we will return to the important theological implications of liturgy and liturgical peace formulas (the "passing of the peace").

18. As we will see, this aspect of peace in the Pauline letters is present only in a surprisingly minimal way.

or benefits of his gospel, and specifically of justification, as the present experience of peace and grace: "Therefore, since we are justified by faith, we have peace with God through our Lord Jesus Christ, through whom we have obtained access to this grace in which we stand" (Rom 5:1–2).[19] This verse suggests that "peace with God," equated also with reconciliation (5:10–11), is at the heart of Paul's gospel. Moreover, rather than foreclosing a horizontal dimension to peace, its centrality to the gospel immediately raises the question, "What does this peace with God have to do with the human condition of injustice and violence depicted in Rom 1:18—3:20, and with the pleas for harmony that run through chapters 9–11 and again through chapters 12–15?" And if Paul (or one of his disciples) calls Jesus "the Lord of peace" (2 Thess 3:16), what does that mean for the role of peace in Pauline theology?[20]

Similarly, if one merely counts the occurrences of "peace" in Luke and Acts, one might conclude that it has a modest role in the Gospel and a minimal role in Acts. If, however, one considers other factors, one might come to a quite different conclusion. For instance, if Luke-Acts is thought of as a unified story, then at the very beginning of the story two major characters announce peace as the purpose of God's sending Jesus (Zechariah in 1:79 and the heavenly host in 2:14), while later on the central character in the first half of Acts, Peter, summarizes both the Gospel narrative itself and the ongoing message of the apostolic gospel in these words: "You know the message he sent to the people of Israel, preaching [the good news of] peace by Jesus Christ—he is Lord of all" (Acts 10:36).[21] That is, the gospel is the gospel of peace, and the Lord of all is the Lord of peace.

19. The notorious textual question about the indicative *eirēnēn echomen*, "we have peace," versus the imperative (hortatory subjunctive) *eirēnēn echōmen*, "let us have peace," cannot be resolved here. Despite the manuscript evidence favoring the latter reading and the presence of a similar construction in Rom 14:19, *ta tēs eirēnēs diōkōmen* ("Let us then pursue what makes for peace"), I think it is unlikely that Paul in Romans 5 is doing anything other than declaring the reality, the "indicative," of what God has done for us in the death of Jesus.

20. Most commentators take the referent of "Lord" here to be Jesus. The chapter will show that it is appropriate to think of Christ for Paul as "the Lord of peace" and even as "our peace" (Eph 2:14) even if Paul himself did not pen the phrases. In fact, if "disciples" of Paul coined such phrases, they will have done so only because they believed the language to represent the apostle accurately. This would make such phrases the first recorded evidence of the reception history of Paul's peace motif. However, for a recent argument in favor of Paul's authorship of 2 Thessalonians, see Foster, "Who Wrote 2 Thessalonians?"

21. My addition in brackets to the NRSV text better conveys the sense of the Greek

As already noted, however, from much Pauline and Lukan scholarship one would hardly know that a fundamental christological claim of these authors is that Jesus is the Lord of peace who proclaims and inaugurates God's *shalom*. Christ as source of peace, much less Christ as peacemaker, is not a prominent theme in New Testament studies generally.

Yet the evidence suggests that peace is a central and critical part of Pauline and Lukan theology about Christ and the community of the new covenant that he created, especially by his death. The new covenant that Jesus came to inaugurate as Messiah, through his ministry and death, and that he continues to administer as the resurrected Lord in the community of the new covenant, is the covenant of peace. For Paul and for Luke, Jesus is both the *source* and the *shape* of God's *shalom*. While this evidence demonstrates the centrality of peace and peacemaking to Pauline and Lukan Christology and soteriology, it also shows that Paul and Luke do not think of Christ as peacemaker in isolation, but only in conjunction with God the Father and the Spirit, on the one hand, and in union with the *ekklēsia*, the church, on the other.

Moreover, both Paul and Luke (as well as other New Testament writers) articulate their vision of peace, quite obviously, in the context of the Roman Empire and the famous *Pax Romana*. This *pax*—which was hardly established nonviolently—may be described as having several dimensions: it is (a) the longed-for "golden age" of peace and security, which has been (b) achieved and maintained by military victory and power over enemies and which (c) imposes Roman law and culture on the conquered, all (d) by the power, and with the approval, of the Roman gods.[22] The peace of Christ will be *quite* different.

---

euangelizomenos eirēnēn and captures the centrality of this text to Luke-Acts, in which the divine message of and about Jesus (in continuity with John the Baptist) is summarized in the verb *euangelizomai* (1:19; 2:10; 3:18; 4:18, 43; 7:22; 8:1; 9:6; 16:16; 20:1). In Acts, the verb is naturally applied to apostolic activity as well (5:42; 8:4, 12; 10:36; 11:20; 13:32; 14:7, 15, 21; 15:35; 16:10). Tannehill (*Narrative Unity*, 2:138) suggests that Acts 10:36 is an echo of Luke 2 (esp. vv. 10–15). These two key references to peace (Acts 10:36; Luke 2:14), then, should be taken as both summative and programmatic statements for Luke. Keener (*Acts*, 2:1798–1801) has an excellent overview of various aspects of peace in antiquity, including Isaiah. He finds it "highly significant" (1800) that in Acts 10:36 Jesus speaks of peace to an officer of the *Pax Romana*.

22. See, e.g., Wengst, *Pax Romana*, 7–51. The New Testament writers refer to this *pax* both explicitly and implicitly. On violence in the Roman Empire, see Gabrielson, *Paul's Non-Violent Gospel*, 7–9.

The thesis I am proposing will be developed in three stages in this chapter and the next, with special attention given to stages one and three:

1. For Paul, the prophetically promised age of eschatological, messianic peace has arrived in the death and resurrection of Jesus the Messiah, an age characterized especially by reconciliation and nonviolence. Jesus' death and resurrection were congruent with his teaching ministry. For Luke, the age of peace has also been inaugurated; for him it arrives not only in Christ's death and resurrection, but in the birth, ministry, death, resurrection, and exaltation of Jesus and in the gift of the Spirit. This new age is characterized by reconciliation and nonviolence, but also especially by justice effected by status-reversal and inclusion. This is peace, *shalom*, as divine promise and divine promise fulfilled.

2. For Paul, God in Christ, on the cross, has made peace with humanity and between humans. This is peace as divine and messianic gift. The centrality of peacemaking to atonement theology is characteristic of Paul, but it is also present in Luke. This is peace as the effect of the cross.

3. For Paul, Jesus is the present Lord of peace, active in his communities by the Spirit to continue making peace in and through those communities, especially through practices of unification and reconciliation internally, and nonretaliation and nonviolence externally. For Luke, Jesus came to create a new people who would walk in the way of peace, and this also defines the Spirit-filled church, "the Way." This is peace as ongoing divine and messianic activity and as ecclesial identity marker.

In both its theological foundations and its outworking in ecclesial practice, this peace will be a creative embodiment of the prophetically hoped-for age of peace, but (to repeat) it will be radically different from the *Pax Romana*.

We will consider the first part of this unfolding thesis in the present chapter, and the other two parts in the next. We begin with Paul.

JESUS, THE PROMISED PRINCE OF PEACE AND THE COVENANT OF PEACE: ISAIAH, EZEKIEL, AND PAUL "IN CONCERT"[23]

In a recent essay summarizing his work on Romans, the Jewish New Testament scholar Mark Nanos concludes with an intriguing and insightful

23. I allude to Wagner's brilliant book on Paul's use of Isaiah, *Heralds of the Good News.*

sentence about the Christ-followers in Rome. Nanos argues that these Christ-followers consist of Jewish subgroups that continue to operate within the larger Jewish community but who also include non-Jews, representing the other nations, as equal members of God's people. "For Paul," Nanos writes, "this communal gathering thereby exemplifies the arrival of the end of the ages, when, according to Scripture, the wolf will graze with, rather than devour, the lamb (Isa 65:25)."[24]

What is intriguing about this concluding sentence is that Paul (as well as other writers in the New Testament)—unlike Christian leaders, musicians, and painters of later generations—nowhere explicitly borrows Isa 2:4 or Isa 65:25 or other go-to images of the age of *shalom*; the wolf and the lamb do not appear in Romans or anywhere else in Paul or the rest of the New Testament, and swords-turned-into-ploughshares do not surface either—not even the precise phrase "the Prince of Peace."[25] Nonetheless, though Nanos is not persuasive with respect to all the specifics of his reconstruction of the Roman communities, he is absolutely right that Paul saw the existence of Jews and Gentiles together, not only as the eschatological ingathering of the nations to worship YHWH, but also as a fundamental and substantive sign that the eschatological age of *shalom* has arrived in Jesus the Messiah. And yet it is seldom, if ever, that Christian commentators associate the wolf and the lamb text, or similar texts, with Paul, much less specifically with Paul and Gentile-Jew relations. Does it perhaps take Jewish eyes to make this connection?

I want to suggest that there is ample evidence that Paul did in fact connect the peace offered in Jesus the Messiah with the *shalom* texts and motifs of Isaiah 2, 11, and 65, as well as similar passages elsewhere in Isaiah. Like other Second Temple writers, Paul was drawn to such texts, as evidenced in quotations and allusions, but—also like many Second Temple writers—he did not utilize some of the images we might have expected.[26]

24. Nanos, "To the Churches within the Synagogues of Rome," 27.

25. As Fowl and others have noted, already in the early centuries of the Christian church diverse theologians pointed to the church as the fulfillment of Isaiah 2. See, e.g., Fowl, *God's Beautiful City*, 10–15.

26. *Jubilees, Psalms of Solomon, 1 Enoch*, the *Testaments of the Twelve Patriarchs*, and *4 Ezra* all point to an eschatological age of peace, echoing Isaiah 2 and 11, for instance, without using the most "famous" Isaianic images. *2 Baruch* 73.6 and the *Sibylline Oracles*, however, do make use of them. *Sibylline Oracles* 3 expects an age when there will be "no sword on earth or din of battle . . . no longer be war or drought on earth . . . great peace throughout the whole earth. King will be friend to king to the end of the age" (3.751–56; cf. 3.707). Also, "wolves and lambs will eat grass together in the mountains. Leopards will

Within the Scriptures of Israel, the future, eschatological, and/or messianic age of peace, when a covenant of peace will be established, is described most frequently and fully in Isaiah.[27] There are several elements that emerge from these texts taken as a cluster, forming a literary composite, a *shalom*-collage, so to speak—or perhaps, in addition, a kind of *shalom*-narrative in the making.[28] We can construct this narrative-collage of peace primarily from parts of Isaiah 2, 9, 11, 32, 52, 54, 55, 60, and 65, without claiming that the prophet Isaiah, or the book's compiler(s), or Paul had such a narrative collage explicitly in mind.[29] Rather, it may be that someone like Paul, who was intimately familiar with this prophet and, it appears, with these thematically connected texts, would naturally allude to their features at various junctures, even as he just as naturally altered or reinterpreted them in light of the actual Messianic event.[30] As Steve Moyise has put it, Paul works within an "overall [Isaiah] narrative framework."[31]

Among the several texts from Isaiah that contribute to this *shalom*-collage, one of the most important, quoted, or echoed in many Second Temple Jewish writers (including Paul, as we will see), is Isaiah 11:

---

feed together with kids. Roving bears will spend the night with calves. The flesh-eating lion will eat husks at the manger like an ox, and mere infant children will lead them with ropes. For he will make the beasts on earth harmless. Serpents and asps will sleep with babies and will not harm them, for the hand of God will be upon them" (3.785–95). For a brief but helpful overview of the use of Isaiah in Second Temple literature, see Hannah, "Isaiah within Judaism." Isaiah, especially chapter 11, was central to Second Temple accounts of the Messiah and the coming age of peace.

27. For a brief overview, see Swartley, *Covenant of Peace*, 15–19; cf. 27–34.

28. See Wagner, *Heralds of the Good News* for the implicit soteriological narrative in the book of Isaiah.

29. If justification is needed for drawing on Isaiah in this way, it would be twofold: (1) the significance of the peace motif in Isaiah and (2) Paul's extensive use of the book of Isaiah to portray God's redemption in Jesus the Messiah and the corresponding mission to the world that Paul finds therein. See, e.g., Wagner, "Isaiah in Romans and Galatians," esp. 129.

30. I imagine something similar to this scenario, described by N. T. Wright, of Paul's rethinking the human plight and the meaning of salvation in light of Christ: "He was asking himself (scrolling through his well-remembered scriptures as he did so): what does *this* 'solution' (the resurrection of the crucified Jesus) have to say to *these* 'problems'?" (*Paul and the Faithfulness of God*, 751). Similar hermeneutical strategies (or natural interpretive moves) in the reading of Isaiah occur in other ancient Jewish literature, including the *Psalms of Solomon* and the Isaiah Targum (Wagner, *Heralds*, 323n63).

31. Moyise, *Evoking Scripture*, 49, summarizing his discussion on 33–48.

¹A shoot shall come out from the stump of Jesse, and a branch shall grow out of his roots. ²The spirit of the Lord shall rest on him, the spirit of wisdom and understanding, the spirit of counsel and might, the spirit of knowledge and the fear of the Lord. ³His delight shall be in the fear of the Lord. He shall not judge by what his eyes see, or decide by what his ears hear; ⁴but with righteousness he shall judge the poor, and decide with equity for the meek of the earth; he shall strike the earth with the rod of his mouth, and with the breath of his lips he shall kill the wicked. ⁵Righteousness shall be the belt around his waist, and faithfulness the belt around his loins. ⁶The wolf shall live with the lamb, the leopard shall lie down with the kid, the calf and the lion and the fatling together, and a little child shall lead them. ⁷The cow and the bear shall graze, their young shall lie down together; and the lion shall eat straw like the ox. ⁸The nursing child shall play over the hole of the asp, and the weaned child shall put its hand on the adder's den. ⁹They will not hurt or destroy on all my holy mountain; for the earth will be full of the knowledge of the Lord as the waters cover the sea. ¹⁰On that day the root of Jesse shall stand as a signal to the peoples; the nations shall inquire of him, and his dwelling shall be glorious. ¹¹On that day the Lord will extend his hand yet a second time to recover the remnant that is left of his people, from Assyria, from Egypt, from Pathros, from Ethiopia, from Elam, from Shinar, from Hamath, and from the coastlands of the sea. ¹²He will raise a signal for the nations, and will assemble the outcasts of Israel, and gather the dispersed of Judah from the four corners of the earth. ¹³The jealousy of Ephraim shall depart, the hostility of Judah shall be cut off; Ephraim shall not be jealous of Judah, and Judah shall not be hostile towards Ephraim. ¹⁴But they shall swoop down on the backs of the Philistines in the west, together they shall plunder the people of the east. They shall put forth their hand against Edom and Moab, and the Ammonites shall obey them. ¹⁵And the Lord will utterly destroy the tongue of the sea of Egypt; and will wave his hand over the River with his scorching wind; and will split it into seven channels, and make a way to cross on foot; ¹⁶so there shall be a highway from Assyria for the remnant that is left of his people, as there was for Israel when they came up from the land of Egypt. (Isa 11:1–16)

A few other texts are worthy of special note:

²In days to come the mountain of the Lord's house shall be established as the highest of the mountains, and shall be raised above the hills; all the nations shall stream to it. ³Many peoples shall

come and say, "Come, let us go up to the mountain of the Lord, to the house of the God of Jacob; that he may teach us his ways and that we may walk in his paths." For out of Zion shall go forth instruction, and the word of the Lord from Jerusalem. [4]He shall judge between the nations, and shall arbitrate for many peoples; they shall beat their swords into plowshares, and their spears into pruning hooks; nation shall not lift up sword against nation, neither shall they learn war any more. (Isa 2:2–4)

[1]But there will be no gloom for those who were in anguish. In the former time he brought into contempt the land of Zebulun and the land of Naphtali, but in the latter time he will make glorious the way of the sea, the land beyond the Jordan, Galilee of the nations. [2]The people who walked in darkness have seen a great light; those who lived in a land of deep darkness—on them light has shined. [3]You have multiplied the nation, you have increased its joy; they rejoice before you as with joy at the harvest, as people exult when dividing plunder. [4]For the yoke of their burden, and the bar across their shoulders, the rod of their oppressor, you have broken as on the day of Midian. [5]For all the boots of the tramping warriors and all the garments rolled in blood shall be burned as fuel for the fire. [6]For a child has been born for us, a son given to us; authority rests upon his shoulders; and he is named Wonderful Counselor, Mighty God, Everlasting Father, Prince of Peace. [7]His authority shall grow continually, and there shall be endless peace for the throne of David and his kingdom. He will establish and uphold it with justice and with righteousness from this time onward and forevermore. The zeal of the Lord of hosts will do this. (Isa 9:1–7)

[1]See, a king will reign in righteousness, and princes will rule with justice . . . [14]For the palace will be forsaken, the populous city deserted; the hill and the watchtower will become dens forever, the joy of wild asses, a pasture for flocks; [15]until a spirit from on high is poured out on us, and the wilderness becomes a fruitful field, and the fruitful field is deemed a forest. [16]Then justice will dwell in the wilderness, and righteousness abide in the fruitful field. [17]The effect of righteousness will be peace, and the result of righteousness, quietness and trust forever. [18]My people will abide in a peaceful habitation, in secure dwellings, and in quiet resting places. (Isa 32:1, 14–18)

[7]How beautiful upon the mountains are the feet of the messenger who announces peace, who brings good news, who announces

salvation, who says to Zion, "Your God reigns." [8]Listen! Your sentinels lift up their voices, together they sing for joy; for in plain sight they see the return of the Lord to Zion. [9]Break forth together into singing, you ruins of Jerusalem; for the Lord has comforted his people, he has redeemed Jerusalem. [10]The Lord has bared his holy arm before the eyes of all the nations; and all the ends of the earth shall see the salvation of our God. (Isa 52:7–10)

For the mountains may depart and the hills be removed, but my steadfast love shall not depart from you, and my covenant of peace shall not be removed, says the Lord, who has compassion on you. (Isa 54:10)

[17] . . . I will appoint Peace as your overseer and Righteousness as your taskmaster. [18]Violence shall no more be heard in your land, devastation or destruction within your borders; you shall call your walls Salvation, and your gates Praise. (Isa 60:17b–18)

[17]For I am about to create new heavens and a new earth; the former things shall not be remembered or come to mind. [18]But be glad and rejoice forever in what I am creating; for I am about to create Jerusalem as a joy, and its people as a delight. [19]I will rejoice in Jerusalem, and delight in my people; no more shall the sound of weeping be heard in it, or the cry of distress. [20]No more shall there be in it an infant that lives but a few days, or an old person who does not live out a lifetime; for one who dies at a hundred years will be considered a youth, and one who falls short of a hundred will be considered accursed. [21]They shall build houses and inhabit them; they shall plant vineyards and eat their fruit. [22]They shall not build and another inhabit; they shall not plant and another eat; for like the days of a tree shall the days of my people be, and my chosen shall long enjoy the work of their hands. [23]They shall not labor in vain, or bear children for calamity; for they shall be offspring blessed by the Lord—and their descendants as well. [24]Before they call I will answer, while they are yet speaking I will hear. [25]The wolf and the lamb shall feed together, the lion shall eat straw like the ox; but the serpent—its food shall be dust! They shall not hurt or destroy on all my holy mountain, says the Lord. (Isa 65:17–25)

Following the strategy proposed in chapter 1 regarding the elements of the new covenant, we may suggest that the elements found in these Isaianic visions include at least the following:

1. Peace as good news (Isa 52:7)

2. Peace as the peaceful reign of God and/or God's son/Davidic king/ delegate (e.g., Isa 9:6–7; 11:1, 10; 32:1; 52:7)

3. Peace as a reconciled covenant relationship with Israel's loving God (Isa 54:10)[32]

4. Peace as deliverance from and/or the defeat of Israel's enemies (Isa 9:4–5; 11:4b, 14–16)

5. Peace as the redemption/restoration of Israel (e.g., Isa 9:2–3; 11:10–13, 16; 52:9; 65:18) and the inclusion of the Gentiles/nations/ends of the earth in God's salvation (e.g., Isa 2:2–3; 9:1–2; 52:10)

6. Peace as the reconciliation of natural enemies/those who have been divided, and resulting harmony (Isa 11:6–9, 13; 65:25)[33]

7. Peace as the absence of violence (e.g., Isa 2:4; 11:9; 60:18; 65:25; cf. 59:6–8)

8. Peace as inclusive of righteousness and justice (e.g., Isa 2:4a; 9:7; 11:3b–4a, 5; 32:1, 16–17; 60:17; cf. 59:6–8)

9. Peace as security/safety (e.g. Isa 11:6–9; 32:18; 54:12; 65:19b–23, 25)

10. Peace as enabled by God/God's Spirit and inclusive of God's presence (e.g., Isa 11:2; 32:15; 52:8)

11. Peace as joyful flourishing and abundance, salvation, and even a new creation (e.g., Isa 52:8; 55:12–13; 60:18; 65:17–18, 21–24)

This *shalom* narrative-collage and vision are most fully expressed in the book of Isaiah, but it can also be found in visionary texts elsewhere in the Scriptures of Israel, sometimes in the poetry of the Psalms (some of which are used by Paul and cited below), sometimes in the voice of another prophet, especially Ezekiel:

> [22]I will save my flock, and they shall no longer be ravaged; and I will judge between sheep and sheep. [23]I will set up over them

32. For the notion of a covenant of peace, see also Num 25:12–13; Ezek 34:25 (cited below); 37:26; Mal 2:4–5; Sir 45:24. For additional promises of a future covenant, see Isa 42:6–7 (with a missional emphasis and cited in the New Testament as such); 49:8 (stressing restoration and security); 55:1–5 (also with a missional focus); 59:21 (highlighting the presence of the Spirit); and 61:8 (stressing restoration).

33. A helpful table of parallels between Isaiah 65 and Isaiah 11 can be found in Paul, *Isaiah 40–66*, 606–7.

one shepherd, my servant David, and he shall feed them: he shall feed them and be their shepherd. ²⁴And I, the Lord, will be their God, and my servant David shall be prince among them; I, the Lord, have spoken. ²⁵I will make with them a covenant of peace and banish wild animals from the land, so that they may live in the wild and sleep in the woods securely. ²⁶I will make them and the region around my hill a blessing; and I will send down the showers in their season; they shall be showers of blessing. ²⁷The trees of the field shall yield their fruit, and the earth shall yield its increase. They shall be secure on their soil; and they shall know that I am the Lord, when I break the bars of their yoke, and save them from the hands of those who enslaved them. ²⁸They shall no more be plunder for the nations, nor shall the animals of the land devour them; they shall live in safety, and no one shall make them afraid. ²⁹I will provide for them a splendid vegetation so that they shall no more be consumed with hunger in the land, and no longer suffer the insults of the nations. ³⁰They shall know that I, the Lord their God, am with them, and that they, the house of Israel, are my people, says the Lord God. ³¹You are my sheep, the sheep of my pasture and I am your God, says the Lord God. (Ezek 34:22–31)

All of the peace-themes we have identified from Isaiah (except [1] the language of "good news") are substantively present here and in Ezek 37:21–28, which was quoted in chapter 1 as a witness to the new-covenant theme and which also has the phrase "a covenant of peace" (37:26). These themes in Ezekiel include (2) the peaceful reign of God and/or God's son/Davidic king/delegate (34:23–24; 37:22, 24a, 25, 26); (3) a reconciled covenant relationship with Israel's loving God (34:24, 30–31; 37:23b, 26); (4) the defeat of Israel's enemies (34:27); (5) the redemption/restoration of Israel (34:22–23; 37:21, 25); (6) the reconciliation of those who have been divided, and resulting harmony (34:22–23; 37:22, 24a); (7) the absence of violence (34:28); (8) righteousness (37:23a, 24b); (9) security/safety (34:25, 28; 37:26); (10) enabled by God and inclusive of God's presence (34:24–25; 37:26–28); and (11) flourishing and abundance (34:26–27, 29; 37:25–26).³⁴

In sum, this new era anticipated by the prophetic tradition of Isaiah and Ezekiel will be an age of peace, indeed a "covenant of peace" (Isa 54:10;

---

34. There are some differences in certain themes between Isaiah and Ezekiel. For instance, righteousness/justice figures more prominently in Isaiah and forsaking idolatry in Ezekiel. Also, Ezekiel does not focus on the inclusion of the Gentiles per se (but see 37:28).

Ezek 34:25; 37:26). That is, in more typically Pauline language, they offer a "gospel of peace" (Eph 6:15; cf. Isa 52:7[35]).

I would propose that each of the eleven elements of peace from Isaiah and Ezekiel identified above appears in the Pauline corpus, scattered throughout but also sometimes clustered, in a way rather similar to what we find in the prophets themselves. The following lengthy table sets these Isaiah/Ezekiel and Pauline parallels out in relationship to one another:[36]

"The Covenant of Peace"
Parallel Peace Texts in Isaiah, Ezekiel, and the Pauline Letters

Note: All texts from Paul contain the noun *eirēnē* (or the verb *eirēneuō* or *eirēnopoieō*) except those preceded by "Cf." (Many of the latter contain *katallassō*, etc.) The English text is taken from the NRSV.

Theme and Isaiah/Ezekiel Texts	Pauline Texts
1. Peace as good news	Eph 6:15 (the gospel of peace)
Isa 52:7	Cf. Rom 10:15 (good news)

35. The connection between gospel/good news and the death of the Messiah in early Christianity generally, and in Paul particularly, is almost certainly due in some measure to the proximity of Isa 52:7–12 to the first Servant Song, which begins at 52:13 (ending at 53:12). Indeed, the announcement of good news of peace in 52:7–12 serves as a kind of preface to that song, which highlights the redemptive death and subsequent exaltation of the servant.

36. The superscript letter refers to the note at the end of the table. All texts from Paul cited in the list below contain the noun *eirēnē* (or the verb *eirēneuō* or *eirēnopoieō*) except those preceded by "Cf." (Many of the latter contain *katallassō* [reconcile], etc.) One could also look at just one or two of these themes in Paul's use of Isaiah; Wagner, for instance, focuses on the restoration of Israel and the inclusion of the Gentiles, without omitting others. There are aspects of Isaiah and the OT more generally that Paul does not include, and they are not included here—especially the subjection of the nations to Israel. (See further below.) Paul can be "quite selective in which details of the Isaianic vision he appropriates" (Wagner, *Heralds of the Good News*, 325n69)—and this is true because his reading of Isaiah is shaped by his Christology as well as his ecclesiology and his own sense of vocation. The subjection of the nations would be antithetical to the gospel. On Rom 15:12 ("The root of Jesse shall come, the one who rises to rule the Gentiles . . .""), see Jewett, *Romans*, 895–97.

Theme and Isaiah/Ezekiel Texts	Pauline Texts
2. Peace as the peaceful reign of God and/or God's son / Davidic king / delegate^A Isa 9:6–7; 11:1, 10; 32:1; 52:7; cf. Ezek 34:23–24; 37:22, 24a, 25, 26	Rom 14:17 (For the kingdom of God is . . . righteousness and peace and joy in the Holy Spirit.) Rom 15:33; 16:20; Phil 4:9; 1 Thess 5:23 (God of peace) 1 Cor 7:15 (It is to peace that God has called you.) 1 Cor 14:33 (God is a God not of disorder but of peace.) 2 Cor 13:11 (the God of love and peace) Col 3:15 (And let the peace of Christ rule in your hearts, to which indeed you were called in the one body.) 2 Thess 3:16 (Now may the Lord of peace himself give you peace at all times in all ways. The Lord be with all of you.)
3. Peace as a reconciled covenant relationship with Israel's loving God Isa 54:10; 34:24, 30–31; 37:23b, 26; Cf. Ezek 34:24, 30–31; 37:23b, 26 For "covenant of peace," cf. Num 25:12–13; Mal 2:4–5; Sir 45:24	Rom 5:1–11 ([1]Therefore, since we are justified by faith, we have peace with God through our Lord Jesus Christ . . . . [10]For if while we were enemies, we were reconciled to God through the death of his Son, much more surely, having been reconciled, will we be saved by his life . . .) Eph 2:17–18 (So he came and proclaimed peace to you who were far off and peace to those who were near; for through him both of us have access in one Spirit to the Father.) Col 1:20–22 (and through him God was pleased to reconcile to himself all things, by making peace through the blood of his cross. And you who were once estranged and hostile in mind, doing evil deeds, he has now reconciled in his fleshly body through death, so as to present you holy and blameless and irreproachable before him) 1 Thess 5:23 (May the God of peace himself sanctify you entirely; and may your spirit and soul and body be kept sound and blameless at the coming of our Lord Jesus Christ.) Cf. 2 Cor 5:18–21 (in Christ God was reconciling the world to himself, not counting their trespasses against them [5:19])

Theme and Isaiah/Ezekiel Texts	*Pauline Texts*
4. Peace as deliverance from and/or the defeat of Israel's enemies Isa 9:4–5; 11:4b, 14–16; cf. Ezek 34:27	Rom 16:20 (The God of peace will shortly crush Satan under your feet.) Cf. 1 Cor 15:24–27, 54–57 (The last enemy to be destroyed is death. [15:26]) Cf. Col 2:13–15 (. . . God made you alive together with him, when he forgave us all our trespasses, erasing the record that stood against us with its legal demands. He set this aside, nailing it to the cross. He disarmed the rulers and authorities and made a public example of them, triumphing over them in it.) Cf. 2 Cor 10:1–6; 1 Thess 5:8, 15; Eph 6:10–18 [believers' participation in spiritual battles]
5. Peace as the redemption/restoration of Israel Isa 9:2–3; 11:10–13, 16; 52:9; 65:18; cf. Ezek 34:22–23; 37:21, 25 *and* the inclusion of the Gentiles/nations/ends of the earth in God's salvation Isa 2:2–3; 9:1–2; 52:10	Gal 6:15–16 (For neither circumcision nor uncircumcision is anything; but a new creation is everything! As for those who will follow this rule—peace be upon them, and mercy, and upon the Israel of God.) Eph 2:14–17 (For he is our peace; in his flesh he has made both groups [Gentiles and Jews] into one and has broken down the dividing wall, that is, the hostility between us. He has abolished the law . . . that he might create in himself one new humanity in place of the two, thus making peace, and might reconcile both groups to God in one body through the cross, thus putting to death that hostility through it. So he came and proclaimed peace to you who were far off and peace to those who were near.) Rom 14:1—15:13 (May the God of hope fill you [all believers, Gentiles and Jews] with all joy and peace in believing. [15:13]) Cf. Rom 9–11 (e.g., 11:15: For if their rejection [referring to unbelieving Israel] is the reconciliation of the world, what will their acceptance be but life from the dead!)

Theme and Isaiah/Ezekiel Texts	Pauline Texts
	Rom 12:18 (live peaceably with all)
	Rom 14:19 (Let us then pursue what makes for peace and for mutual upbuilding.)
	2 Cor 13:11 (agree with one another, live in peace; and the God of love and peace will be with you.)
	Eph 2:14–16 ([14]For he is our peace; in his flesh he has made both groups into one and has broken down the dividing wall, that is, the hostility between us. [15]... that he might create in himself one new humanity in place of the two, thus making peace, [16]and might reconcile both groups to God in one body through the cross, thus putting to death that hostility through it.)
	Eph 4:2–3 (with all humility and gentleness, with patience, bearing with one another in love, making every effort to maintain the unity of the Spirit in the bond of peace)
6. Peace as the reconciliation of natural enemies/those who have been divided, and resulting harmony	Eph 6:23 (Peace be to the whole community)
	Col 1:20 (and through him God was pleased to reconcile to himself all things, whether on earth or in heaven, by making peace through the blood of his cross)
Isa 11:6–9, 13; 65:25; cf. Ezek 34:22–23; 37:22, 24a	Col 3:15 (And let the peace of Christ rule in your hearts, to which indeed you were called in the one body.)
	1 Thess 5:13, 15 (Be at peace among yourselves . . .); see also 1 Thess 5:23 (May the God of peace himself sanctify you entirely . . .)
	Cf. Gal 5:20 ([works of the flesh:] enmities, strife, jealousy, anger, quarrels, dissensions, factions)
	Cf. Phlm 15–16 (Perhaps this is the reason he was separated from you for a while, so that you might have him back forever, no longer as a slave but more than a slave, a beloved brother— especially to me but how much more to you, both in the flesh and in the Lord.)

Theme and Isaiah/Ezekiel Texts	Pauline Texts
7. Peace as the absence of violence Isa 2:4; 11:9; 60:18; 65:25 (cf. 59:6–8); cf. Ezek 34:28	1 Thess 5:15 (See that none of you repays evil for evil, but always seek to do good to one another and to all.) Rom 12:14–21 ([14]Bless those who persecute you; bless and do not curse them . . . [17]Do not repay anyone evil for evil . . . [19]Beloved, never avenge yourselves . . . [20]No, "if your enemies are hungry, feed them . . ." [21]Do not be overcome by evil, but overcome evil with good.) Cf. Rom 3:13–17 ([15]"Their feet are swift to shed blood . . . [17]and the way of peace they have not known.") Cf. Rom 5:6–11 (For if while we were enemies, we were reconciled to God through the death of his Son . . . [5:10])
8. Peace as inclusive of righteousness and justice Isa 2:4a; 9:7; 11:3b–4a, 5; 32:1, 16–17; 60:17 (cf. 59:6–8); cf. Ezek 37:23a, 24b	Rom 5:1 (justified by faith . . . peace with God) Rom 12:17, 21 (Do not repay anyone evil for evil, but take thought for what is noble in the sight of all . . . Do not be overcome by evil, but overcome evil with good.) Rom 14:16–19 ([16]So do not let your good be spoken of as evil. [17]For the kingdom of God is . . . righteousness and peace and joy . . . [19]Let us then pursue what makes for peace and for mutual upbuilding.) 1 Thess 5:15 (See that none of you repays evil for evil, but always seek to do good to one another and to all.) 2 Tim 2:22 (Shun youthful passions and pursue righteousness, faith, love, and peace) Cf. Rom 3:13–17 ([15]"Their feet are swift to shed blood . . . [17]and the way of peace they have not known.") Cf. 2 Cor 5:21 (For our sake he made him to be sin who knew no sin, so that in him we might become the righteousness of God.)

Theme and Isaiah/Ezekiel Texts	Pauline Texts
9. Peace as security/safety Isa 11:6–9; 32:18; 54:12; 65:19b–23, 25; cf. Ezek 34:25, 28; 37:26	1 Cor 16:11 (Send him on his way in peace) Phil 4:7 (And the peace of God, which surpasses all understanding, will guard your hearts and your minds in Christ Jesus.) 1 Thess 5:3 (When they say, "There is peace and security")
10. Peace as enabled by God/ God's Spirit and inclusive of God's presence Isa 11:2; 32:15; 52:8; cf. Ezek 34:24–25; 37:26–28	Benedictions: peace from God/Christ (Rom 1:7; 15:13, 33; 1 Cor 1:3; 2 Cor 1:2; Gal 6:16; etc.) Rom 8:6 (to set the mind on the Spirit is life and peace) Rom 14:17 (For the kingdom of God is . . . joy in the Holy Spirit.) Rom 15:13 (May the God of hope fill you with all joy and peace in believing, so that you may abound in hope by the power of the Holy Spirit.) Rom 15:33 (The God of peace be with all of you.) 2 Cor 13:11 (the God of love and peace will be with you) Gal 5:22 (the fruit of the Spirit is love, joy, peace) Eph 4:2–3 (with all humility and gentleness, with patience, bearing with one another in love, making every effort to maintain the unity of the Spirit in the bond of peace) Phil 4:7–9 ([7]And the peace of God, which surpasses all understanding, will guard your hearts and your minds in Christ Jesus . . . [9]and the God of peace will be with you.) 2 Thess 3:16 (Now may the Lord of peace himself give you peace at all times in all ways. The Lord be with all of you.)

Theme and Isaiah/Ezekiel Texts	*Pauline Texts*
	Rom 2:10 (glory and honor and peace for everyone who does good)
	Rom 8:6 (to set the mind on the Spirit is life and peace)
	Rom 14:17 (For the kingdom of God is . . . joy in the Holy Spirit.)
	Rom 15:13 (May the God of hope fill you with all joy and peace)
11. Peace as joyful flourishing and abundance, salvation, and even a new creation Isa 52:8; 55:12–13; 60:18; 65:17–18, 21–24; cf. Ezek 34:26–27, 29; 37:25–26	Gal 6:15–16 (a new creation is everything! As for those who will follow this rule—peace be upon them)
	Phil 4:4–7 ([4]Rejoice in the Lord . . . Rejoice [6]Do not worry . . . but . . . let your requests be made known to God. [7]And the peace of God . . . will guard your hearts and your minds in Christ Jesus.)
	Col 1:20 (and through him God was pleased to reconcile to himself all things, whether on earth or in heaven, by making peace through the blood of his cross)
	Cf. 2 Cor 5:17 (So if anyone is in Christ, there is a new creation)

A. We must keep in mind that Paul was unaware that David "plays no role in the future according to Deutero-Isaiah [chaps. 40–55]" (Paul, *Isaiah 40–66*, 607) because Paul did not divide Isaiah into parts but read it as a narrative whole (while drawing heavily on chapters 40–55).

In what follows, we will focus our discussion of these themes on the Isaiah texts because of the already noted importance of the book of Isaiah to Paul. Nevertheless, it is important to recognize that there may also be echoes of Ezekiel (and of other texts from Scripture, or from Second Temple writings indebted to Scripture) in Paul's writings.

Of course all of the prophetic themes identified above are transformed in the Pauline corpus as they are reworked in light of the reality of the crucified and resurrected Jesus as Messiah.[37] But it is also important to note two of the Isaianic themes that receive particularly radical reinterpretation in Paul, especially vis-à-vis certain other texts in Second Temple Judaism.

37. On the New Testament's deconstruction and reconstruction of received traditions in light especially of the cross, see Harrisville, *Fracture*.

Most significantly, regarding theme 4, Paul has no interest in the literal destruction of human enemies, whereas there appears to be a strong desire precisely for that in some of the Dead Sea Scrolls and the *Psalms of Solomon*, for instance.[38] In addition, with respect to theme 5, unlike Isaiah Paul does not focus on the restoration of Israel as a nation per se or on Jerusalem as a city,[39] and he does not pick up on the prophetic notion of the subjugation of the Gentiles as part of the future peace (e.g., Isaiah 60).[40]

Space does not permit extensive development of these various dimensions, but some of them will emerge in the discussion below.

I am proposing, therefore, that Paul himself understood that the "peace of God/Christ/the Messiah" (Phil 4:7; Col 3:15) about which he spoke was in fact the peace promised by Isaiah (and Ezekiel) in the texts from which we have drawn our narrative-collage, and this despite the absence of certain key images.

The question naturally arises, Did Paul himself know what he was doing?[41] He certainly does not provide us with an in-depth exegesis of any of Isaiah's peace passages. Indeed, there are probably only three marked citations of relevant Isaiah texts, so we are dealing largely with allusions and echoes.[42]

---

38. E.g., the following excerpts from 1QSb (= 1Q28b) (*Rule of the Blessings*) cols. 3, 5, messianic interpretations of Isaiah 11 and related texts: "May He grant you everlasting [peace] ... May He fight [at the head of] your Thousands [until the generation of falsehood is ended] ... [to bend] many people before you ... [May you smite the peoples] with the might of your hand and ravage the earth with your scepter; may you bring death to the ungodly with the breath of your lips!" See also 4Q285 (*War Rule*) frag. 5, which almost certainly says that the Branch of David will kill the king of the Kittim. See also 1QM (*War Scroll*) as well as parts of *Psalms of Solomon* 17–18, in which Isa 11:4b and Psalm 2:9 are sources for images of the destruction of sinners and the rebuking of the nations by means of the Lord's anointed. Although *some* of this language may be metaphorical, the attention to the destruction of sinners and oppressors is striking in contrast to Paul's interpretations of the same texts. See the discussion in Hannah, "Isaiah within Judaism," 11–16.

39. On the importance of the restoration of Israel in Isaiah 40–66, see the commentary by Paul, *Isaiah 40–66*.

40. On these sorts of themes in the interpretation of Isaiah in Second Temple Judaism, see Mallen, *Reading and Transformation of Isaiah*, 29–59. Mallen notes, for example, that Isaiah is generally read very "nationalistically" (esp. 57–59) and as predicting the judgment of the nations.

41. "Peace" is not one of the aspects of Paul's use of Isaiah discussed in Moyise, *Paul and Scripture*. Moyise treats such themes as creation, Abraham, Moses, the law, the Gentiles, and the life of the Christian community (the last without reference to peace).

42. The marked citations (those Paul explicitly indicates as scriptural quotations) are Rom 3:17 = Isa 59:8; Rom 10:15 = Isa 52:7; and Rom 15:12 = Isa 11:10.

And in one instance—when Paul explicitly cites Isa 52:7, about good news of peace and salvation (Rom 10:15)—he omits the LXX reference to peace:

> *hōs hōra epi tōn oreōn hōs podes euangelizomenou akoēn eirēnēs*
> *hōs euangelizomenos agatha hoti akoustēn poiēsō tēn sōtērian sou*
> *legōn siōn basileusei sou ho theos* (Isa 52:7 LXX)

> like season upon the mountains, like the feet of one bringing good news of a report of peace, like one bringing good news of good things, because I will make your salvation heard, saying to Zion, "Your God shall reign" (translation of Isa 52:7 LXX)[43]

> And how are they to proclaim him unless they are sent? As it is written, "How beautiful are the feet of those who bring good news!" (Rom 10:15)

But Paul also omits the LXX references to salvation and to the reign of God in Isa 52:7, not because he discounts either of those realities—or the reality of peace—but because his immediate focus in the context of Romans 10 is the word "gospel/good news" (Rom 10:16) and the corollary imperative to mission symbolized by "feet."

More positive evidence that Paul does find the promised peace of Isaiah fulfilled in Jesus comes in another marked citation. In Rom 15:12, as Paul concludes his admonition to, and celebration of, unity among Gentiles and Jews in Messiah Jesus within the Roman house churches, he quotes, in abbreviated form, Isa 11:10:

> [A]gain Isaiah says, "The root of Jesse shall come, the one who rises to rule the Gentiles; in him the Gentiles shall hope." (Rom 15:12)

The LXX Of Isa 11:10 actually reads "and there shall be on that day [*en tē hēmera ekeinē*] the root of Jesse . . ."

What interests us is Paul's omission of the underlined phrase *en tē hēmera ekeinē*, "in that day," referring back to the poetic prophecy of vv. 1–9. It is likely that Paul omits this phrase because he believes that the hoped-for coming day is no longer future but present;[44] the root of Jesse, the hope of the nations, has inaugurated that which vv. 1–9 anticipate:

---

43. Adapted from the translation of Moisés Silva in Pietersma and Wright, *New English Translation of the Septuagint.*

44. So also Wagner, *Heralds of the Good News*, 318.

> [1]A shoot shall come out from the stump of Jesse, and a branch shall grow out of his roots. [2]The spirit of the Lord shall rest on him, the spirit of wisdom and understanding, the spirit of counsel and might, the spirit of knowledge and the fear of the Lord. [3]His delight shall be in the fear of the Lord. He shall not judge by what his eyes see, or decide by what his ears hear; [4]but with righteousness he shall judge the poor, and decide with equity for the meek of the earth; he shall strike the earth with the rod of his mouth, and with the breath of his lips he shall kill the wicked. [5]Righteousness shall be the belt around his waist, and faithfulness the belt around his loins. [6]The wolf shall live with the lamb, the leopard shall lie down with the kid, the calf and the lion and the fatling together, and a little child shall lead them. [7]The cow and the bear shall graze, their young shall lie down together; and the lion shall eat straw like the ox. [8]The nursing child shall play over the hole of the asp, and the weaned child shall put its hand on the adder's den. [9]They will not hurt or destroy on all my holy mountain; for the earth will be full of the knowledge of the Lord as the waters cover the sea. (Isa 11:1–9)

Righteousness and faithfulness, peace and security: these are the traits of the messianic age. In 11:10–11 Isaiah extends these benefits beyond Israel to the Gentiles; he internationalizes the messianic peace.[45]

Paul's omission of "in that day" indicates that he has read the verse he cites in context. For him, the inclusion of the Gentiles is an essential part of the peace of God that the Messiah Jesus has inaugurated. As N. T. Wright says, it is "no accident" that Rom 15:7–13 quotes both Deuteronomy 32 and Isaiah 11 in a summary of "the entire narrative of God's saving purposes."[46] In Rom 15:9–13, therefore, Paul is not merely creating a catena of texts testifying to the inclusion of the Gentiles, or nations, in God's salvation. He is telling his audience that the inclusion of the nations is part of the great divine, messianic peace initiative to bring together Israel and non-Israel, to reconcile and unite those who are at odds in one way or another. The inclusion of the Gentiles also means the reconciliation of the Gentiles with Jews and with one another. It is this conviction that drives Rom 15:7–13, the letter's peroration, with the opening admonition to "[w]elcome one another, therefore, just as Christ has welcomed you, for the glory of God" (15:7), as well as the closing benediction, "May the God of hope fill you with all joy and peace in believing, so that you may abound in hope by the power of the Holy Spirit"

---

45. Brueggemann, *Isaiah 1–39*, 104–5.
46. Wright, *Paul and the Faithfulness of God*, 399.

(15:13)—both rooted in the reality that the peacemaking Messiah has come and is still here in the powerful, peaceable presence of the Spirit. Indeed, the previous passage (15:1–6) indicates that the Messiah's cruciform love is both the source and the shape of people's reconciliation with God and with one another, so that the purpose of human existence may come to fruition:

> May the God of steadfastness and encouragement grant you to live in harmony with one another, in accordance with Christ Jesus, so that together you may with one voice glorify the God and Father of our Lord Jesus Christ. (Rom 15:5–6)[47]

Themes and visions of peace similar to those of Isaiah may be found elsewhere in the Bible. One that resonates well with the Isaianic texts, and with Paul, is Psalm 85 (LXX 84), which includes the following lines:

> [4(5)]Restore us again, O God of our salvation, and put away your indignation toward us.

> [5(6)]Will you be angry with us forever? Will you prolong your anger to all generations?

> [6(7)]Will you not revive us again, so that your people may rejoice (*euphranthēsetai*) in you?

> [7(8)]Show us your steadfast love, O Lord, and grant us your salvation.

> [8(9)]Let me hear what God the Lord will speak, for he will speak peace (*eirēnēn*) to his people, to his faithful, to those who turn to him in their hearts.

> [9(10)]Surely his salvation is at hand for those who fear him, that his glory may dwell in our land.

> [10(11)]Steadfast love and faithfulness will meet; righteousness (*dikaiosynē*) and peace (*eirēnē*) will kiss each other.

I would propose that Paul echoes and summarizes this Psalm in Rom 14:17 as a kind of synopsis of his convictions about the peace of God in Christ: "For

---

47. I owe this insight in part to Andy Johnson, who also suggests that "glorifying God 'with one mouth' [15:6] looks almost like a gloss on the end of the Christ hymn [Phil 2:6–11] and graphically illustrates the (triangular) peace God brings through Jesus, i.e., peace between God and humanity and between people at odds with each other, in this case, probably Jews and Gentiles" (personal correspondence, Aug. 25, 2013). On the theological significance of this on-the-ground harmony for Paul, see my "Romans: The First Christian Treatise on Theosis."

the kingdom of God is not food and drink but righteousness and peace and joy in the Holy Spirit (*dikaiosynē kai eirēnē kai chara en pneumati hagiō*)." This, in turn, is not far from being a summary of Rom 5:1–11, in which Paul claims that what God has lovingly done in the crucified and resurrected Messiah is to offer humanity righteousness/justice and peace/reconciliation, known now experientially by the presence of the Spirit: "Therefore, since we are justified by faith, we have peace with God through our Lord Jesus Christ (*Dikaiōthentes oun ek pisteōs eirēnēn echomen pros ton theon dia tou kyriou hēmōn Iēsou Christou*)."[48] Indeed, Isaiah had written, "The effect of righteousness will be peace" (Isa 32:17; *estai ta erga tēs dikaiosynēs eirēnē*). The phrase "Peace and righteousness (or justice)" is frequently shorthand for the eschatological or messianic age in both the OT—including Isaiah specifically—and in at least some Second Temple texts.[49] Paul both knows this slogan and develops it, as Rom 5:1, 14:17, and several other texts make clear.

For Paul, then, Jesus is indeed the Prince of Peace, the one through whom God has made and is making the messianic *shalom* a reality, the covenant of *shalom* to which the Scriptures of Israel bear witness.

Of course, as all interpreters of Paul recognize, this reality is not yet here in its fullness. Paul, of all people, is painfully aware of that reality, as he experiences anxiety, strife, and even violence in his own life (see, e.g., 2 Cor 11:22–30)—quite the opposite of security and reconciliation. Paradoxically, Paul can associate even this aspect of believing existence with the peace of Christ. He writes to the Philippians as follows:

> [16]It is by your holding fast to the word of life that I can boast on the day of Christ that I did not run in vain or labor in vain. [17]But even if I am being poured out as a libation over the sacrifice and the offering of your faith, I am glad and rejoice with all of you—[18]and in the same way you also must be glad and rejoice with me. (Phil 2:16–18)

The phrase "labor in vain" (*eis kenon ekopiasa*) appears to be based on Isa 65:23, "They shall not labor in vain [LXX *ou kopiasousin eis kenon*] or bear children for calamity; for they shall be offspring blessed by the Lord—and

---

48. As noted earlier, in Rom 5:1–2 Paul connects peace and grace as fundamental aspects of the church's present experience. The presence of the Spirit (5:5) means that justification and peace include the experience of love, hope, and something approaching joy (5:2–4, "boasting" in future glory and even present suffering; cf. RSV "rejoice"). Paul's language of justification and reconciliation reappears at the end of Rom 5:1–11 (vv. 9–11).

49. E.g., Isa 32:16; 60:17. See also, e.g., *Test. Judah* 24.1.

their descendants as well," part of the glorious vision of the coming new creation. Paul, who knows the new creation has begun (2 Cor 5:17; Gal 6:15), understands in light of the narrative of Jesus that the new creation does not come without a price. His suffering will have been worth the cost if his churches remain faithful to the gospel, with the result that he can then know that his work of proclaiming the good news of reconciliation and new creation was not in vain.[50] Even in the present struggles, however, those in the Messiah can know the peace of the Messiah, as Paul reminds the Philippians (Phil 4:7, 9).

To summarize: for Paul, Jesus is the prophetically promised Prince of Peace, the Lord of Peace, who inaugurates the age and the covenant of peace. The echoes we have considered were available to Paul; they recur; cohere, and have sufficient volume to be heard; and they are both historically plausible and satisfying.[51]

The Covenant of Peace in Luke

As noted above, the word "peace" does not occur frequently in Luke-Acts. Nevertheless, peace is critical to the narrative; it is announced at highly significant moments, and it is woven into the very fabric of Luke's two-volume work, especially the Gospel.[52] Willard Swartley rightly claims that the way Luke uses the vocabulary of peace indicates that peace "expresses the very heart of the gospel."[53] Like Paul, Luke is quite fond of Isaiah, and the *sha-lom*—God's peace and justice—promised in the book of Isaiah is one of several complementary Isaianic themes (including especially the theme of

50. One even wonders if Paul feared, with respect to the Galatians at least, that he sometimes did "bear children for calamity" (Isa 65:23; see, e.g., Gal 4:11, 19–20).

51. I refer to six of the seven chief criteria proposed by Hays (*Echoes of Scripture*, 29–32) for discerning the presence of scriptural echoes. The other criterion, history of reception, also lends some support to my thesis, but it is also precisely part of the problem I am addressing.

52. For a thorough treatment, see Swartley, *Covenant of Peace*, 121–76, who does an excellent job of relating peace to salvation and justice. See also, inter alia, Yoder, *Politics of Jesus*, esp. 21–111; and Neville, *A Peaceable Hope*, 91–117, who also deals at length with the issue of judgment versus restoration in Luke's eschatology (119–73).

53. Swartley, *Covenant of Peace*, 130.

a new Exodus[54]) that work together to convey Luke's understanding of the salvation wrought by God through Jesus and in the power of the Spirit.[55]

The word "peace" makes its first appearance in the Benedictus, which ends on the word "peace"; it is the culmination of Zechariah's hope/prophecy—the reality that his son John (the Baptist) will prepare and that the Messiah will bring:

> [68]"Blessed be the Lord God of Israel, for he has looked favorably on his people and redeemed them. [69]He has raised up a mighty savior for us in the house of his servant David, [70]as he spoke through the mouth of his holy prophets from of old, [71]that we would be saved from our enemies and from the hand of all who hate us. [72]Thus he has shown the mercy promised to our ancestors, and has remembered his holy covenant, [73]the oath that he swore to our ancestor Abraham, to grant us [74]that we, being rescued from the hands of our enemies, might serve him without fear, [75]in holiness and righteousness before him all our days. [76]And you, child, will be called the prophet of the Most High; for you will go before the Lord to prepare his ways, [77]to give knowledge of salvation to his people by the forgiveness of their sins. [78]By the tender mercy of our God, the dawn from on high will break upon us, [79]to give light to those who sit in darkness and in the shadow of death, to guide our feet into the way of peace." (Luke 1:68–79)

At several points, these words echo Mary's Magnificat (Luke 1:46–55), suggesting that the way of peace the Messiah brings will, paradoxically, not be so peaceful—at least not in the sense of calm.[56] It will involve reversal of the

54. See especially Pao, *Acts and the Isaianic New Exodus* and Green, *Gospel of Luke*. Hahn, *Kinship by Covenant* (217–37) argues that for Luke Jesus brings a restored and transformed Davidic covenant and kingdom. There is no reason to see any of these themes as mutually exclusive. Hahn, in fact, stresses the expectation of a renewed Davidic kingdom and covenant in the text and context of Jeremiah 31 (226).

55. There are many studies of Luke's indebtedness to Isaiah. See, e.g., Mallen, *Reading and Transformation of Isaiah* and the bibliography there, though (as noted above) I disagree sharply with him about the role of peace in Luke's theology; Mallen is generally right in what he affirms about Luke's use of Isaiah but wrong in what he unnecessarily denies. He is certainly right that Isaiah provides the interpretive framework for Luke's portrayal of both Jesus and Paul, and for the overall narrative of his two-volume work (e.g., 60). It should be obvious, therefore, that claiming that peace is a cardinal dimension of Luke's theology, and of his appropriation of Isaiah, in no way exhausts either Luke's theology or his interpretation of Isaiah. There are various (generally) complementary themes both in Isaiah and in Luke's interpretation of Isaiah.

56. See also, of course, the words of Jesus in Luke 12:51: "Do you think that I have come to bring peace to the earth? No, I tell you, but rather division!"

status quo (so especially Mary in 1:52–53) and defeat of enemies, even if Luke later makes it clear that Jesus the Messiah will not deal with enemies as certain other Second Temple Jews would have wanted to do.

Furthermore, both the Magnificat and the Benedictus refer to God's covenantal promise to Abraham (1:54–55, 72–73), suggesting that what is about to happen in the Messiah Jesus is the renewal of the covenant. Although neither poetic text uses the language of "new" covenant, Luke is making it clear that what is about to transpire is covenantal, and when Jesus announces at the Last Supper that his death is effecting the "new covenant in my blood" (Luke 22:20), we are brought back to these opening announcements. (We shall return to this in the next chapter.)

Following the words of Zechariah, we have almost immediately the words of the heavenly host at the birth of the "dawn from on high," their burst of praise confirming the promise of Zechariah:

> [10]But the angel said to them, "Do not be afraid; for see—I am bringing you good news of great joy for all the people: [11]to you is born this day in the city of David a Savior, who is the Messiah, the Lord. [12]This will be a sign for you: you will find a child wrapped in bands of cloth and lying in a manger." [13]And suddenly there was with the angel a multitude of the heavenly host, praising God and saying, [14]"Glory to God in the highest heaven, and on earth peace among those whom he favors!" (Luke 2:10–14)

In implicit but clear contrast to Caesar Augustus,[57] Lord and Messiah Jesus, the Son of David and Son of the Most High God, is the bringer of God's peace to those who are the recipients of divine benefactions.

The truth of these promises is quickly reconfirmed in the praise of Simeon as he holds the infant savior: "'Master, now you are dismissing your

---

57. Luke's text can usefully be contrasted with the famous calendar inscription from 9 BCE that was put forth in Priene and elsewhere to honor Caesar Augustus and to re-order the calendar in light of him: "It seemed good to the Greek cities in Asia, on the recommendation of the high priest Apollonius, son of Menophilos from Arcadia, since providence, in divinely ordering our existence, has shown esteem and a lavish outlay has embellished the good—perfection—onto life by displaying Augustus, whom virtue has filled for the benefit of humankind, while graciously giving us and those after us a *Savior* who has *ended war, setting things right in peace*, and since Caesar when revealed surpassed the hopes of all who had anticipated the *good news* [*euangelia*], not only going beyond the benefits of those who had preceded him, but rather leaving no hope of surpassing him for those who will come, because of him *the birthday of God began good news* [*euangelia*] for the world." (Elliott and Reasoner, *Documents and Images*, 35, translating lines 32–41; emphasis added.)

servant in peace, according to your word; for my eyes have seen your salvation'" (Luke 2:29–30). The covenant of peace has arrived.

agree

These first three peace texts in Luke—first the promise of imminent peace to be brought by the Messiah (Luke 1:79); then, immediately, the inauguration of peace in the birth of the Messiah (Luke 2:14); and then, immediately, the confession of Simeon (Luke 2:29–30)—are programmatic for Luke's Gospel and his entire theological project. They tell us what the ministry of the Messiah consists of: inaugurating the age of peace and thereby creating a community, a people, of *shalom*—a covenant community that experiences and practices God's peace and justice. Indeed, these initial texts establish the context for the additional indications of Jesus' ministry that emerge in the rest of chapter 2, in chapters 3 and 4, and beyond: being about his Father's business (1:49), baptizing with the Holy Spirit (3:15–17), announcing the good news of liberation for the oppressed (4:14–21), bringing God's healing and delivering power to all in need of liberation from oppression (4:31–44 and afterwards), and teaching the way of peace (e.g., 6:20–49). These are cardinal aspects of the messianic reign of *shalom*, of peace and justice and wholeness.[58]

If the Gospel of Luke begins on a repeated note of peace, it also culminates on such a note. When Jesus, who has "set his face to go to Jerusalem" (Luke 9:51) less than halfway through the narrative, arrives in Jerusalem—where he is to die—he is greeted by a "multitude of the disciples" (Luke 19:37) saying, "Blessed is the king who comes in the name of the Lord! Peace in heaven, and glory in the highest heaven!" (Luke 19:38). This clear echo of the angels in Luke 2:14 establishes a literary inclusio and a theological claim: the good news of peace Jesus was born to bring is being brought to a new level, a fuller conclusion, with his imminent death.[59]

58. Borgman, *The Way according to Luke*, is particularly good at showing the connections between peace and justice in biblical theology and specifically in Luke.

59. The specific sense of Luke 19:38 is a bit unclear. Joel Green remarks that "peace in heaven," in contrast to "on earth" in 2:14, refers to God's intention for peace that has been partly thwarted by opposition to Jesus and is therefore still future (*Gospel of Luke*, 687). If Green is correct, then my point still holds: the death will reaffirm the divine intention and bring about that peace, even if opposition to Jesus continues (as it does in Acts). De Villiers sees it this way: "These two exclamations in Luke 2:14 and 19:38, taken together, portray the whole of Jesus' ministry and death as a cosmic peace that encompasses earth and heaven. Luke thus plots his narrative to reflect the cosmic peace that has become a reality in the life of Christ" ("Peace in Luke and Acts," 5; cf. 7–8). That does not mean, however, that everyone has accepted or will accept this peace, or that Rome's version of peace has been fully and finally dismantled, as Luke 19 also makes clear, when Jesus weeps over Jerusalem for not recognizing "the things that make for peace" (19:42).

All of this is why Peter, in Acts 10:36, can rightly summarize God's activity in Jesus as "preaching the good news of peace by Jesus Christ" (MJG). Here and throughout Acts, preaching the good news (using the verb *euangelizomai*) is expressed in various ways: preaching [the good news of] the Messiah, Jesus (Acts 5:42); preaching [the good news of] the kingdom of God and the name of Jesus (Acts 8:12); preaching [the good news of] the Lord Jesus (Acts 11:20); preaching [the good news of] God's promises fulfilled in Jesus' resurrection (Acts 13:32). These are obviously not different gospels but one gospel, which can be called first and foremost, according to Luke's narrative, the gospel of peace.

It therefore makes sense for us to look at Luke-Acts as a narrative of the arrival of the prophetically promised covenant of peace, as we did with Paul. The table below provides a sampling of texts from Luke-Acts that correspond to the eleven thematic aspects of the peace motif from Isaiah and Ezekiel. This of course is not a separate covenant from the new covenant, but one and the same, with *shalom* being highlighted.

The Prophetic Peace Themes in Luke-Acts[60]

Prophetic Theme	Sample Texts in Luke-Acts
1. Peace as good news	Luke 2:10, 14 ("good news of great joy for all the people . . . on earth peace")
	Acts 10:36 ("preaching [the good news of peace] by Jesus Christ")
2. Peace as the peaceful reign of God and/or God's son / Davidic king / delegate	Luke 1:31–33, 69 ("the Lord God will give to him the throne of his ancestor David, of his kingdom there will be no end")
	Luke 2:11 ("to you is born this day in the city of David a Savior, who is the Messiah, the Lord")
	Luke 18:38–39; 20:41–44 (Son of David)
	Acts 8:12 (proclaiming the good news about the kingdom of God and the name of Jesus Christ)
	Acts 13:32–37 ("For David, after he had served the purpose of God in his own generation, died, was laid beside his ancestors, and experienced corruption; but he whom God raised up experienced no corruption.")

60. The table is not exhaustive. Many of the texts are deliberately taken from the programmatic statements early in the Gospel. Additional texts could be provided to demonstrate each of the themes. Unlike the table for Paul, however, the word "peace" does not appear in every text cited; Luke's vocabulary of *shalom* is larger than the word "peace." Superscript letters refer to notes at the end of the table.

The Death of the Messiah and the Birth of the New Covenant

Prophetic Theme	Sample Texts in Luke-Acts
3. Peace as a reconciled covenant relationship with Israel's loving God, including especially forgiveness^	Luke 1:16–17 ("He [John] will turn many of the people of Israel to the Lord their God.") Luke 1:76–79 ("you [John] will go before the Lord to prepare his ways, to give knowledge of salvation to his people by the forgiveness of their sins. By the tender mercy of our God, the dawn from on high will break upon us . . . to guide our feet into the way of peace.") Luke 7:50; 8:48 ("Your faith has saved you/made you well; go in peace.") Acts 2:38 ("Repent, and be baptized every one of you in the name of Jesus Christ so that your sins may be forgiven.")
4. Peace as deliverance from and/or the defeat of Israel's enemies	Luke 1:71, 74 ("that we would be saved from our enemies and from the hand of all who hate us. . . . that we, being rescued from the hands of our enemies, might serve him without fear") Luke 10:17–19 ("Lord, in your name even the demons submit to us!" He [Jesus] said to them, "I watched Satan fall from heaven like a flash of lightning. See, I have given you authority to tread on snakes and scorpions, and over all the power of the enemy; and nothing will hurt you.") Acts 9:23–25 ([T]he Jews plotted to kill him, but their plot became known to Saul. They were watching the gates day and night so that they might kill him; but his disciples took him by night and let him down through an opening in the wall, lowering him in a basket.) Acts 12:11 (Then Peter came to himself and said, "Now I am sure that the Lord has sent his angel and rescued me from the hands of Herod and from all that the Jewish people were expecting.")
5. Peace as the redemption/restoration of Israel *and* the inclusion of the Gentiles/nations/ends of the earth in God's salvation	Luke 1:54–55, 68 ("He has helped his servant Israel . . . according to the promise he made to our ancestors, to Abraham and to his descendants forever . . . he has looked favorably on his people and redeemed them.") Luke 2:25, 29–32 ("Master, now you are dismissing your servant in peace, my eyes have seen your salvation, a light for revelation to the Gentiles and for glory to your people Israel.") Cf. Luke 7:1–17, in which the healing of a Gentile centurion's slave and the raising of a Jewish woman's son from the dead are paired Acts 11:17–18 ("If then God gave them the same gift that he gave us when we believed in the Lord Jesus Christ, who was I that I could hinder God?" When they heard this, they were silenced. And they praised God, saying, "Then God has given even to the Gentiles the repentance that leads to life.")

Prophetic Theme	Sample Texts in Luke-Acts
6. Peace as the reconciliation of natural enemies/those who have been divided, and resulting harmony	Luke 12:57–59 ("Thus, when you go with your accuser before a magistrate, on the way make an effort to settle the case.") Acts 10, which narrates the acceptance of Cornelius and the Gentiles/Romans (10:36 = "peace by Jesus Christ") Acts 15:1–35, which narrates the Jerusalem meeting and acceptance of Gentiles (after which Judas and Silas are "sent off in peace" [15:33]) Acts 15:8–9 ("And God, who knows the human heart, testified to them by giving them the Holy Spirit, just as he did to us; and in cleansing their hearts by faith he has made no distinction between them and us.")
7. Peace as the absence of violence[B]	Luke 6:27–29, 35 ("Love your enemies, do good to those who hate you, bless those who curse you, pray for those who abuse you. If anyone strikes you on the cheek, offer the other also . . . [L]ove your enemies . . . Luke 9:54b–55 ("Lord, do you want us to command fire to come down from heaven and consume them?" But he turned and rebuked them.); cf. 22:36–38, 49–51. Luke 23:34 ("Father, forgive them; for they do not know what they are doing.")[C] Acts 7:60 ("Lord, do not hold this sin against them.") Acts 9:31 (Meanwhile the church throughout Judea, Galilee, and Samaria had peace and was built up.)
8. Peace as inclusive of righteousness and justice	Luke 1:17 ("he [John] will go before him, to turn the hearts of parents to their children, and the disobedient to the wisdom of the righteous") Luke 1:74–75 ("that we . . . might serve him without fear, in holiness and righteousness before him all our days")
9. Peace as security/safety	Luke 1:74 ("that we, being rescued from the hands of our enemies, might serve him without fear") Luke 10:19 ("See, I have given you authority to tread on snakes and scorpions, and over all the power of the enemy; and nothing will hurt you.") Acts 9:31 (Meanwhile the church throughout Judea, Galilee, and Samaria had peace and was built up.)

Prophetic Theme	Sample Texts in Luke-Acts
10. Peace as enabled by God/God's Spirit and inclusive of God's presence	Luke 4:18–19 ("The Spirit of the Lord is upon me, because he has anointed me to bring good news to the poor. He has sent me to proclaim release to the captives and recovery of sight to the blind, to let the oppressed go free, to proclaim the year of the Lord's favor.") Acts 2:1–18 ("I will pour out my Spirit upon all flesh.")[D] Acts 2:38–39 ("Repent, and be baptized every one of you in the name of Jesus Christ so that your sins may be forgiven; and you will receive the gift of the Holy Spirit. For the promise is for you, for your children, and for all who are far away, everyone whom the Lord our God calls to him.")
11. Peace as joyful flourishing and abundance, salvation, and even a new creation	Luke 2:10 ("good news of great joy for all the people"); cf. 1:41, 44 Luke 10:17 (The seventy returned with joy, saying, "Lord, in your name even the demons submit to us!") Luke 15:7, 10 (joy in heaven/the presence of the angels of God over one sinner who repents) Acts 8:7–8 (unclean spirits, crying with loud shrieks, came out of many who were possessed; and many others who were paralyzed or lame were cured. So there was great joy in that city.)

A. I have added "forgiveness" to the table in the consideration of Luke-Acts because of its prominence in Luke's theology. The connection of forgiveness to healing and wholeness can be found in, e.g., Isa 33:24; 40:2; 52:13—53:12.

B. The point here, for Luke, is not the absence of violence in the world, but the absence of violence in Jesus and his community, even in the face of violence.

C. I assume that this verse, omitted from some manuscripts, is part of the original text of Luke. See chapter 2, n. 17.

D. Although Peter's speech quotes from Joel 2:28–32 rather than from Ezekiel or Isaiah, it is the theme of the promised Spirit that connects the Pentecost account with the new covenant, too (see the discussion in chapter 2) and hence with the covenant of peace.

This table enables us to see, as suggested earlier, not only that the covenant of peace arrives in Jesus, but that this covenant of peace is the will and activity of God the Father, that it is empowered by the Spirit, and that it takes shape not only in the ministry of Jesus, but also in the life of his disciples and in the life of the church as narrated in Acts. This is Luke's perspective on peace.

CONCLUSION

In this chapter we have argued that for Paul and Luke, two of the New Testament's chief theologians, the prophetically promised era of peace, the covenant of peace, has come in the Messiah Jesus, and that this is a significant part of the theological project of each author. We have done this by looking at specific texts from the writings of Paul and Luke that use the word "peace" and/or contain echoes of the principal themes about peace drawn from the prophets Isaiah and Ezekiel. More could still be explored (as others such as Swartley have done), but it is now time to move on to two topics that flow from the argument of this chapter.

We turn, then, in the next chapter to consider Jesus' death as the means of effecting the covenant of peace, and to the ecclesial practices of peace that, according to Paul and Luke, are constituitive of the new-covenant community.

―7―

Baptized into the Messiah's Death
New-Covenant Practices of Cruciform Peace

MOST TREATMENTS OF THE atonement, as noted in the introduction to this book, focus on what may be called the "mechanics" of atonement. The New Testament's focus, I have been suggesting, is on the purpose or results of Jesus' death, and specifically on the creation of a new-covenant people who continue to participate in the event that has brought them into existence as a people. In chapters 4 and 5, we saw how the people of the new covenant participate in Jesus' death by embodying its covenant structure of faithfulness and love in various practices that give expression to that faithfulness and love. In this chapter, we turn from faith and love to hope—by turning to peace. Building on the claim of chapter 6 that the covenant brought to birth by Jesus' death is the prophetically promised covenant of peace, we consider new-covenant practices of peace as the means of ongoing participation in the once-for-all, hope-fulfilling, peacemaking death of Jesus. As in chapter 6, we consider the contributions of Paul and of Luke.

CHRIST THE PEACEMAKER: RECONCILIATION AS DIVINE/MESSIANIC INITIATIVE AND GIFT

We noted in chapter 6 that 2 Thessalonians and Ephesians employ christological titles to indicate the peacemaking role of Jesus as Messiah. We find this elsewhere in the New Testament, too, sometimes explicitly, sometimes implicitly. As we have seen, Luke implies that Jesus is the Davidic Prince of

Peace, whose liberating activity (Luke 4) and resurrection (Acts 13) inaugurate the reign of God, the age of *shalom*. Matthew implies that Jesus is the peacemaking Son of God in his earthly ministry, who teaches his disciples that those who make peace will similarly be called children of God (Matt 5:9). The letter to the Hebrews affirms that Jesus is the king of peace and righteousness (Heb 7:1–3). Revelation attests to Jesus as the reigning (Rev 1:4) and coming king of peace, in spite of (or, better, because of) its use of graphic scriptural images of war to portray Jesus as God's peacemaker (e.g., Rev 19:11–21).[1]

In other words, the New Testament recognizes Jesus as a peacemaker before and after his death as well as in his death. Indeed, the witness of the New Testament as a whole is that there is a close connection between Jesus' teaching and ministry, on the one hand, and his death, on the other.[2] The canonical witness, taken as a whole, is that the covenant-of-*shalom*-making activity of Jesus spans his entire ministry in the broadest sense of that term, that is, his activity from birth to *parousia*. He enacts and inaugurates the promised peace of Isaiah and other prophets throughout the span of his work.

But in the New Testament, the central time and place in which Jesus makes peace is at his crucifixion outside Jerusalem, the city of peace. This is widely acknowledged as true for Paul, but less so for Luke. We begin with the Pauline corpus before also considering Luke-Acts.

The Peacemaking Death of Jesus in Paul

The letter to the Colossians sums up the Pauline perspective quite nicely:

> For in him all the fullness of God was pleased to dwell, and through him God was pleased to reconcile to himself all things, whether on earth or in heaven, by making peace (*eirēnopoiēsas*) through the blood of his cross. (Col 1:19–20)[3]

This peace was effected in the hard reality of the real world of Roman crucifixion: "through the blood of his cross," "in his fleshly body through death" (Col 1:20b, 22a). Moreover, this was not, says Colossians, the act of

---

1. On Jesus as peacemaker in Revelation, see Swartley, *Covenant of Peace*, 324–55; Johns, "Leaning toward consummation"; and my forthcoming "*Shalom* in the Book of Revelation."

2. On this, see my forthcoming article "The Work of Christ in the New Testament."

3. Cf. Matt 5:9, "Blessed are the peacemakers (*eirēnopoioi*)."

an independent contractor, but the messianic expression of the divine will: "through him [Christ] God was pleased to reconcile to himself all things" (Col 1:20a). The human race was in a state of disrepair, enmity, and anti-*shalom* toward God, within itself, and vis-à-vis the rest of creation. On the Messiah's cross God graciously and lovingly addressed that human and cosmic predicament; it was God's peace initiative. The letter to the Colossians celebrates this act of redeeming love (together with the prior act of creation) in some of the most beautiful poetry in the New Testament (Col 1:15–20), and it is altogether appropriate that Christian hymnody down through the ages has similarly celebrated the death of Jesus on our behalf. But the emotive doxological poetry of Col 1:15–20 leads immediately and seamlessly into the reflective theological prose of the following verses, which suggest that the death itself, as critical as it is, is not the ultimate point.

The immediate purpose and result of God's peacemaking, redemptive act in Jesus' death was the creation of a new community of reconciled and righteous people:[4] "And you who were once estranged and hostile in mind, doing evil deeds, he has now reconciled in his fleshly body through death, so as to present you holy and blameless and irreproachable before him" (Col 1:21–22). Paul (or his disciple[5]) does not dwell on the "how" of this reconciliation but on the "that" and on the result. The rest of the letter sets forth the theological and existential consequences of the claim that God the Father chose to dwell fully in the Jesus the Son (Col 2:9) in order to "[rescue] us from the power of darkness and [transfer] us into the kingdom of his beloved Son, in whom we have redemption, the forgiveness of sins" (Col 1:13–14). Those who are part of this kingdom, this community, are united as one diverse body, chosen by God (the language of covenant), forgiven and practicing forgiveness, clothed with God's love and peace, and called to let that love create a harmonious (peace-filled) community as they allow the peace of Christ (Col 3:15) to rule in their hearts (Col 3:8–15).[6]

4. I say "immediate" because the ultimate purpose is the reconciliation of "all things" (Col 1:20a).

5. Colossians remains one of the disputed Pauline letters, though I judge it to be from the mind and heart of Paul, if perhaps with some secretarial assistance in its written form.

6. "[8]But now you must get rid of all such things—anger, wrath, malice, slander, and abusive language from your mouth. [9]Do not lie to one another, seeing that you have stripped off the old self with its practices [10]and have clothed yourselves with the new self, which is being renewed in knowledge according to the image of its creator. [11]In that renewal there is no longer Greek and Jew, circumcised and uncircumcised, barbarian, Scythian, slave and free; but Christ is all and in all! [12]As God's chosen ones, holy and beloved, clothe yourselves with compassion, kindness, humility, meekness, and patience.

Romans and 2 Corinthians, from the undisputed Pauline letters, tell us essentially the same thing as does Colossians about the cross and peacemaking. The "love of Christ" mentioned in Rom 8:35 cannot be anything other than the embodiment of the *pro-nobis* act of God's giving rather than withholding his Son (Rom 8:31–32), and thus also of the surprising love of God for enemies (Rom 5:6–10). Even the brief formulaic statements like "Christ died for us/for our sins" (Rom 5:6, 8 and elsewhere in Paul) are quite likely references not only to Christ's death as atonement by substitution or (more likely) representation, but also to his death as an act of dying for enemies rather than for fellow combatants, friends, or the state.[7] Accordingly, the love of the Messiah must refer, at least in part, to his love of enemies expressed on the cross, even if Paul refers to this love in Romans 8 primarily to remind the Roman believers that the resurrected and reigning Messiah Jesus, who is one with the crucified Messiah Jesus, continues to love him and them in the present, particularly in their experience of tribulation. Unlike 1 John, Paul never says, "God is love," but if actions reveal character (and even being, ontology), then Paul clearly thinks that God *is* love because God *does* love. And this love comes to its fullest expression in the gift of Christ to make peace between a rebellious world and this loving God, a gift that is nothing other than the richest expression of divine grace while at the same time the most profound self-gift of both the Father and the Son.

This interweaving of God's grace/love and initiative (a theological claim properly speaking) and Christ's grace/love and self-gift (a christological claim) is certainly one of the richest and most profound contributions of Paul to Christian theology, found here in Romans and elsewhere. Indeed, this interweaving leads almost inevitably to Trinitarian conclusions, as we see already in Romans 5. The love and peacemaking of God are revealed in the death of the Son and communicated by the indwelling Spirit, who is the mark of the new covenant, as we saw in chapter 1:

---

[13]Bear with one another and, if anyone has a complaint against another, forgive each other; just as the Lord has forgiven you, so you also must forgive. [14]Above all, clothe yourselves with love, which binds everything together in perfect harmony. [15]And let the peace of Christ rule in your hearts, to which indeed you were called in the one body. And be thankful" (Col 3:8–15).

7. See Gibson, "Paul's Dying Formula." Gibson rightly suggests that Paul's use of dying formulae is therefore implicitly a challenge to his culture's understanding of the glory of dying in battle allegedly to effect peace and salvation.

> [1]Therefore, since we are justified by faith, we have peace with God through our Lord Jesus Christ, [2]through whom we have obtained access to this grace in which we stand; and we boast in our hope of sharing the glory of God . . . [5]and hope does not disappoint us, because God's love has been poured into our hearts through the Holy Spirit that has been given to us. [6]For while we were still weak, at the right time Christ died for the ungodly. [7]Indeed, rarely will anyone die for a righteous person—though perhaps for a good person someone might actually dare to die. [8]But God proves his love for us in that while we still were sinners Christ died for us. [9]Much more surely then, now that we have been justified by his blood, will we be saved through him from the wrath of God. [10]For if while we were enemies, we were reconciled to God through the death of his Son, much more surely, having been reconciled, will we be saved by his life. [11]But more than that, we even boast in God through our Lord Jesus Christ, through whom we have now received reconciliation. (Rom 5:1–2, 5–11)

The remainder of Romans spells out the consequences of this death: to form a reconciled people of holiness, hospitality, love, and peace (see further below). This is the people of the new covenant, the covenant of peace.[8]

So too in 2 Corinthians 5, we find in the cross God's initiative, Christ's love, and the purpose/result of transformation into God's new-covenant people:

> [14]For the love of Christ urges us on, because we are convinced that one has died for all; therefore all have died. [15]And he died for all, so that those who live might live no longer for themselves, but for him who died and was raised for them. [16]From now on, therefore, we regard no one from a human point of view; even though we once knew Christ from a human point of view, we know him no longer in that way. [17]So if anyone is in Christ, there is a new creation: everything old has passed away; see, everything has become new! [18]All this is from God, who reconciled us to himself through Christ, and has given us the ministry of reconciliation; [19]that is, in Christ God was reconciling the world to himself, not counting their trespasses against them, and entrusting the message of reconciliation to us. [20]So we are ambassadors for Christ, since God is making his appeal through us; we entreat you on behalf of Christ, be reconciled to God. [21]For our sake he made him to be sin who knew no sin, so that in him we might become the righteousness of God. (2 Cor 5:14–21)

8. See Whittle, *Covenant Renewal*.

The love of the Messiah that "urges us on" (v. 14a), or perhaps "directs" us (whoever "us" refers to[9]) is the present, ongoing experience of the Messiah's loving death on the cross (v. 14b), which is precisely the reconciling love of God embodied in that death (vv. 18–21), for "God was in the Messiah, reconciling the world to himself" (v. 19a; MJG). As in Colossians and Romans, the christological and the properly theological are inseparably woven together. The theology of the atonement here is clearly very rich, as we saw in chapter 3. The primary point for us now is the singularity and purpose of what is both God's act and Christ's: reconciliation with God, which unleashes both the new creation and the ongoing, ambassadorial ministry of reconciliation.[10] That Paul cannot divorce the work of Christ from the work of God is clear as well in 2 Corinthians 8 and 9, where he speaks of both "the generous act (or "grace"; *charin*) of our Lord Jesus Christ, that though he was rich, yet for your sakes he became poor, so that by his poverty you might become rich" (2 Cor 8:9) and the "grace (*charin*) [and] . . . indescribable gift (*dōrea*)" of God (2 Cor 9:14–15).

This love the Messiah had and has for the world and for the church is not, for Paul, only a reference to Jesus' deep concern for individuals' salvation in the sense of their reconciliation to God—though it is clearly and emphatically that. Indeed, everything Paul thinks and says about peace is grounded in and flows from his theology of the cross. For him, there can be no true and lasting peace among humans without reconciliation with God, without a common embrace of the cross. Yet there can be no doubt that for Paul "the love of Christ" manifested on the cross refers not only to his compassionate desire to restore humanity to fellowship with God, but also to Jesus' deep concern to effect reconciliation of people to one another. That is, the purpose of Christ's death on the cross is to create a people of the covenant—the new covenant promised by the prophets in which people live in peace with God and with one another.

The texts of Romans 5 and 8 and of 2 Corinthians 5 do not say this explicitly, but—as with Colossians—their respective contexts make it clear that this is the case. The subject of Romans 9–11, and indeed all of Romans

9. The numerous occurrences of second-person-plural pronouns and verbs in 2 Corinthians are challenging to interpret. The narrower reference (i.e., to Paul and his colleagues) may be in view here, though that does not necessarily mean that Paul would exclude others in the spiritual reality to which the text bears witness.

10. Again, the possibly narrower reference (i.e., to Paul and his colleagues) may be in view in some sentences in this passage, but we should not therefore exclude others from participation in the ministry of reconciliation.

9–15, is the unity of Jews and Gentiles in the Messiah Jesus, the realization of the Isaianic dream. In chapters 9–11 Paul spells out the reasons for his hope for a future peaceful unification of Gentiles and Jews in the Messiah, while warning Gentiles not to be arrogant about the grace they have received. That is, the new covenant has not nullified the original covenant but is rather its continuation, reworked around the Messiah and the Spirit.[11] In chapters 12 to 15 of Romans, Paul describes what that peaceful coexistence should look like *now*, for those who are already united in the Messiah. As Reta Halteman Finger has put it, "in chapters 12–15, Paul discusses how the reconciliation introduced in 5:1–11 is worked out on the horizontal level."[12] In other words, Romans 12–15 is an overview, tailored to the Roman house churches, of the meaning of Jesus' death for Jews and Gentiles alike (the theme-litany of the entire letter) in the concrete realities of daily life as the people of the new (renewed) covenant, the covenant of peace. Paul does not need to use those precise terms to express what he is about because he repeatedly quotes or alludes to the texts and themes that constitute the structure and contents of these covenantal realities.[13]

With respect to 2 Corinthians, the subject of all of chapters 1–7 and 10–13 is reconciliation between Paul and the Corinthians, and among the Corinthians, while chapters 8 and 9 are, at least in part, about the reconciliation of Gentiles and Jews as embodied practically in the collection for Jerusalem. As my colleague Brent Laytham has said, the collection is the churches' way of enacting both its liturgy, in which it receives and passes on the grace and peace of God, and its international identity.[14] The reconciled/ justified people have a mission of reconciliation and justice. These lines of investigation suggest that the late Ralph Martin was not off the mark when he argued that reconciliation was the center of Paul's theology.[15]

The soteriological logic embedded in Romans and 2 Corinthians is that those who respond in the affirmative to the gospel of the Messiah's death as God's act of peacemaking are drawn by the Spirit, in their act of

11. I am here echoing the language of Wright in his approach to Pauline theology, particularly in *Paul: In Fresh Perspective* and in *Paul and the Faithfulness of God*.

12. Halteman Finger, "'Reconciled to God through the Death of his Son,'" 151.

13. On the theme of covenant renewal/new covenant and the consecration and transformation of God's people in Romans, see Whittle, *Covenant Renewal*.

14. In a presentation on Pauline theology and practice, St. Mary's Seminary & University, November 9, 2012.

15. Martin, *Reconciliation*. As noted earlier, N. T. Wright has now made reconciliation central to his construal of Pauline theology, too.

faith and in baptism, into the Messiah—not merely to exist in the Messiah as individuals, but to constitute a corporate entity, a body, a covenant people. It is a body that transcends both the most local and the most global differences, uniting people who would otherwise at least remain distant from one another, and perhaps live in a state of hostility or even be violent enemies. This, in the words of Thomas Stegman, is *the miracle of the gospel.*[16] These individuals and groups are formed into one, whether or not they know it and, to put it bluntly, whether or not they like it. "Is the Messiah divided?" (1 Cor 1:13; MJG). Of course not! All who are baptized are one in the Messiah, both Gentile and Jew, male and female, slave and free, etc., as Gal 3:28 puts it.

This soteriological logic of people's reconciliation with God including also reconciliation among people becomes fully explicit in Ephesians: in the Messiah (recall the many occurrences of the phrase "in Christ" in Ephesians) Gentiles have been brought near to the God of Israel and thus also to Jews who are also already in the Messiah. This is not a matter, then, of a theological shift from reconciliation as Pauline *potential* to reconciliation as post-Pauline *realization* (as if there were no Gentile-Jewish unity before Paul's death and no Gentile-Jewish tensions in the church by the time Ephesians was written) but, rather, a more explicit statement of fact that has already appeared in the letters of Paul implicitly.

Moreover, in both the undisputed letters and in Ephesians, the fact, or indicative, of God's act of reconciliation in the Messiah yields an imperative to embody the reconciliation, to put unity into practice. At the nitty-gritty level, even Ephesians starts with humanity's relationship with God, with the "vertical," so to speak (Eph 2:1–10), and then moves to the "horizontal" (Eph 2:11–22).[17] For Pauline audiences, this inclusion of the "horizontal" may mean beginning to practice that which is currently absent (as reflected in, say, 1 and 2 Corinthians, as well as Romans); maintaining that which has been established (as in Ephesians); or radically reconfiguring an existing relationship in a dramatic act of reconciliation because both parties are now "in the Messiah" (as in Philemon).[18] In each case, however, the imperative is a natural and necessary dimension of reconciliation with God,

16. In a presentation on Pauline theology and practice, St. Mary's Seminary & University, November 9, 2012.

17. Brueggemann (*Isaiah 1–39*, 105) suggests that this pattern is an echo of the theological movement in Isaiah 11.

18. On Philemon, see my discussion of the letter in *Apostle of the Crucified Lord*, 454–70; and Wright's in *Paul and the Faithfulness of God*, 3–74.

a constitutive part of the soteriology of messianic peace. This reflects the general prophetic (and specifically Isaianic) vision of the cessation of hostility among natural or normal enemies, and specifically, at least in Romans and Ephesians, the prophetic vision of the rapprochement of the nations and Israel. This is what the new covenant looks like.

For Paul, then, Jesus is "the Messiah, our peace" (cf. Eph 2:14) by virtue of his peacemaking death that has made God's enemies into God's friends, and has also made people who are naturally quite different and even estranged into one body, one reconciled people of the (new) covenant. This is a reality, a divine and messianic gift. The promised peace has arrived, in all of its dimensions. At the same time, however, it has not arrived in its fullness and, for that reason, it is a peace that needs to be embraced and embodied day to day. That is, Jesus the Lord of peace continues the work of peace in the present. We need, then, to consider Jesus as the *present* Lord of peace, and thus to peace as ecclesial practice. To that subject we will turn after looking at the cross and peace in Luke's theology.

The Peacemaking Death of Jesus in Luke

For Luke too the cross is the place of God's making peace, even though it is less explicitly developed than in the Pauline corpus.[19] In his Gospel, we see Luke's connecting of the cross to peace in several ways.

First of all, we learn in the first mention of peace in Luke's Gospel (1:79, Zechariah's prophecy) that peace is associated with the forgiveness of sins (1:77—along with much else in 1:68–79). To be sure, Jesus forgives sins throughout his ministry, but the pinnacle of this aspect of his ministry is on the cross itself (see further below). Forgiveness of sins is an essential aspect of the new covenant according to the prophets; it is one of the cardinal elements of peace for Luke (see especially 7:36–50), as we noted in the table in chapter 6, and it will also be one of the chief aspects of peacemaking as an ecclesial practice, as we will see.

Second, as the Spirit-empowered gospelizer and liberator who reverses the hierarchical status quo and breaks down the horizontal walls of

---

19. This does not mean that peacemaking is Luke's only theological interpretation of the cross, but as we will see, as God's act of peacemaking it includes many other dimensions of Luke's soteriology, not least the inauguration of the new covenant. For the interpretation of Jesus' death in Luke more broadly, see Carroll and Green, *Death of Jesus*, 60–81; and for a survey of recent interpretations, see Reardon, "Recent Trajectories and Themes."

separation that would otherwise keep out Gentiles, the poor, lepers, and so on, Jesus engages in risky behavior that will get him into trouble. There are hints of this already in Simeon's words about Mary's soul being pierced by a sword (1:34–35), and then it becomes explicit already after the Nazareth inaugural sermon (4:16–30), when the crowds want to stone Jesus (4:29). Jesus is certainly more than a prophet for Luke, but he is not *less* than a prophet, and his activity in fulfillment of the prophetic dream of *shalom* will lead, in part, to his rejection and death—in keeping with the prophetic tradition (4:24; 6:23, 26; 11:47–51; 13:33–34).

Third, then, the entire narrative of Luke's Gospel leads of course to the cross, his *exodos* (9:31; cf. 13:33–34). The journey to and ministry in Jerusalem occupies more than half of the Gospel. As noted in the previous chapter, the angelic announcement of peace (2:14) is echoed as Jesus enters Jerusalem (19:38). Accordingly, we should see continuity among the various events and phases of Jesus' ministry. His death is a direct consequence of his birth and life, and an integral part of his prophetic ministry.

This is in no small measure the case because he and his ministry—especially his proclamation of good news—pose a threat to the Roman *pax*.[20] In his death at the hands of Roman officials, he will again challenge the imperial claims of peace that began with the angelic announcement of his birth, only this time the challenge will be much more obvious and tangible. Ironically, then, the one who seeks peacefully to bring good news to all will be perceived as, and eventually crucified as, bad news—a threat to peace and security. This is, paradoxically, both true and false. On the one hand, because Jesus' way of the cross, in all its counterintuitive and countercultural dimensions, challenges the very notion of Roman peace and power to its core, that Roman "peace" and power will have to deal with the threat. On the other hand, the very thing Rome needs in order to have true peace and security is the nonviolent, topsy-turvy power of God that arrives in Jesus. He is, in other words, both Rome's problem and Rome's solution.

Fourth, if it is true that Luke seeks in his work to show how the community of the new covenant came into being, then it will be clear from the teaching on discipleship during the journey to Jerusalem that sharing in Jesus' death is a necessary and integral dimension of discipleship. Luke gives voice to this costly dimension of discipleship both by using the traditional

---

20. The older idea that Luke is a defender of the Roman Empire will simply not stand up to the evidence of Luke and Acts. See, e.g., Evans, "King Jesus and his Ambassadors" (on Luke-Acts as a whole). On the Empire and Acts, see also n34 in the discussion of Acts below.

passion prediction-summonses he takes from Mark (inserting one at the Last Supper; see the discussion in chapter 5) and by placing certain parts of the sermonic material that is similar to Matthew 5–7 in the context of the journey to Jerusalem (e.g., the Lord's prayer, with its challenge to forgiveness [11:2–4]; the word about possessions and treasures [12:33–34]; the word about serving two masters [16:13]). The new community is defined by the road to Jerusalem and all that it entails; if the community of the new covenant (the disciples) is so defined, then also the Lord of the covenant is defined by how and why he goes to Jerusalem. He goes in peace to make peace, and he instructs the disciples to follow (culminating in 22:38).

Fifth, at the Last Supper, in Gethsemane, and after the arrest, Jesus interprets his death as a peaceful, nonviolent, creative act of covenant- and community-creation, and he does so in several ways[21]:

- Jesus announces his willingness to suffer (22:15); he has accepted his cup, even if he will later struggle with that decision (22:42).

- Jesus identifies the cup as "the new covenant in my blood" (22:20). In this statement and his acceptance of suffering just noted, Jesus is forswearing the use of violence to bring about the kingdom of God; he is prepared to shed his own blood, rather than that of his enemies, to accomplish God's plan for salvation, for peace. By sharing his body and his blood, his very self in its crucified reality, he invites his disciples to share in his mission and his fate. "There is 'no communion' between partaking of the bread and cup, sharing in the body and blood of Jesus, and drawing the sword."[22] The new covenant is coming about through nonviolent means, by Jesus' accepting rather than inflicting violence.[23]

- The very fact, therefore, that in this Gospel Jesus says that the new covenant is going to be effected by means of his death must be taken with the utmost seriousness. It means that the new covenant (and

21. See also Swartley's excellent analysis of the Last Supper/Lord's Supper, in Luke and elsewhere, as Jesus' establishment of the covenant of peace (*Covenant of Peace*, 177–88).

22. Ibid., 180.

23. This is not at all to deny what Fitzmyer (*Gospel according to Luke X—XXIV*, 1390–91) describes as the "vicarious and soteriological character of Jesus' reinterpretation" of the Passover meal "in terms of himself" as "an allusion to the covenantal sacrifice of Exod 24:3–8," even if the reference is less explicit than Mark's because it is "overlaid now with an allusion to Jer 31:31." Moreover, Fitzmyer rightly adds that because this is a *new* covenant, "the pact is concluded not with the blood of sacrificed oxen, but 'with my blood.'" This is obviously also the main theological point of Hebrews regarding atonement.

thus the community of the new covenant) could not be birthed in any other way. It also means that the community of the new covenant is also the community of the covenant of peace; the two covenants and communities are inseparable; they are, in fact, one. To share in the benefits of Jesus' death is to share in its peaceable means as well as its peaceful results.

- This connection between new covenant and covenant of peace emerges clearly in the disciples' misunderstanding about the sword, and in Jesus' response (22:35–38). Jesus is in the process of fulfilling the Isaianic text about being numbered among—but not as one of—the lawless (22:37, citing Isa 53:12). His metaphorical summons to prepare for the events about to unfold (22:36), and for future hostility more generally, is taken by the disciples as a call to (literal) arms (22:38a)— which Jesus firmly rejects with the words, "It is enough" (22:38b) or, more colloquially, "Enough already!"[24]

- When one of the disciples cuts off the ear of the high priest's slave, there is Jesus rejecting violence (22:51a) and making *shalom*, bringing the healing that has characterized his ministry to the party of his enemies (22:51b). Luke alone records this healing. It is not merely an enacted parable of peacemaking but an instantiation of the kind of peaceful new covenant his death brings about.

- When Jesus is insulted and beaten, he does not make any effort to retaliate (22:63–65).

- Finally, the man who is traded for Jesus is a man of great violence—accused of insurrection and murder (23:19). Jesus is not merely innocent (23:22); he is the one who can challenge the peace and justice of the empire in a way radically different from that of Barabbas.

Sixth, the peacemaking dimension of the Messiah's death is captured perhaps most poignantly in the first word Jesus speaks from the cross: "Father, forgive them; for they do not know what they are doing" (23:34a).[25]

---

24. Nearly all commentators interpret the Greek *(hikanon estin;* "it is enough," not "they are enough") as an expression of Jesus' exasperation with the disciples, not a statement suggesting that literal swords are good or that two such swords will suffice. See, e.g., ibid., 2:1432–34; Green, *Gospel of Luke,* 774–75.

25. As noted in chapter 2, I find the arguments for this text being in the original gospel of Luke compelling. To repeat the key bibliography listed there: Brown, *Death of the Messiah,* 2:975–81; Carroll, *Luke,* 466, with additional bibliography.

This merciful, gracious pronouncement is significant because it embodies, at the ultimate point of testing and temptation to betray one's most deeply held convictions, Jesus' teaching about enemy-love and his practice of forgiveness throughout his ministry. Furthermore, we must assume that for Luke the "them" in "forgive them" includes Jewish leaders as well as Roman soldiers and officials,[26] ironically furthering the theme of the gospel's being for both Jews and Gentiles. The words of Jesus are equally important, moreover, as a prayer to the Father, for Jesus the Prophet-Messiah-Son has come into the world, and has come to this unjust place on earth, precisely to bring God's *shalom*, God's peace and justice, to the earth.[27] That was the plan of God announced by Zechariah (esp. 1:76–79) and by the heavenly host (2:14). It is particularly telling that Zechariah's prophecy included specifically the forgiveness of sins (1:77), which is now being brought to fruition on the cross in the most dramatic way possible: forgiveness not only for God's people, but even for the Lord's enemies. The penitent thief is surely sorry for his sins, and his words (23:40–42) certainly underscore one more time in the Gospel the Lukan themes of repentance for salvation and Jesus' innocence. But the main point is christological, even (properly) theological: the grace of Jesus on behalf of the Father, even on the cross. This man will be with Jesus, with God (23:43).

Seventh, with this sort of dying, Jesus can breathe his last with the psalmist's intimate prayer of peace and trust, the prayer of the suffering righteous: "Father, into your hands I commend my spirit" (23:46, citing Ps 31:5).

Finally, in his death on the cross, Jesus demonstrates his solidarity with the lowly to whom he has been bringing peace since his birth. But the cross is not the end of the story, because the story of God's *shalom* is a story of the exaltation of the lowly. Thus the resurrection, for Luke, is God's act of exalting the crucified Messiah Jesus (Acts 2:24, 32; 3:15; 4:10; etc.) and God's renewed promise to exalt the lowly and the humble, which now includes bringing them, with Jesus, into the kingdom and presence of God—into God's *shalom* (Luke 22:40–43). But this experience of God's peace is not limited, for Luke, to a post-mortem future. For those who remain alive,

---

26. So also, e.g., Brown, *Death of the Messiah*, 2:972–75.

27. See Green, *Gospel of Luke*, 812: "From the cross Jesus twice addresses God in familial terms as Father, confirming that he regards his passion as fully congruent with his status as God's son."

the gift of the Spirit at Pentecost brings the future, eschatological age and kingdom of peace into the here and now.[28]

It should be stressed that Luke does not portray Jesus' death as an act of peacemaking *rather than* an atoning sacrifice. It is both, with forgiveness of sins being the factor common to both aspects, and to the death's effectiveness in inaugurating the new covenant.[29] Indeed, the identity of the new-covenant community depends on its participants receiving forgiveness and peace, and then sharing forgiveness and peace with others (see below on ecclesial practices).

Three final brief but important points remain to be made. First, the death itself is not the only, or the final, peacemaking action in Luke's Gospel. To repeat our point from above: the resurrection is the confirmation of the validity of Jesus' peaceful death and the ultimate source of peace. Accordingly, even before Pentecost, the risen Jesus greets his gathered disciples with the words, "Peace be with you" (24:36).[30] Second, this resurrection episode illustrates the truth of another point made earlier: that Jesus' death on the cross is not an isolated act of peace- or covenant-making for Luke; it is, rather, his part of a larger narrative, a larger reality—the story of Jesus from birth to resurrection, exaltation, and beyond—into Acts and the period of the church. And third, then, Jesus' death, and all that has led up to it, has begun the creation of a new, alternative community that will embody the peaceful practices that have been taught and narrated in Luke's passion narrative.

In the book of Acts, as we have already noted, the word "peace" does not appear frequently. In fact, four of the seven references are primarily to corporate or personal tranquility, while two occur in narratives about past events involving reconciliation that are not given particular emphasis.[31] The remaining reference, however, is more significant and is particularly relevant to our concerns in this chapter. In Acts 10:34–43 we find a speech by Peter that eloquently sums up the gospel of peace as Luke presents it:

---

28. See the discussion of Pentecost in chapter 2.

29. See the succinct but helpful discussion in Green, *Gospel of Luke*, 763.

30. Cf. John 20:21, 26. "From a theological perspective, it is dumbfounding that one who was betrayed, scorned, shame, vilified, and tortured to death should then make his presence felt among his own without so much as a hint of recrimination of retribution on his lips but rather with a greeting of peace" (Neville, *A Peaceable Hope*, 95).

31. Calm: Acts 9:31; 15:33; 16:36; 24:2. Reconciliation: Acts 7:26; 12:20 (and usually translated with the "reconcile" word–family).

³⁴Then Peter began to speak to them: "I truly understand that God shows no partiality, ³⁵but in every nation anyone who fears him and does what is right is acceptable to him. ³⁶You know the message he sent to the people of Israel, preaching peace (*euangelizomenos eirēnēn*) by Jesus Christ—he is Lord of all. ³⁷That message spread throughout Judea, beginning in Galilee after the baptism that John announced: ³⁸how God anointed Jesus of Nazareth with the Holy Spirit and with power; how he went about doing good (*euergetōn*),³² and healing all who were oppressed by the devil, for God was with him. ³⁹We are witnesses to all that he did both in Judea and in Jerusalem. They put him to death by hanging him on a tree; ⁴⁰but God raised him on the third day and allowed him to appear, ⁴¹not to all the people but to us who were chosen by God as witnesses, and who ate and drank with him after he rose from the dead. ⁴²He commanded us to preach to the people and to testify that he is the one ordained by God as judge of the living and the dead. ⁴³All the prophets testify about him that everyone who believes in him receives forgiveness of sins through his name."

Key Lukan themes are present in this speech: inclusivity, good news, peace, Jesus' Messiahship and Lordship, the Holy Spirit and power, Jesus' ministry of doing good (benefaction, in contrast to Gentile rulers—Luke 22:24–30) and healing/exorcising, Jesus' crucifixion, God's resurrection of Jesus, witnessing, judgment, fulfillment of prophecy, and forgiveness.

The speech reinforces the way in which Luke sees Jesus' death as God's act of peacemaking that we have explored at length with respect to the Gospel's passion narrative. That is, Jesus' entire ministry was one of inaugurating the reign and the peace of God. The healings, exorcisms, deeds of mercy, pronouncements of forgiveness, and death were all of a piece—the peace of God.

Furthermore, the emphasis on the resurrection as God's answer to human violence is also a critical dimension of this speech. Of particular note is the "They" of v. 39b. It conveys a generalized charge, perhaps implying Jewish leaders and/or Romans—Luke's speeches can certainly also use "you" in such charges³³—but also suggesting a universality that has now been answered in the universality of the gospel, in the impartiality (v. 34)

32. This is the only occurrence of this word in the New Testament, and almost certainly an echo of rulers' claims to be the people's benefactors. See the related noun *euergetēs*, "benefactor," which also occurs only once in the New Testament, in Luke 22:25, in the plural.

33. Acts 2:23; 3:14; 7:52.

of the God who raised Jesus from the dead in response to human evil. This violent evil may have come to expression in the murderous power of the so-called *Pax Romana*, but it is a violence that stretches beyond the officials and soldiers of Rome, beyond the cooperating Jewish leaders and the people they represented, to include all of humanity: "they"—even "we."

In other words, God has made peace with rebellious humanity in the life, death, and resurrection of Jesus. The consequences are enormous: the new covenant is a covenant of peace, calling a people to walk in the way of peace (Luke 1:79), or simply "the Way" (Acts 9:2; 19:9, 23; 22:4; 24:14, 22; cf. 18:25–26 [Way of the Lord/of God]). And this is not the way of Rome; it is not the way of violence and domination.[34] It is the way both to and from Jerusalem, the way of the cross, the way of peace.

THE WAY OF PEACE: DIMENSIONS OF THE ECCLESIAL PRACTICE OF PEACE

We have now explored the basis of peace in Paul and Luke: the death of Jesus as the critical moment in God's peacemaking initiative. In the words of Stanley Hauerwas, "God, through the cross, refuses our refusal of friendship."[35] We turn now to the ongoing practice of peace in the communities that have been birthed by that death. The phrase "the way of peace" appears three times in the Bible: in Isaiah 59:8, Luke 1:79, and Rom 3:17. It summarizes the thesis we have been arguing in this and the previous chapter: that Paul and Luke, in particular, give expression to the Isaianic hope for peace, being convinced that it has arrived in Jesus and that it continues in the life of the community that calls Jesus the Lord of peace. The covenant of peace obliges (and permits!) the community to participate in a journey of discipleship in the way of peace. Thus we will consider dimensions of the ecclesial practice of peace in the letters of Paul and in Luke-Acts, with an additional brief note on Hebrews. Once again, we begin with Paul.

---

34. Swartley (*Covenant of Peace*, 164–70) has a balanced survey of the evidence for and against Acts as an apologia for Rome and its *pax*. He concludes that "Acts subverts the claims of the Pax Romana by letting them [the Roman officials] 'play' a role in the narrative, only to show the limited nature and insustainability of the Pax Romana" (170). See also Rowe, *World Upside Down*.

35. *Cross-Shattered Church*, 65.

Ecclesial Practices of Peace in Paul

For Paul, Jesus is the present Lord of peace, present in his communities by the Spirit to continue making peace in and through those communities. Although this present work has numerous forms, it is especially manifested as unifying and reconciling activity within the churches, and as nonretaliatory and nonviolent love for all, even enemies, outside the churches. Peace, then, is a critical marker of ecclesial identity—not merely as an ethical principle but as a sign of the presence of Jesus and of the church's fellowship with him.[36]

The epistolary greetings and benedictions in Paul's letters remind us that God the Father, Jesus the Lord, and the Holy Spirit remain for Paul the one, gracious divine provider of peace; the work of peace is not yet complete. By grace the church is always receiving the gift of *shalom*. At the same time, it is clear that for Paul peaceableness and peacemaking are ecclesial practices, even obligations. The *shalom* that was promised through Isaiah held peace and righteousness together. Just as Paul sees close ties between righteousness and peace in the action of God in Christ, so also does he see close connections between them in his discussion of messianic peace as ecclesial practice.

One place where this connection emerges explicitly is 2 Corinthians 5, where God's peacemaking is intended to create a community of reconciled people who practice *dikaiosynē*—they are intended to become the righteousness, or justice, of God (2 Cor 5:21).[37]

Another place where the righteousness-peace connection appears is Romans 14, which we considered earlier. Here Paul calls the Roman house churches to practice peace and unity. To do so, he uses another psalm (in addition to Psalm 85[84], discussed in chapter 6): Psalm 34 (LXX 33), which speaks of the practices of the righteous, including the pursuit of peace. Psalm 34:11–15 (LXX 33:12–16) reads as follows:

> [11(12)]Come, O children, listen to me; I will teach you the fear of the Lord.

> [12(13)]Which of you desires life, and covets many days to enjoy good?

> [13(14)]Keep your tongue from evil, and your lips from speaking deceit.

36. In addition to the discussion of Pauline ecclesial practices of peace here, see also Swartley, *Covenant of Peace*, 211–21 and the bibliography there.

37. See Grieb, "'So That in Him,'" as well as the discussion on 60–62 and 174–75.

¹⁴⁽¹⁵⁾Depart from evil, and do good; seek peace, and pursue it (*zētēson eirēnēn kai diōxon autēn*).

¹⁵⁽¹⁶⁾The eyes of the Lord are on the righteous, and his ears are open to their cry.

The psalm refers to the practices of "the righteous" (*hoi dikaioi*), not only in v. 15 (LXX v. 16), but also again in vv. 17, 19, and 21 (LXX vv. 18, 20, 22); it is the subject of this section of the psalm. In the same spirit, Paul admonishes the Romans believers to pursue peace because it belongs with righteousness/justice, and they of course now constitute the justified in the Messiah who have peace with God (Rom 5:1); they are thereby the community of the just and peaceful, as Romans 14 makes clear[38]:

> For the kingdom of God is not food and drink but righteousness and peace (*dikaiosynē kai eirēnē*) and joy in the Holy Spirit . . . Let us then pursue what makes for peace and for mutual upbuilding (*ara oun ta tēs eirēnēs diōkōmen kai ta tēs oikodomēs tēs eis allēlous*). (Rom 14:17, 19)

Interestingly, Paul transforms Psalm 34's two second-person-singular imperative verbs ("seek peace, and pursue it"; *zētēson eirēnēn kai diōxon autēn*) into a single first-person-plural hortatory verb ("Let us . . . pursue"; *diōkōmen*) with two grammatical objects ("what makes for peace" [*ta tēs eirēnēs diōkōmen*] and "[what makes] for mutual upbuilding" [*ta tēs oikodomēs tēs eis allēlous*]), the second of which explains the first.[39] The pursuit of peace is above all a communal practice expressed concretely in mutual edification.

For Paul, furthermore, pursuing peace is a manifestation of walking according to love (*kata agapēn peripateis*; 14:15[40]), which, in turn, means walking according to the Messiah (*kata Christon Iēsoun*; Rom 15:5, summarizing the call to please [= love] the neighbor in the interest of community unity).[41] To work for peace in the church requires the kind of self-giving,

38. On the connections between justification and justice, see my "Justification and Justice in Paul."

39. That is, the *kai* introducing *ta tēs oikodomēs tēs eis allēlous* is epexegetical. The *kai* in the original LXX line (v. 14 [15]) was already functionally epexegetical, joining two short parallel phrases.

40. Paul actually negates this phrase in the text, warning the Roman believers that their current practices are not loving or peaceable.

41. The connection between love and edification is clear also in 1 Corinthians, especially summarized in the phrase "love builds up" (*hē de agapē oikodomei*; 1 Cor 8:1).

others-regarding love that Jesus displayed on the cross; such love edifies and unifies. It is the ongoing work of God in the Messiah by the Spirit.

In other words, for Paul the reconciled and justified community will practice and pass on the peace it has received; the divine/messianic gift becomes divine, messianic, pneumatological, ecclesial practice.

When Paul calls the church to be at peace, whether addressing the competing factions in Corinth, the contentious women in Philippi, or the diverse house churches in Rome, he is calling them to put on Christ, to adopt the mindset—the dispositions and corollary practices—of the crucified Messiah (Phil 2:1–8; Rom 15:1–6). We see this in whole letters, such as 1 and 2 Corinthians, in short snippets, such as Phil 4:2–3, and in focused but well-developed texts such as Rom 14:1—15:13—and elsewhere. Paul does not merely hold out Christ as an example, but points to him as a living presence with and in whom the church has *koinōnia* inasmuch as it practices peace—the peace of the crucified and resurrected Messiah. He is the Lord of peace, the Son of the God of peace.

Peaceableness/peacemaking is, therefore, practicing the presence of God and of Christ or, more precisely, it is allowing the present Christ, the Lord of peace, to do in the community that which he has done and wishes to continue doing for the sake of the people of God and for the entire world. For Paul, the church is, or should be, a "sphere of interrupted violence in the midst of a violent world"—a sign of hope.[42]

Peaceableness and peacemaking are, accordingly, ecclesial practices that are both internal and external, acts of both *koinōnia* and *martyria*.

We see the former, peace in the church, in many texts, both explicitly and implicitly, and we have already at least briefly noted some of these. Paul takes this communal responsibility so seriously that he finds an inseparable connection between practicing peace toward others and experiencing the promised peace of God, as we see in the conclusion of 2 Corinthians:

> Finally, brothers and sisters, farewell. Put things in order, listen to my appeal, agree with one another, live in peace (*to auto phroneite, eirēneuete*); and the God of love and peace will be with you. (2 Cor 13:11)[43]

There are of course many similarities (though also differences) between 1 Cor 8:1—11:1 and Rom 14:1—15:13.

42. The quote is from Wengst, *Pax Romana and the Peace of Jesus Christ*, 88.

43. This connection is reminiscent of the teaching of Jesus summarized in the Lord's prayer and the brief interpretation of it in Matthew's gospel: "And forgive us our debts, as we also have forgiven our debtors . . . For if you forgive others their trespasses, your

We see the latter, peace in the world, less often but no less poignantly, with references to outsiders sometimes as "all" and sometimes as "enemies." The peace of the church is not simply for its members, for those "in Christ." From what is likely his earliest surviving letter (1 Thessalonians), we see that Paul urges believers to practice peacemaking (1 Thess 5:13b) by "not repay[ing] evil for evil" and by "do[ing] good to one another and to all" (1 Thess 5:15)—that is, to believers and to non-believers, even to persecutors. This pair of admonitions re-emphasizes the prayer of 1 Thess 3:12: "And may the Lord make you increase and abound in love for one another and for all." Making peace, not retaliating, and doing good (we might substitute the word "justice") are all of a piece—an integrated vision of practicing *shalom*. Paul echoes Ps 34:14 (LXX 33:15) quoted above: "Depart from evil, and do good; seek peace, and pursue it." It is highly unlikely that Paul is making these connections among love, goodness, and peace for the first time as he writes 1 Thessalonians. Rather, it is virtually certain that Paul is reminding the Thessalonians about his previous teaching and encouraging them to continue to pursue the ways they have been taught and they have practiced to date.[44]

In Romans we find a similar exhortation in a similar context. After Paul instructs the believers in Rome to excel in mutual love, honor, and practical care toward one another, as well as hospitality to strangers (Rom 12:9–13), he turns to the topic of the treatment of those outside the community, specifically persecutors: "Bless those who persecute you; bless and do not curse them" (Rom 12:14, echoing Matt 5:44 and Luke 6:27–28). A few lines later, Paul returns to the subject of appropriate practices toward "all," as in 1 Thess 3:12 and 5:15, including (once again) especially opponents and persecutors:

---

heavenly Father will also forgive you; but if you do not forgive others, neither will your Father forgive your trespasses" (Matt 6:12, 14–15). The other significant connection is the one among unity, peace, and love, which we have seen also in Romans and Philippians. The phrase *to auto phronein* ("to have the same mind") refers to practicing the others-oriented mind of Christ, not to having homogeneity.

44. See 1 Thess 4:1–12, which suggests that (1) Paul and his colleagues gave initial moral instruction about the practices of Christian love, (2) the Thessalonians have generally followed those teachings, (3) Paul sees God as their ultimate teacher in these matters, and (4) the Thessalonians nonetheless need gentle apostolic reminders to sustain their practices. Paul also believes they need ongoing mutual support within the community to live appropriately as God's holy ones (see 1 Thess 5:11).

[17]Do not repay anyone evil for evil, but take thought for what is noble in the sight of all. [18]If it is possible, so far as it depends on you, live peaceably (*eirēneuontes*) with all. [19]Beloved, never avenge yourselves, but leave room for the wrath of God; for it is written, "Vengeance is mine, I will repay, says the Lord." [20]No, "if your enemies are hungry, feed them; if they are thirsty, give them something to drink; for by doing this you will heap burning coals on their heads." [21]Do not be overcome by evil, but overcome evil with good. (Rom 12:17–21)

The echoes of 1 Thessalonians in Romans 12 reveal a Pauline pattern of peacemaking toward outsiders ("all"). This means both refraining from evil—cursing, retaliation, and so on—and doing good—blessing, feeding, etc. The admonition to practice non-retaliation and peace toward outsiders receives special attention, no doubt, because of the frequent hostility toward believers practiced by certain members of the universal set that Paul calls "all." Practicing peace is therefore a form of bearing witness to the gospel in the most difficult circumstances, the expression of the teaching and example of both Jesus and Paul to refrain from retaliation and to love one's enemies.[45] By obeying and imitating both their apostle and their Lord in this regard, believers would become a living exegesis of the gospel of peace.[46] Such peaceful relations with outsiders would include the rejection of violence toward them, apparently even in self-defense, for as Richard Hays has put it, "There is not a syllable in the Pauline letters that can be cited in support of Christians employing violence."[47] Non-retaliation, for Paul, is not an *option* for peacemakers in Christ; rather, it is the way of Christ.

We should also emphasize, however, that Paul does not limit peacemaking to reactionary measures of doing good instead of evil. On the contrary, Paul admonishes his communities to be proactive peacemakers, to *initiate* good and not just to *avoid* reactionary evil. Gordon Zerbe has shown that Paul's "ethic of nonretaliation and peace" appears in general

---

45. See Zerbe, *Citizenship*, 148–50, for a discussion of Romans 12 and love, and see Gabrielson, *Paul's Non-Violent Gospel*, 56–62, for the most recent treatment of the Pauline texts on nonretaliation as indebted to the church's memory of Jesus. Gabrielson also rightly focuses on the "behavioral correspondence" between Paul and Jesus (63–68).

46. On enemy-love in Paul, see Swartley, *Covenant of Peace*, 213–15 and, for more detail, Zerbe, "Paul's Ethic of Nonretaliation and Peace" (now reprinted in Zerbe's *Citizenship*, 141–68). Zerbe refers to "passive" and "active" responses to enemies (143–44).

47. Hays, *Moral Vision*, 331. See also my *Inhabiting the Cruciform God*, 129–60.

exhortations on the topic (e.g., Rom 12:9–21), in catalogs of Paul's hard-ships (e.g., 1 Cor 4:12–13a), in lists of virtues and vices (e.g., Gal 5:16–24), in reference to a concrete situation (1 Cor 6:1–8), and in his poem on love (1 Corinthians 13). That is to say, *for Paul peacemaking is a normal and on-going ecclesial practice, a sign that the community is part of the new covenant of peace and is practicing the presence of the Lord of peace.*[48] In so being and doing, the community follows not only Jesus, but Paul himself.[49]

Such admonitions to *shalom*-making are hardly "conventional" (Schnelle's word noted at the beginning of chapter 6) in Paul's letters or in other New Testament writings, even if parallels can be found, as they can be, in Jewish or pagan literature. For Paul these admonitions are grounded in two assumptions. The first assumption is that the world does not normally operate according to the norms of peace (and neither does the church, he would probably add); it is, in fact, a place of strife, violence, and bloodshed. The "proof text" here is certainly the catena of Scripture passages in Romans 3:

> [10][A]s it is written: "There is no one who is righteous, not even one; [11]there is no one who has understanding, there is no one who seeks God. [12]All have turned aside, together they have become worthless; there is no one who shows kindness, there is not even one." [13]"Their throats are opened graves; they use their tongues to deceive." "The venom of vipers is under their lips." [14]"Their mouths are full of cursing and bitterness." [15]"Their feet are swift to shed blood; [16]ruin and misery are in their paths, [17]and the way of peace they have not known." [18]"There is no fear of God before their eyes." (Rom 3:10–18)[50]

Paul's second assumption is that the gospel of God's peacemaking activity in Jesus the Messiah is the ultimate manifestation of divine universal love and divine enemy-love. The foundational text here is found in Romans 5:

> [6]For while we were still weak, at the right time Christ died for the ungodly. [7]Indeed, rarely will anyone die for a righteous

48. See also Paul's words in 1 Cor 7:15 about God's general calling of believers to peace, with specific application to non-believing spouses.

49. Gabrielson (*Paul's Non-Violent Gospel*, 63–68) rightly connects 1 Cor 4:12–13a to the memory of Jesus' teaching in Matt 5:11 and Luke 6:28, and to Jesus' example.

50. The last sentence comes from Psalm 36:1 (LXX 35:2). It is significant that fear of the Lord is associated with the righteous/just who practice peace, according to Psalm 34:7, 9, 11 (LXX 33:8, 10, 12). The biblical mindset refuses to separate appropriate relations with God from appropriate relations with others.

person—though perhaps for a good person someone might actually dare to die. [8]But God proves his love for us in that while we still were sinners Christ died for us. [9]Much more surely then, now that we have been justified by his blood, will we be saved through him from the wrath of God. [10]For if while we were enemies we were reconciled to God through the death of his Son, much more surely, having been reconciled, will we be saved by his life. (Rom 5:6–10)

This twofold assumption—the human practice of violence versus the divine, messianic practice of peace—certainly reflects the realities of the world in general for Paul. But clearly we should also hear an echo of the realities of the *Pax Romana*, the "realized eschatology" of the imperial myth that Augustus and his heirs brought the world true peace and justice.[51] *From Paul's perspective, however, if peace and justice come through violence and war (whether then or now), then Rome was right and Christ died in vain.*[52] Indeed, for Paul the Messiah came to undo humanity's propensity to practice bloodshed by shedding his own blood once and for all. Accordingly, "the way of peace they have not known" is, or should be, the antithesis of the life of those who have been justified and brought into the peace of God by God's own enemy-loving, peacemaking act in Christ. The new way, the way of the Messiah and his people, is the way of peace.

What God has done and is doing in Christ, therefore, is an act of radical pacification,[53] of radical transformation. God has made friends out of enemies.[54] Reconciliation is not merely a pronouncement of forgiveness but

51. The reference to Rome's own version of realized eschatology is from Wright, *Paul and the Faithfulness of God*, 305; 1265. Wright also speaks of a Roman *Heilsgeschichte*, or salvation history, that even has its own "climax"—Augustus and his golden age (xv; 383). On Paul and Rome, see (among many) Wright, *Paul and the Faithfulness of God*, 279–347, 1271–1319; Wengst, *Pax Romana*; and Elliott, *Arrogance of Nations*.

52. Paraphrasing Gal 2:15–21. For the peace of Christ in Paul as the antithesis of Roman peace, see (among others) Gabrielson, *Paul's Non-Violent Gospel*, 125–38 (on Galatians), 140–58 (on 1 Thessalonians).

53. I use the term "radical pacification" cautiously, even hesitantly, but deliberately—in order to indicate the antithetical character of the divine peace initiative over against the Roman program of pacification.

54. It should be recalled, as noted above, that both in Rom 5:1–11 and in 2 Cor 5:14–21 justification/righteousness language and reconciliation/peace language appear, the former more so in Romans and the latter more so in 2 Corinthians. Justification and reconciliation are two ways of referring to the same reality. See further Dunn, *Theology of Paul the Apostle*, 386–89; Gorman, *Apostle of the Crucified Lord*, 364–66; Gorman, *Inhabiting the Cruciform God*, 52–57; de Villiers, "Peace in the Pauline Letters," 11–14.

an event of conversion, an act of new creation, as Paul knew from his own experience of conversion away from hatred and violence,[55] and as he makes clear in 2 Corinthians: "So if anyone is in Christ, there is a new creation: everything old has passed away; see, everything has become new! All this is from God, who reconciled us to himself through Christ" (2 Cor 5:17–18a). Jeremy Gabrielson has rightly drawn the connection between Paul's violent past and his new mission. Paul's language and practices of peace are not indebted primarily to a general Jewish ethic but to his "experience of being a violent persecutor of Jesus' followers whose violent life was shattered on the road to Damascus." Gabrielson continues: "Enlivened by the risen Jesus from this point on, Paul's task of announcing the gospel to the nations involved calling and equipping assemblies of people whose common life was ordered by a politics (by which I mean, chiefly, a mode of corporate conduct) characterized by peaceableness."[56] Paul's violent self, we might say, was co-crucified with Christ.[57] All those who are similarly reconciled to God through Christ are now—because they are *in* him, clothed by him, reshaped by him—being transformed away from violence and into the righteousness/justice of God (2 Cor 5:21). That is, they are not only *benefiting* from God's reconciling love but *participating* in it.

To be sure, the age of peace, the new creation, is not here in its fullness. But because it *has* in fact been inaugurated we should think of Paul's "spirituality" and ethics as one of *anticipatory participation*, and not merely anticipation. To participate now in the inaugurated new creation promised

---

55. Acts 7:58—8:1; 9:1–2; 22:3–5; 26:9–12; Gal 1:13–14; 1 Cor 15:9; 1 Tim 1:13. See Gorman, *Inhabiting the Cruciform God*, 129–60; and Gabrielson, *Paul's Non-Violent Gospel* (esp. 91–101). A number of scholars have proposed that Paul himself was violent, in his use of language, his imposition of control, and so on. See my response to this perspective in *Inhabiting the Cruciform God*, 129–60, and, for a more thorough analysis, with a theologically nuanced way forward, Zerbe, *Citizenship*, 169–80. A few scholars have also questioned whether Paul was in fact violent; see Gabrielson, *Paul's Non-Violent Gospel*, 83–91, for a cogent argument that he was—before his conversion (Gabrielson: before "the apocalypse" [91]).

56. Gabrielson, *Paul's Non-Violent Gospel*, 2. Paul's conversion was not by itself, however, the sole source of his nonviolence. Paul's politics, Gabrielson also argues, were in contrast to those of violent Rome and necessarily nonviolent because they were "built . . . on the shoulders of the politics of Jesus" (5–6). Gabrielson argues convincingly that Paul knew, and in his letters embeds parts of, early traditions about Jesus' nonviolence (79–138). These traditions may have confirmed what he had come to believe after his encounter with the risen Christ.

57. Ibid., 93. His whole discussion of Gal 2:19–20 in relation to Paul and violence/nonviolence is illuminating (93–98).

in Isaiah, with anticipation and hope about its consummation in the future, means that the church is called to live peaceably with God, with others, and with the entire creation. Humanity's reconciliation with, and within, the creation/environment is an integral part of *shalom*. Care for God's creation is a manifestation of peace with God and with neighbor; it is an act of love toward both the creator and fellow creatures, as well as the creation. Justice and peace can truly flourish only when the *entire* creation in which humans participate is treated justly and peaceably.[58] For this reason, too, peace for Paul includes concrete expressions of mutual aid that bring about some semblance of equality and justice within and among the various communities in Christ (e.g., especially, 2 Corinthians 8).[59] Shalom is possible only when words and theologies of reconciliation express themselves in concrete practices that affect the daily lives of all involved. This is hope—the hope for God's future—in action.

N. T. Wright insists now that we see the theology of reconciliation at the heart of Paul's ecclesiology, his vision of the church:

> I want . . . to argue that Paul's practical aim was the creation and maintenance of particular kinds of communities; that the means to their creation and maintenance was the key notion of reconciliation; and that these communities, which he regarded as the spirit-inhabited Messiah-people, constituted at least in his mind and perhaps also in historical truth a new kind of reality, embodying a new kind of philosophy, of religion, and of politics, and a new kind of combination of those . . . a new kind of Jewishness, a community of new covenant, a community rooted in a new kind of prayer.[60]

The death of the Messiah, then, is the non-negotiable foundation of Christian behavior both in the church and in the world; there can be no separate practices for separate spheres. "Pursue and practice peace" is an admonition both internal (2 Cor 13:11) and universal (Rom 12:18) in scope. One fundamental imperative, representing one Lord of peace, fits all, though what this practice looks like concretely will of course vary from inside to outside the church, and from place to place and time to time. But peacemaking,

---

58. On the inclusion of the entire creation in the Pauline perception of *shalom*, texts such as Romans 8 and Colossians 1 have become important to interpreters. See, among others, Horrell et al, *Greening Paul.*

59. See Swartley, *Covenant of Peace*, 219–21.

60. Wright, *Paul and the Faithfulness of God*, 1476; see the entire discussion on 1473–1519.

rather than its opposite, is the messianic way. And because it is the messianic way of a particular messiah, namely *Jesus*, it will always be linked to and expressive of his particular way of making peace—on the cross. This means for Paul, and for those who read Paul as Scripture, that evangelization and peacemaking (including both reconciliation among peoples and "creation care"), rather than being at odds with each other, are in reality inseparable from each other.

Ecclesial Practices of Peace in Luke-Acts

For Luke the faithful, Jesus-like community will be, by necessity, a countercultural, status-quo-challenging community because its Lord, both in his life and teachings and on his cross, turned everything topsy-turvy. Status- and power-reversal were the order of the day, as Jesus challenged his own Jewish culture's evaluations of worth and status even as he called into question the entire ethos and structure of the Roman social and political order. He did so by calling for absolute loyalty to YHWH alone (rather than Rome and its gods) and displaying what that meant by his life of liberation and service to all, especially the poor and oppressed, that culminated in his death.[61] Luke can sum up this counter-cultural, or alter-cultural, existence in various ways, but the one most relevant for our purposes is "the way of peace" (Luke 1:79).

Practically speaking, for Jesus' disciples in Luke, for the apostles and others in Acts, and for those who read or hear Luke-Acts as witness to Jesus, walking in the way of peace is defined by the gospel narrative, by Jesus' own words and, especially, deeds. These words and deeds belong together, intended to be as inseparable for Jesus' followers as they were for Jesus himself throughout his ministry and culminating on the cross. Moreover, they consist of both prohibitions and positive admonitions. Those who are *beneficiaries* of God's peace become *instruments* of God's peace. This peace, we must remember, is the comprehensive *shalom* promised by the prophets, inclusive of restorative justice and coterminous with the kingdom of God.[62]

---

61. Of many treatments of Luke's theology, see the excellent overview in Green, *Theology of the Gospel of Luke* and, focusing on peace, Swartley, *Covenant of Peace*, 121–51. Green points out Luke's opposition to Roman ways, including violence (120–21). He also discusses Jesus' challenge to certain Jewish conventions (76–94). On the cultural revolution to which the book of Acts bears witness, see Rowe, *World Upside Down*.

62. See Hays, *Moral Vision*, 120–28; Swartley, *Covenant of Peace*, 152–76.

We may analyze the practices of *shalom* in Luke-Acts as consisting of seven basic practices, grouped into four categories: (1) evangelizing, liberating/welcoming the poor and oppressed, and healing and exorcising; (2) forgiving enemies and others, reconciling, and refraining from violence; (3) trusting in God; and (4) sharing material possessions.

The first category—evangelizing, liberating/welcoming the poor and oppressed, and healing/exorcising—includes both words and deeds, both "spiritual" and "social" ministry. Jesus' followers, both during and after his lifetime, are called to share in the Spirit-empowered mission of liberation and service that defines Jesus himself (Luke 4:16–30). Thus the Twelve (Luke 9:1–6), and then the Seventy (Luke 10:1–12), are sent out to share in Jesus' ministry. It is a ministry of peace because Jesus' ministry is a ministry of peace (7:50; 8:48), restoring people to wholeness and community (e.g., 8:26–39; 9:37–43a), to right relations with God (e.g., the penitent thief; Luke 23:39–43) and with others (e.g. Zaccheus; Luke 19:1–10). In Acts, Spirit-empowered apostles continue these forms of ministry, especially healing and exorcism,[63] as well as constantly offering reconciliation with God to all. Inviting people to repent (whether in the Gospel or in Acts), therefore, is a profound form of peacemaking, of restoring relationships and establishing justice.

For Jesus, this kind of ministry meant service to the point of death, even death on a cross, and so it will be for the disciples and apostles. To practice the peace of Jesus is to take up the cross—*daily* (Luke 9:23)—in costly service that brings about God's *shalom*, God's wholeness. This is itself revolutionary, a challenge to every status quo. This challenge is particularly clear in Jesus' summons to his disciples not to engage in Gentile-like domination and (so-called) benefaction (Luke 22:24–27), which were allegedly acts of peacemaking performed by rulers. Rather, the disciples are to practice a different kind of peace, a different politic.

The challenge to the status quo leads naturally to the second category of peacemaking—forgiving enemies and others, reconciling, and refraining from violence. This too grows out of Jesus' teaching and practice, once again culminating on the cross. Jesus taught enemy love and nonretaliation (Luke 6:20–36) and then practiced them throughout his passion. Thus to follow his teaching is not merely to imitate him but to participate in his life-giving cross, symbolized, as noted in chapter 2, in Simon the Cyrene (Luke 23:26). At least some of the Twelve (and others) apparently did not

63. E.g., Acts 3:1–10; 4:12–16; 9:36–43 (raising the dead!); 16:16–18; 19:11–12.

fully understand, or at least did not fully comply with, this teaching, as the passion narrative itself indicates (Luke 22:49–50). It means to refrain from even the most justifiable revolutionary, retaliatory, or Roman-like practices of violence and thus, positively, practicing forgiveness, mercy, and practical love even toward enemies. As Joel Green has written, "To take up arms, to exert coercive force, would be to adopt a style of life consistent with the Roman way, not with the way of this new kingdom breaking into the world."[64]

It has sometimes troubled interpreters of Luke that in Luke 6 he does not have a version of the Matthean beatitude "Blessed are the peacemakers, for they will be called children of God" (Matt 5:9). But this is less troubling than it first appears. For one thing, Luke's beatitudes function as pronouncements, not as admonitions to virtue. Accordingly, Luke also does not have beatitudes about the merciful—despite the importance of mercy to his overall theological project—or the pure in heart. We should hardly conclude that Luke feels negatively about any of these missing beatitudes or the virtues they enshrine. For another, in Luke 6 there is a high concentration of peacemaking imperatives (Luke 6:27–36), including a double mention of enemy-love (Luke 6:27, 35) and an apparent interpretation of perfection (Matt 5:48) as Godlike mercy: "Be merciful, just as your Father is merciful" (Luke 6:36), the concluding words on enemy-love. They function as Luke's call to Godlike peacemaking; mercy and peacemaking are thus closely connected in Luke's mind.

We see this mind of mercy and peacemaking on display in the passion narrative. The visual images of the healing, restoring Jesus in the garden and the forgiving, welcoming Jesus on the cross are, for Luke, icons of the new-covenant community constituted by the Lord's death. Jesus had already indicated, at the Supper, that his death would not be a solo experience, but something to be shared. It is shared not only in literal death, but especially in life—a life of peacemaking, forgiveness, and nonviolence.

But some will also be called to a literal sharing in Jesus' suffering and death on behalf of the peace of God. The ongoing significance for the community birthed by that passion is forcefully portrayed in another iconic image, this one from Acts:

> [54]When they heard these things, they became enraged and ground their teeth at Stephen. [55]But filled with the Holy Spirit, he gazed into heaven and saw the glory of God and Jesus standing at the right hand of God. [56]"Look," he said, "I see the heavens opened and

64. Green, *Theology of the Gospel of Luke*, 121.

the Son of Man standing at the right hand of God!" [57]But they covered their ears, and with a loud shout all rushed together against him. [58]Then they dragged him out of the city and began to stone him; and the witnesses laid their coats at the feet of a young man named Saul. [59]While they were stoning Stephen, he prayed, "Lord Jesus, receive my spirit." [60]Then he knelt down and cried out in a loud voice, "Lord, do not hold this sin against them." When he had said this, he died. (Acts 7:54–60)

The story of this Jesus-like figure is immediately contrasted, of course, with the figure of Saul, approving of the murder and seeking to end the nascent movement (Acts 8:1–3; 9:1–2). Paradoxically and ironically, however, this violent figure is transformed—by the same Jesus who forgave his ignorant executioners—into nothing less than a new icon of peace. Paul will abandon violence when he is embraced by Jesus, and he will suffer like Jesus as an agent of the reign of God's peace. This is not to say that Paul was anything less than a troublemaker according to Acts (as well as his own letters). But the divisions he created, the worlds he and others turned upside down and the empires they subverted (Acts 17:6–7),[65] were all the consequence of participating in the topsy-turvy *shalom* promised by the prophets, celebrated by Mary and Zechariah and Simeon and the angels, and inaugurated by Jesus.

Once again, by participating in this kind of *shalom*-making the disciples and others take up the cross daily in service that participates in the inbreaking of God's *shalom*, God's wholeness. As Richard Hays observes, "to join 'the Way' is to volunteer for risky duty."[66] When this service leads to literal suffering and death, there can be calm—the third category of peace for Luke—in the midst of chaos through trust in God. The superficially innocuous references to peace in Acts (Acts 9:31; 15:33; 16:36; 24:2) convey this message clearly. More forceful and iconic is, once again, the Jesus-like figure of Stephen, who imitates his crucified Lord at prayer: "Lord Jesus, receive my spirit" (Acts 7:59; cf. Luke 23:46). He does so while being stoned by his enemies.

The fourth category of peace practices in Luke-Acts is the sharing of possessions, meaning both being generous (e.g., Luke 6:38; 11:41; 12:33) and having goods in common (Acts 2:44; 4:32). As Luke Johnson and others have shown, for Luke the treatment of possessions is highly symbolic

---

65. See Rowe, *World Upside Down.*

66. Hays, *Moral Vision*, 122.

of one's spiritual health or lack thereof.[67] But it is more than that, for the two practices of giving and holding in common have the same goal: the justice and flourishing that the prophets promised would obtain with the arrival of the new covenant. This is achieved, says Luke, through sacrificial generosity, on the one hand, and through mutual aid and responsibility, on the other. Whether or not this was idealized—"not a needy person among them" (Acts 4:34) certainly sounds hyperbolic—Luke's vision of possessions is part of his vision of peace-with-justice.[68]

Ecclesial Practices of Peace Elsewhere in the New Testament: Hebrews

Paul and Luke were not alone, of course, in their commitment to practices of peace and peacemaking. Others have looked more broadly at the New Testament; we will limit ourselves here to the homiletical letter to the Hebrews, since it, like Paul and Luke, uses the term "new covenant."

Although Hebrews implies that Jesus is the king of righteousness (7:1–3), for twelve chapters and more it does not appear to make much of his death, explicitly, as Christ's or God's means of peacemaking. Nonetheless, there are at least two elements of divine peacemaking that are implied throughout the document. First, the renewal of the covenant by sacrifice, which involves the forgiveness of sins (8:12; 9:22, 26–28; 10:5–10, 17–18), is an aspect of peacemaking. Second, the very notion of a sanctified people of the new covenant implies a people at peace—in right covenantal relations—with God and one another. This assumption becomes both more explicit and explicitly christological, as we will see below, in the exhortation to peace in chapter 12.

Perhaps of greatest significance, however, is a single sentence at the very end of Hebrews:[69]

> Now may the God of peace, who brought back from the dead our Lord Jesus, the great shepherd of the sheep, by the blood of the eternal covenant, make you complete in everything good so that

67. See Johnson, *Literary Function of Possessions*.

68. See the discussion in Swartley, *Covenant of Peace*, 173–75; and Hays, *Moral Vision*, 123–24, who connects Acts 4:34 to the ideal covenant community described in Deut 15:4–8, in which there will be "no one in need among you" (15:4).

69. There has been debate about whether Hebrews 13 is part of the original document (homily?) or a supplement for epistolary purposes. Although I lean toward the latter perspective, its presence in the canonical form of the text is what matters most.

you may do his will, working among us that which is pleasing in his sight, through Jesus Christ, to whom be the glory forever and ever. Amen. (Heb 13:20–21)

This benediction identifies God as the God of peace, as does the Pauline tradition. More than just a liturgical or epistolary flourish (as also in Paul's letters), this benediction is theologically rich. In announcing God as the God who makes peace, the writer connects this identity to the act of Jesus' death that effected the new covenant. Although the precise connection of the phrase "by the blood of the eternal covenant" to the rest of the passage is a bit unclear, the writer clearly connects the identity of God as the God of peace to Jesus' death, but also to his resurrection. That is, God has made peace and effected the new covenant by means of Jesus' death and resurrection, the former being Christ's act of obedience (e.g., 5:8; 10:5–10), the latter being (it would appear) God's completion and confirmation of it.[70] There would be no atonement, no covenant of peace, without both the death and the resurrection.[71]

Hebrews contains an imperative to peacemaking issued in an instance of believers encountering hostility from outsiders that is similar to, and perhaps even more grave than, the situations reflected in most of the Pauline letters and in the Gospels. Like Paul, the author points his audience of persecuted (and apparently fragile—more fragile than the Thessalonians or the Romans) believers toward Jesus (12:1–3, discussed in chapter 3), and also therefore toward faithfulness toward God and peaceableness toward others. After pointing to Jesus in 12:1–3 and then interpreting suffering as divine moral formation (12:4–11), the author offers the following admonition: "Pursue peace with everyone (*eirēnēn diōkete meta pantōn*), and the holiness without which no one will see the Lord" (Heb 12:14).

It is within the context of focusing on Jesus' faithful suffering, rewarded with glory, and the formative function of suffering for those becoming like Christ, that the call to pursue peace makes sense as both a form of *imitatio Christi* and as a manifestation of covenant faithfulness—fidelity to the new covenant of peace inaugurated by the new king of *shalom*, Jesus,

70. I understand Heb 5:7 ("In the days of his flesh, Jesus offered up prayers and supplications, with loud cries and tears, to the one who was able to save him from death, and he was heard because of his reverent submission") as a reference to the resurrection; God did not save him *from* death but *out of* (Greek *ek*) death, by resurrection. So also Attridge, *Hebrews*, 150. The exaltation is more prominent in Hebrews than the resurrection per se (e.g., 1:3, 8, 13; 2:9; 4:14; 6:20; 7:26; 10:12).

71. See Moffitt, *Atonement and the Logic of Resurrection*.

who was the ultimate and paradigmatic faithful one.[72] One aspect of Jesus' faithfulness was his peaceableness—he endured the cross and its associated hostility (12:2–3). *That is to say, Hebrews, like Paul and Luke, understands the practice of peace as participation in the peaceable story of Jesus.*

CONCLUSION

For Paul (and for the early Pauline tradition, if there was such an entity), Luke, and Hebrews, Jesus is the Lord of peace, the fulfillment of the prophetically promised Prince of Peace. For Paul, we have seen, peace and peacemaking are constitutive of Jesus' identity, his Father's identity, the Spirit's identity, the kingdom's identity, and the church's identity. That is, the Triune God is the God of peace, and the peace of God is a fundamental mark of God's reign and God's people. To make peace, empowered by the Spirit and in the shape of the cross, is to be like Christ and thereby like God. It is to participate in the mission and identity or, better, the missional identity, of God. Paul is fully in sync, therefore, with the words of Jesus in Matthew: "Blessed are the peacemakers, for they will be called children of God" (Matt 5:9, similar in vocabulary to Col 1:20). This Jesus is, for Paul, the Lord of peace, the one who made and who makes peace on behalf of the Father and in the power of the Spirit.[73] Similarly, for Luke, Jesus is the one who inaugurates God's reign of shalom and invites his followers, both before and after his nonviolent, peacemaking death, to follow in "the Way"—the way of God, salvation, and peace: the way of Jesus himself.

What might this say to those who continue to read Paul and Luke (as well as Hebrews and other parts of the New Testament that are not discussed in these chapters) as canonical voice? "What it [the world] needs," said Karl Barth, "is not to be confirmed and strengthened by another variation of its own way, but to be pointed beyond it in unambiguous practice." The church exists (he continues), in obedience to and imitation of Jesus, "to set up in the world a new sign which is radically dissimilar to its [the world's] own manner and which *contradicts it in a way which is full of promise . . .*

---

72. The exegesis of the biblical story of Melchizidek in Heb 7:1–3 implies that Jesus, the eternal high priest, is also the king of righteousness and of peace.

73. If there is any sense in which believers share in Christ's rule in the present for Paul (something Wright says repeatedly in *Paul and the Faithfulness of God* but does not explain clearly), it must be in this sense of embodying the kingdom of cruciform justice, peace, and love.

The true community of Jesus Christ does not rest in itself . . . It exists as it actively reaches beyond itself into the world."[74]

I would suggest that Paul and Luke had a similar vision of the church. To be more specific: the peaceable and peacemaking church was, and could once again be, a sign full of promise and hope, a witness to the world of radical dissimilarity to personal, corporate, and ecological strife and violence, whether ancient or modern. It is difficult to imagine something more needed, whether in the first century or the twenty-first. With such an ecclesial existence in the world, I submit, Paul and Luke would be satisfied—and with nothing less. This is true not because they believed in peace or pacifism (or, for Paul, eco-theology) as a principle, but because they believed that the Lord of the church was the Lord of peace who brought reconciliation with God and among enemies, in the real world that is moaning and groaning (Rom 8:18–25), by his self-gift on the cross. "Every church a peace church" is not merely an Anabaptist slogan; it is the christocentric, messianic, death-and-resurrection reality to which Paul and Luke bear witness. It is an essential and non-negotiable aspect of life in the new covenant, the new covenant of peace.

74. Barth, CD 4/3.2:779; emphasis added.

–8–

Conclusion

The Integrative New-Covenant Model of the Atonement: Participation and Performance

IN THIS CONCLUDING CHAPTER we look back at where we have been and what we have found, contemplate some of the theological advantages and practical implications of our proposed model, consider the new-covenant model in relation to other models of the atonement, and connect our discussion to the Christian church's central activity of worship.

SUMMARY OF THE THESIS AND CONCLUSIONS

The purpose of this book has been to propose a new model of the atonement that is not really new: the new-covenant model. The following is a summary of the proposal:

> *The purpose of Jesus' death was to effect, or give birth to, the new covenant, the covenant of peace; that is, to create a new-covenant community of Spirit-filled disciples of Jesus who would fulfill the inseparable covenantal requirements of faithfulness to God and love for others through participation in the death of Jesus, expressed in such practices as faithful witness and suffering (cruciform faith), hospitality to the weak and servant-love for all (cruciform love), and peacemaking (cruciform hope).*

I have offered this proposal as a response to the lack of a formal new-covenant model in the Christian tradition, and as an outgrowth of my conviction that most of the traditional and recent models of the atonement address the atonement in partial and penultimate ways, rather than in a comprehensive and ultimate way. I have therefore argued that the new-covenant model is more than another ancient model in need of reappropriation, but also that it is a more comprehensive model, addressing ultimate as well as penultimate concerns about the purpose of Jesus' death. Furthermore, I have argued that this proposed new-covenant model is a much more integrated, participatory, communal, and missional model than any of the major models in the tradition. It overcomes the inherent rift in many interpretations of the atonement between the *benefits* of Jesus' death and the *practices of discipleship* that his death both enables and demands. I have contended throughout the book that in the New Testament the death of Jesus is not only the *source*, but also the *shape*, of salvation. It therefore also determines the shape of the community—the community of the new covenant—that benefits from and participates in Jesus' saving death.

With this emphasis on participation, and therefore transformation, I have argued that the New Testament is far more interested in *what* Jesus' death does for and to humanity than in *how* it does it (the "mechanics"). In the New Testament, Christ's death as God's act of faithfulness, love, and reconciliation is portrayed in many images and metaphors. Nevertheless, I have suggested, this rich variety creates a remarkably coherent overall picture of his death as that which brings about the new covenant, in all of its dimensions, that we find promised in the prophets. Each of these dimensions of the promised new covenant is reconfigured, of course, around the death and resurrection of Jesus.

It will be helpful at this point, before considering the advantages and implications of this model, to review the concerns and claims of each chapter.

CHAPTER SUMMARIES

To review our progress through the book, we may begin with a refresher on the chapter titles thus far:

Introduction: Refocusing the Atonement

1. The Promise of the New Covenant

2. Cross and New Covenant in the New Testament: The Gospels and Acts

3. Cross and New Covenant in the New Testament: From Paul to Revelation

4. Baptized into the Messiah's Death: New-Covenant Practices of Cruciform Faithfulness

5. Baptized into the Messiah's Death: New-Covenant Practices of Cruciform Love

6. The (New) Covenant of Peace

7. Baptized into the Messiah's Death: New-Covenant Practices of Cruciform Peace

Chapter 1, "The Promise of the New Covenant," began by noting the curious absence of new-covenant language and theology from discussions about the atonement, especially the absence of a full-blown model called "the new-covenant model of the atonement" or something similar. We noted hints of movement in this direction, however, in the work of biblical scholars and theologians such as Joel Green, David Brondos, Larry Shelton, the late T. F. Torrance, and Kevin Vanhoozer. We also critiqued the proposal of Ted Grimsrud, who argued essentially to do away with traditional atonement theology. We then identified four problems with traditional models of the atonement that need to be remedied. Those models tend to be isolationist, non-integrative, individualistic, and underachieving. The hints about the importance of the new covenant for understanding the atonement and the problems with other models suggest, we argued, that the time is ripe for a new, more comprehensive model of the atonement focused on the new covenant. The chapter continued with a summary of the various dimensions of the new covenant promised by the prophets Jeremiah and Ezekiel: that it would create a liberated, restored, forgiven, sanctified, covenantally faithful, empowered, missional, peace-filled, and permanent people of God. Chapter 1 concluded with a brief overview of the new-covenant obligations to God and to neighbor, and raised the question of how all of this is connected to the death of Jesus.

Chapters 2 and 3 ("Cross and New Covenant in the New Testament") surveyed various parts of the New Testament for their contributions to the proposed new-covenant model, with chapter 2 focused on Mark, Matthew, Luke-Acts, and John, and chapter 3 devoted to Paul, Hebrews, and Revelation. Two major topics were addressed for each New Testament author or writing: (1) the way in which the cross gives birth to the new covenant in its various dimensions and (2) the nature of participation in Jesus' saving and exemplary death as an integrated life of cruciform vertical and horizontal covenant-fulfillment.

Among the many discoveries in these two chapters was the significance for Jesus' disciples of the three passion predictions in Mark, which include (a) cruciform witness and suffering, (b) cruciform hospitality to the weak, and (c) cruciform service, rather than domination, to all. (Hence we referred to these as passion prediction-summonses.) These practices of faithfulness toward God (a) and love toward others (b and c) provide the structure of chapters 4 and 5. Furthermore, we discovered that in all of the Gospels, Jesus' death effected forgiveness (one aspect of the new covenant) but also much more, including the creation of a community that, empowered by the Spirit, peaceably practices faithfulness and love, participating in the mission of God that is embodied in Jesus' life and death. As we said about the Gospel of John, *"To embrace the Son's death is to embrace God's world-mission and thus to embody God's love in the world."*

Regarding Paul, we built on the observation of T. J. Deidun that Paul has a "new-covenant morality," and we sought to show its connections to Jesus' death. We saw in the occurrences of the phrase "new covenant" in 1 and 2 Corinthians the wide-ranging effects of the cross as that which establishes the multi-dimensional new covenant. We also observed, especially in 2 Corinthians, Ephesians, and Romans, the inseparability of reconciliation with God and with others in Pauline theology and practice. Noting the connections between the cross and both faith and love, we suggested that *"Paul's most innovative and important contribution to the theology of the new covenant"* may well be the claim that *"the 'new spirit' that comes to dwell in the people is the Spirit of the crucified Messiah; it is, therefore, the cruciform Spirit, the spirit of cruciformity."* With respect to Hebrews and Revelation, we emphasized that each writing is a call to covenant faithfulness, with Hebrews stressing permanence and Revelation once again blending christologically grounded faithfulness and love.

The conclusion to chapters 2 and 3 focused on the importance of concrete practices to express the reality of the new covenant, and it was to those practices that chapters 4 through 7 were devoted. Chapters 4 and 5 considered the discipleship implications of the three passion prediction-summonses, with chapter 4 looking at the first of the three, faithfulness to Christ and the gospel, even to the point of suffering (the "vertical" component of the new covenant), and chapter 5 treating the second and third, hospitality to the weak and servant-love to all (the "horizontal" component). Chapters

6 and 7 took up the topic of the new covenant as the covenant of peace, as well as practices of peace understood as practices of hope, complementing those of faith and love.

Chapter 4 ("Baptized into the Messiah's Death: New-Covenant Practices of Cruciform Faithfulness") began with the vivid, generative images of participation in Jesus' death found in the Gospels and Paul, especially baptism and co-crucifixion, as well as the three practices (corresponding to the three Markan passion predictions) of taking up one's cross. We suggested that there is a cruciform thread connecting Jesus to Paul and to the rest of the New Testament. The bulk of chapter 4 focused on participation in Christ's sufferings, as found in Jesus' words in the Synoptic Gospels (especially Mark), Paul, and John as well as 1 Peter, Hebrews, and Revelation. Close parallels between Jesus in Mark and Paul, on the one hand, and between the Synoptics and John, on the other, were uncovered. Five principal conclusions about faithful witness and participatory suffering emerged.

In chapter 5 ("Baptized into the Messiah's Death: New-Covenant Practices of Cruciform Love"), we shifted from the primarily "vertical" to the primarily "horizontal" practices of cruciform hospitality to the weak and cruciform servanthood—cruciform love. In the Synoptic witness to Jesus, especially Luke, this derives not only from participation in the cross, but also from Jesus' entire ministry. In Paul, concern for the weak is grounded in the cross as the revelation of God's powerful weakness and Christ's love for all. Similar concerns for the weak and lowly as expressions of the symbiosis of new-covenant faithfulness and love were noted in Hebrews, James, and 1 John. In considering the more general practice of participatory service rather than domination, we noted the strong contrast between Jesus' teaching and imperial policies and practices, as well as the similarities once again between Jesus in Mark (chap. 10) and Paul, due in part to their connection to Isaiah 53. We noted as well the way Luke strengthens the call to such service and its connection to Jesus' death by placing it at the Last Supper. And we looked also at John's presentation of radical, participatory servant-love in John 13.

Chapter 6, titled "The (New) Covenant of Peace," began by connecting the prophetic new covenant to the prophetic "covenant of peace." The chapter, which focuses on Paul and Luke, then notes the general lack of scholarly attention to peace in the New Testament, including especially the writings of those two authors. It then sets out the thesis of chapters 6 and 7: for Paul and Luke, the prophetically promised age of eschatological, messianic peace (*shalom*) has arrived in the death and resurrection of Jesus the

Messiah, which means that the promised new covenant is also the promised covenant of peace. Therefore, both Paul and Luke portray the church as a community of peace, nonviolence, and reconciliation. The remainder of the chapter makes the case that there is a discernible prophetic *shalom* "narrative-collage," especially in Isaiah but also in Ezekiel, with particular features (e.g., security, nonviolence, reconciliation, justice), and that both Paul and Luke demonstrate in numerous texts their belief that this age of peace has arrived. Of special importance is Paul's use of particular Scripture citations and Luke's construction of the entire gospel narrative around the theme of peace.

In chapter 7, "Baptized into the Messiah's Death: New-Covenant Practices of Cruciform Peace," we turned first to Jesus' death as God's means, according to Paul and Luke, of effecting the covenant of peace. Special attention was paid to Paul's theology of reconciliation and to Luke's connecting the cross to peace throughout his Gospel, leading up to the Passion narrative. We then considered the ecclesial practices of peace that, for Paul and Luke, are constituitive of the new-covenant community. In examining Paul's writings, we saw his emphasis on peace and peacemaking in various key texts in several letters. We then looked carefully at the many aspects of Luke's passion narrative that reveal the peacemaking dimensions of Jesus' death for him. The resulting christologically grounded practices of peace we considered were, for Paul, unifying and reconciling activity within the churches, and nonretaliatory and nonviolent love for all, even enemies, outside the churches. For Luke, the practices of peace included several kinds of activity: evangelizing, liberating/welcoming the poor and oppressed, and healing and exorcizing; forgiving enemies and others, reconciling, and refraining from violence; trusting in God; and sharing material possessions. The chapter included a brief note on peacemaking in Hebrews before concluding that for Paul, Luke, and those who embrace their work as Scripture, peace/peacemaking is a christocentric and essential aspect of life in the new covenant, the new covenant of peace.

THEOLOGICAL ADVANTAGES AND IMPLICATIONS OF THE MODEL

If the arguments we have been making for the new-covenant model are convincing, or at least provocative and plausible, then there are some major theological conclusions, and some major advantages to the proposed model, that are implied. Among these are some that we will describe rather succinctly, as well as two that we will consider more fully.

1. The first and most obvious theological advantage is the model's comprehensive and integrated character. Whereas other models of the atonement, I have argued, are isolationist and non-integrative, the new covenant model is just the opposite. Our theology of Jesus' death becomes inseparable from our ethics, spirituality, ecclesiology, pneumatology, missiology, and even politics—the very dimensions of Christian theology and practice that are often unconnected, or only loosely connected, to the various theories and models of the atonement. In this model, the cross shapes each of these aspects of Christian thought and life, weaving them together into a comprehensive and integrated whole.

2. Another important advantage of the new-covenant model is that as the cross pulls the various aspects of the prophetic vision of the new covenant together, the rifts between faith and works (especially faith and love), evangelism and social justice/peacemaking, and spirituality and politics that should have never occurred can be mended, and perhaps in a permanent way. These various aspects of Christian existence are all integral and interrelated aspects of the new-covenant reality envisioned by the prophets and inaugurated by Jesus' death.

3. The model also incorporates and integrates the various aspects of other models of the atonement that are part of the Christian tradition. The words of Kevin Vanhoozer cited in chapter 1 bear repeating: "While the sundry conceptualities championed by the various atonement theories do not, strictly speaking, cohere, they are nevertheless *compatible* thanks to the integrative framework of the covenant—a complex, multilevel reality that combines the judicial and relational aspects of Jesus' death 'for us' in a garment as seamless as the one for which the soldiers cast lots."[1]

   In fact, we can attribute the existence of the various models, both traditional and newer, not only to the multi-faceted nature of Jesus' death, but also to the multi-faceted nature of the new covenant promised by the prophets. Yes, the cross provides forgiveness; yes, the cross provides liberation; yes, it offers an example of self-giving love; and so on. *The cross does all these things because it is God's mysterious*

---

1. Vanhoozer, *Drama of Doctrine*, 391.

way of bringing about the multi-dimensional new covenant that was supposed to consist of these very realities. Traditional theories of the atonement, as well as some contemporary ones, concentrate too much on the *mechanics* of atonement—on *how* God brings about our justification or forgiveness or transformation through Jesus' death. I have been arguing that the New Testament writers are far less interested in the *mechanics* of atonement than they are in the *results* of atonement. In fact, I would suggest that the mechanics are largely a mystery and will always be precisely that.

To some, my claim that the new-covenant model of the atonement is less interested in the mechanics—the *how*—of atonement will suggest that it is insufficient as a model because it only claims *that* the cross effected atonement, not *how* it did so, when in fact the *how*—or at least the why—is the purpose of a theory or model of the atonement.

In response to this concern, two things can be said. First, the new-covenant model welcomes what I call penultimate theories or models that say something about "how" as long as they correspond to aspects of the covenant and are not offered in a "take-it-or-leave-it" fashion. The new-covenant model simply refuses to limit the meaning of the atonement to one mechanical explanation. Second, however, the new-covenant model contains within it an implicit answer to the question "how." If the purpose of Jesus' death was to bring about a people of the new covenant who would embody the covenant life expected by God, then we can assume Jesus himself embodied that covenant life, and he did so most fully in his faithful and loving death. In a profound way, then, Jesus was the *incarnation* of the new covenant, culminating in his new-covenant-effecting death. By virtue of his resurrection and the gift of the Spirit, now we can both benefit from and participate in Jesus' death and the new-covenant life it brings about.

Thus the "how" of atonement would include not only the objective accomplishment of Jesus on the cross, but also the subjective aspect, participation in that faithful and loving death. This understanding of atonement, sometimes called the participatory model, has its roots in Jesus and Paul, comes to vibrant expression in some of the church fathers, and is enjoying a revival today. It says Christ became what we are so we could become what he is. The new-covenant model would focus on this ancient soteriology, stressing its connection to the covenant-fulfilling death of Jesus. When we participate in Jesus' faithful and loving death by the power of the Spirit, we both benefit from and embody Jesus' covenant-fulfilling love for God and neighbor. We have been not only forgiven, but also reconciled and transformed. But even the "how" of participation remains, in the end, somewhat mysterious. Some parts of the Christian tradition will emphasize spirituality, some will stress the sacramental life, some will focus on ethics, and some will attend to all of these.

This emphasis on participation should not, however, be mistaken for a soteriology of human effort, a Pelagianism through the back (or front) door. It is rather the nature of God's relationship with humanity, and the nature of the relationship God *desires* with people and among people, that causes participation to make sense. God has created human beings to be in intimate fellowship—a relationship of loyalty and love—with their creator and with one another; the death of Jesus does not just make that relationship with God and others possible; it makes it actual, real. To do so, *that death must be something more than a substitution, representation, declaration, victory, or example that does not directly involve the intended beneficiaries.*

It might be useful to think of the atonement as creating a marriage, as St. John of the Cross interpreted it.[2] Marriage is, of course, an intimate, personal relationship, a relationship of self-involving loyalty and love. The only appropriate response to Jesus' death, says Adam Johnson in his study of atonement in John of the Cross, is not to like it or even to imitate it, but to participate in it—but only because this cross, in light of the resurrection, is life-giving.[3] In connection with the marriage metaphor, furthermore, we should perhaps also think of the cross as creating not just a couple but a paradoxical, suprahuman set of relationships in which one bridegroom (Christ) can be the faithful spouse of many brides, all of whom are siblings to one another. The Christian tradition has generally referred to this reality in terms of the one bride of Christ, namely the church as a whole.[4]

4. Yet another theological advantage of the new-covenant model, then, is its communal emphasis. Rather than being largely or exclusively

2. See Johnson, "The Crucified Bridegroom." Luther also spoke of the marriage between Christ and the believer.

3. Johnson, "The Crucified Bridegroom," 407.

4. We will return to the subject of incorporating other, penultimate models below.

individualistic, this model is inherently corporate without giving up the personal dimension of relationship and discipleship. The promise of a new covenant was not merely that individuals would have a new relationship with God—though that is true—but that God would create a people, a community, that would experience this new covenant together while also giving corporate witness to the new covenant, and to the God who made it, in the public arena. This is not to discredit the importance of individual faith, but to contextualize it. The existence of Christian community, then, is not an *addition* to atonement theology, nor a way of superficially joining together myriads of individuals who each happen to have received the forgiveness of their sins. Rather, Christian community is part of atonement theology's very essence. There is no atonement without ecclesiology, and no ecclesiology without a comprehensive account of the atonement.

5. Still another theological advantage of the new-covenant model is the centrality it gives to the Holy Spirit. The Christian doctrine of the atonement needs to include the role of the Spirit more explicitly and comprehensively. In the words of Kevin Vanhoozer:

> [Here is] my thesis: the saving significance of Jesus' death consists in making possible God's gift of the Holy Spirit. "The 'wonderful exchange' is thus not economic but thoroughly eschatological: *Jesus gives his body and blood for us, and in return we receive the Spirit, the operative principle of the new covenant and the new age.*[5]

It is the work of the Spirit, promised by the prophets and sent following the death of Jesus, that makes the death of Jesus an existential reality within and among the community of the new covenant. The reality of the Spirit addresses head-on the "under-achievement" of other models. The close relationship of the Spirit to the cross, that is, to atonement, means that, whatever else the cross does, it connects people to God and to one another in a transformative way. To be saved by the cross of Christ is not only to be forgiven but also to be changed; it is not merely to believe in a past one-time act but to participate in its ongoing, transformative effects—all by the workings of the Spirit.

5. Vanhoozer, "Atonement in Postmodernity," 398–399. I would disagree, however, with Vanhoozer's previous sentence in this passage, in which he unfortunately equates the kingdom of God with "the reign of God in human hearts" (398), which is far too narrow in scope. I do not find this same narrowness in his *Drama of Doctrine*.

Thus the people of the new covenant effected by God's action in Jesus' death are empowered by the Spirit to fulfill the horizontal and vertical demands of the Law, also reconfigured by the cross into a cruciform shape, and to live peaceably.

6. In the new-covenant model, not only does Jesus remain connected to the Spirit, but also Jesus' death remains connected to his life. The cross remains central, though not isolated from the incarnation, birth, life/ministry, resurrection, and exaltation of Jesus as the Son of God. As we have seen at numerous junctures in this book, what Jesus did on the cross is intimately connected to the rest of his ministry, both before and after his death.

7. Furthermore, the prophetically promised new covenant is realized, but also reconfigured, in and through the life, death, and resurrection of Jesus. The cross, still central (though not isolated), must be understood not only as the *source* but also as the *shape* of salvation. As we have seen, three fundamental practices of this cruciform community of the new covenant are provided by the synoptic passion prediction-summonses: courageous, self-giving witness to Christ and the gospel; hospitality to the weak and marginalized; and service, rather than domination, as the Christian expression of love and power. These are not be understood as restrictive but as open-ended and generative practices that can and must take specific forms in particular times and situations. Similarly, peaceableness and peacemaking flow directly from the new covenant effected by the cross, and are not optional add-ons for certain kinds of Christians; peace is at the heart of the gospel and of Christian practice. That is, peace (including nonviolence) is not a minor or peripheral aspect of Christian theology and life but a cardinal dimension of it because the very act of Jesus' death is his "no" to violence and his "yes" to faithful suffering and to reconciliation, both of humanity to God and of people to one another.[6]

8. Another significant point to be made is this: speaking of a "new covenant" is not inherently dismissive of the old or former covenant, and is to be understood in terms of both continuity and discontinuity. The notion of a new covenant is obviously fundamentally prophetic and Jewish, and the idea of that new covenant being somehow effected and embodied in a community is also Jewish—and not unique to the early

---

6. On this point, I am in agreement with Grimsrud, *Instead of Atonement*.

Jesus movement/church; it was found as well at Qumran. Historically, it should not surprise us that claims about the identity of the community of the "new covenant" were disputed, just like claims about the identity of the "Messiah." Theologically, it is critical that Christians who embrace the claims of the New Testament about the identity of this community recognize its Jewishness and therefore its continuity with Israel, with Israel's covenants and promises, and with Israel's Scriptures. The new covenant means the fulfillment of the original, valid, enduring covenantal obligations.

At the same time, the often implicit and sometimes explicit claim of the New Testament writings is that something decidedly new has happened before, during, and after the death of Jesus that inaugurated this new covenant. To call this new covenant "more glorious" (2 Corinthians) or "better" (Hebrews) is above all to use the criteria of comparison provided by the covenants, promises, and Scriptures of Israel themselves. It is not—or at least it does not have to be—an act of religious superiority. The promises of the Spirit, internalization, permanence, and so forth come from the prophets. The New Testament claims to "newness" and "superiority" are made by *Jewish* writers who believe that they are the recipients of those promises; accordingly, they compare two legitimate covenants by means of internally generated criteria (i.e., criteria from within the tradition). Their primary intent in these comparisons is not to criticize an earlier covenant or its adherents, but rather to promote (new-) covenant faithfulness among their audiences, whether ancient or contemporary.

Christians, therefore, may and indeed must assert the reality of the "new" covenant without disparaging the "old." As Paul says,

> [26]And so all Israel will be saved; as it is written, "Out of Zion will come the Deliverer; he will banish ungodliness from Jacob." [27]"And this is my covenant with them, when I take away their sins." [28]As regards the gospel they are enemies of God for your sake; but as regards election they are beloved, for the sake of their ancestors; [29]for the gifts and the calling of God are irrevocable. (Rom 11:26–29)

Paul expects that ethnic Israel, or the Jewish people, will be renewed and transformed because of God's faithfulness, and he draws on Isa 27:9 and 59:20–21 to say so. The context in both places is covenant renewal, and there are almost certainly echoes of Jer 31:31–34 here in

Romans as these texts are merged.[7] The theological consequences are at least three: (1) Israel (i.e., the Jewish people) remains God's people; (2) God's faithfulness to Israel (so understood) is guaranteed; and (3) Israel too will one day be transformed and participate in the new covenant. Participants in the new covenant, in the meantime, remain grateful to and for the people Israel, even as they proclaim and embody the gospel for Jew and Gentile alike—as did Paul.

9. Finally, the spirituality of the new covenant, as a participatory spirituality, is decidedly a this-worldly spirituality. It is this-worldly, first of all, because it is fundamentally Jewish and therefore affirms the goodness of creation. It is this-worldly also because it is grounded in, and is a means of sharing in, the events of a very this-worldly reality: a Roman crucifixion that Christians confess to be the divine "medicine for the world" (*crux est mundi medicina*, a saying of the ancient church). Here the gospel images of "cup" and "baptism" and walking in the "Way" overlap with the Pauline images of dying with Christ. These images only make sense as indicators of the spiritual life, however, if they are constantly paired with images of resurrection. The paradox of Christian existence, in the words of Paul (and in the context of the new covenant) is that in dying we are both recipients and channels of Christ's resurrection life: "For while we live, we are always being given up to death for Jesus' sake, so that the life of Jesus may be made visible in our mortal flesh. For while we live, we are always being given up to death for Jesus' sake, so that the life of Jesus may be made visible in our mortal flesh. So death is at work in us, but life in you" (2 Cor 4:12–13). Furthermore, because this spirituality of the new covenant is this-worldly, it is also inherently political—that is, it is a form of life in the public square.

Much more could be said about each of these nine claims. But this last point especially deserves some additional attention. So does the third point, referring to the new-covenant model's incorporation of other models of the atonement into it. We will address these two matters in that order.

---

7. On the scriptural texts Paul uses here, see, e.g., Jewett, *Romans*, 702–9 and especially Dunn, "Did Paul Have a Covenant Theology?," 15–18.

THE THIS-WORLDLY, MISSIONAL, POLITICAL CHARACTER OF NEW-COVENANT SPIRITUALITY[8]

New-Covenant Spirituality

The word *spirituality* is open to various definitions, even in the context of Christian faith. For many people, including Christians of various kinds, the word "spirituality" connotes an experience of the transcendent, even specifically of God or Jesus, that is not connected to life in the world. Its purpose, so to speak, is to transport people out of the trials and tribulations of this world through mystical experience(s), an interiority focused on the self or the god/God within, or an eschatological ("heavenly") orientation that pays scant if any attention to social ills. ("She is so heavenly minded, she is of no earthly good.") Although recent scholarly interpretation of Christian existence has opposed such approaches to spirituality, much popular spiritual writing and some Christian music (both traditional and contemporary) reinforce such sentiments. The resulting spirituality is often other-worldly, escapist, and even narcissistic. But a spirituality associated with the death of the Messiah can never be any of these things. *It is inherently a this-worldly spirituality, a missional and even a political spirituality.*

To speak of Christian spirituality as "this-worldly" is first of all to make a theological claim about the Christian faith itself, a claim related directly to the death of Jesus. This claim was articulated eloquently in the inaugural lecture of one of my teachers and my original doctoral supervisor at Princeton Theological Seminary, the late Paul W. Meyer. His 1979 inaugural lecture at Princeton was entitled the "The This-Worldliness of the New Testament." In that address, which has since been published, Meyer acknowledges that the term "this-worldliness" is awkward.[9] He insists on its use, however, in deliberate opposition to the term "otherworldliness" and all attempts to understand Christian faith as flight from this world. Meyer contends that for the earliest Christian communities, and for us, the very this-worldly crucifixion of Jesus—as historical fact, as God's means of redemption, as hermeneutical (interpretive) key—renders Christian faith inevitably this-worldly. For the New Testament writers, everything they

---

8. This section draws freely from my essay entitled "The This-Worldliness of the New Testament's Other-Worldly Spirituality" and from my inaugural lecture, "The Death of the Messiah: Theology, Spirituality, Politics."

9. Meyer, "This-Worldliness," 7.

know about God and life, Meyer contends, "has been *stamped with the branding iron of the crucifixion.*"[10] He continues:

> All has become irreversibly this-worldly, because the transcendence and authority of God himself now underscore and authorize that this-worldliness. And there is something on the stage of history that was not there before: a community that calls itself by the name of the crucified Messiah. It is one that can say now with integrity that it has been brought into being not by a flight into another world or by visions of things yet to be, but by its experience of life and by God's confirmation of the same.[11]

Returning to the question of spirituality: one standard definition of Christian spirituality among those who study it formally is "the lived experience of Christian belief"[12] or "of Christian faith and discipleship."[13] This definition, though useful, may be too general. Another proposal is "a transformative relationship with God," with emphasis less on experience and more on transformation.[14] In our context, and in light of Meyer's important comments, we might define spirituality this way: *"Spirit-enabled, this-worldly, transformative participation in the life-giving death of the Messiah such that the cross is not only the source, but also the shape, of our life in the new covenant."*

It is, in other words, our theology of atonement (or the Paschal Mystery[15]) embodied in daily life. If it is true that when we sing, we pray twice, then it is even more true that when we live, we theologize twice. Kevin Vanhoozer has described the church as "a form of reconciliatory theater: a theater of faith, hope, and love" that *performs* the atonement.[16] The church is called to "speak, act, live—and . . . suffer—in ways that correspond and cohere with the cross of Christ, the climax of the theo-drama."[17] Inde-

---

10. Ibid., 14; emphasis added.

11. Ibid. Meyer also rightly stresses that only with the resurrection does the crucifixion have any theological or existential import (11–14, 17–18).

12. The substance of the "working definition" used in the preparation of McGinn et al., *Christian Spirituality: Origins to the Twelfth Century*, xv.

13. The operative definition in *The Blackwell Companion to Christian Spirituality*. See Holder, "Introduction," 1, 5.

14. See especially Waaijman, *Spirituality: Forms, Foundations, Methods*, 305–591.

15. So, e.g., Schneiders, "Biblical Spirituality," 136–37.

16. Vanhoozer, *Drama of Doctrine*, 426–44, esp. 427. See also McKnight (*Community Called Atonement*, 28–31), who follows Vanhoozer and speaks of reciprocal performance, participation, and (later) "missional praxis" (117–56).

17. Vanhoozer, *Drama of Doctrine*, 428.

pendently of the line of argumentation in this book, Vanhoozer comes to similar conclusions: that the church must live in atonement-shaped faith and hope that includes faithful *martyria* even to the point of martyrdom, and love that "bear[s] witness to the reconciliation that the cross has made possible among human beings."[18]

The prophets had indicated that the new covenant would be one in which the law of God would be inscribed within the people so that they could and would do God's will. This internalization can also be described as God's *Spirit* being put within God's people. Thus life within the new covenant involves an intimate union of ourselves with the very self of God. It is participatory, and since in the New Testament the Spirit of God is also the Spirit of Jesus, new-covenant spirituality is participation in the event that brought about the new covenant and created the new-covenant people. That is, the death of the Messiah: the cup of suffering, serving, self-giving, and peacemaking we are privileged to share. In Vanhoozer's words:

> Truly to understand the atonement, the church must have recourse to more than theories and explanations: *Understanding is demonstrated through fitting participation, that is, by engaging in the right theo-dramatic practices.*[19]

For example, Vanhoozer writes in reflecting on Ephesians, "The church demonstrates her understanding of atonement by breaking down the dividing walls of racial and ethnic hostility."[20]

Thus atonement and mission are inseparable. The church becomes a living exegesis of the this-worldly reality of the cross when it lives the practices of faithfulness, love, and hope (i.e., *shalom*—peace, justice, wholeness for all people and all creation). As Darrin Belousek has put it, simply but accurately, "God's purpose to redeem the world, worked in and through the life, death, and resurrection of Christ, continues in and through the mission of the church."[21] Furthermore, he continues, "*neither* the cross of Christ *nor* the salvation of humanity through the cross is an end in itself; rather, both are for God's purpose of bringing about the redemption of the world."[22]

---

18. Ibid., 434. He discusses faith and hope (witness, suffering) on 428–34, love (reconciliation, forgiveness, peacemaking, enemy-love) on 434–38.

19. Ibid., 436.

20. Ibid., 440.

21. Belousek, *Atonement, Justice, and Peace*, 608.

22. Ibid., 610.

New-Covenant Politics

If the new-covenant community is active in the world, if it has practices, it is inherently a *political* entity. I do not mean political in the sense of political parties or leanings (e.g., conservative or liberal), nor even in the more generic sense of "the structuring of human life for human flourishing." Rather, for our purposes, by "politics" I mean this: if spirituality is our theology embodied in daily life, then politics is our spirituality embodied in the public square. It is our public life together, our corporate way of being in the world and thus also our corporate practices and witness.

The New Testament proclaims that the reign of God has already begun in the life, death, and resurrection of Jesus. Therefore members of the new-covenant community formed by his death constitute an alter-culture (an alternative culture) within whichever host culture they find themselves. This theme runs through the New Testament, from each of the Gospels, through Acts and Paul and other letters, to Revelation. Members of the new covenant live in a kind of exile, as resident aliens, constituted by a different charter, the word of the cross.[23] That is, we *are* a politic before we *have* a politics. Our primary political activity is to be the church, the new-covenant community shaped by the cross: to worship God truly and to live out the demands of the kingdom of God and the lordship of Jesus.

The primary group identity of all members of the new-covenant community is that they belong to their common Lord and to one another across the globe. Thus their primary allegiance is to that common Lord and to one another, not to any other group or entity, including any nation-state. In other words, *the death of Jesus means, for his followers, the death of every form of nationalism*. Participation in the new covenant means a change of loyalty. The Epistle to Diognetus (5.5) was on the right track in the second century: "[Christians] live in their own countries as though they were only passing through. They play their full role as citizens, but labor under all the disabilities of aliens. Any country can be their homeland, but for them their homeland, wherever it may be, is a foreign country." Christians, once again, are resident aliens, having a distinctive loyalty and allegiance.

For all kinds of reasons, members of the new-covenant community should operate with a hermeneutic, an interpretive posture, of suspicion vis-à-vis the powers, since those powers crucified Jesus. The Gospel of John reminds us that political power is often blind to the truth of God and, we should probably say, to truth more generally. In John's passion narrative

23. See Hauerwas and Willimon, *Resident Aliens*.

we have the famous scenes of Pilate coming in and out as he exercises his political power, in deference to the crowds and the emperor, by questioning Jesus and having the innocent man flogged and eventually crucified (John 18:28—19:16a). But when Jesus identifies himself as being on a divine mission to witness to truth, Pilate asks, "What is truth?" (John 18:38). For readers of John, this is not the sincere question of a philosopher-king but the question of a blind politician so caught up in the web of imperial untruth that he cannot recognize truth when it is standing in front of him, the incarnation of truth, the one who is the way, the truth, and the life (John 14:6). Thus, as Raymond Brown said, "the tables are turned; and Pilate, not Jesus, is the one who is really on trial," for his question about truth is "in reality a decision for falsehood."[24]

Readers and hearers of this narrative should henceforth know that politics is often the sphere of spiritual blindness, where power can prohibit the perception of truth and lead to persecution of witnesses to the truth. Paul speaks in a similar vein when he tells the Corinthians that the apostolic gospel is about the revealed wisdom of God, but that "[n]one of the rulers of this age understood this; for if they had, they would not have crucified the Lord of glory" (1 Cor 2:8).

This political blindness to the truth and wisdom of God is hardly limited to the first century or the crucifixion of Jesus. In addition, political power of course often leads to a search for more power, and that search often results in mistreatment of the powerless, as Jesus told his disciples: "You know that among the Gentiles those whom they recognize as their rulers lord it over them, and their great ones are tyrants over them" (Mark 10:42). Instead of the kind of cruciform hospitality and service seen in Jesus' death and expected by Jesus of his disciples, possessors of political power—at least to the degree that their power is Rome-like—are more likely to practice exclusion and oppression, seeking to be served rather than to serve, even if they frequently do so in the name of serving the greater good.

Thus it is no surprise that the earliest known articulation of the case for Christian civil disobedience is related to the death of the Messiah. When Peter and the other apostles are told not to preach the truth of the crucified and resurrected Messiah, they respond by saying, "We must obey God rather than any human authority" (Acts 5:29b). We have already seen that most of the New Testament writers expected suffering from public officials as a routine part of the life of faith.

24. Brown, *A Crucified Christ in Holy Week*, 10.

Now one might expect that the logical conclusion of this line of thinking is for the Christian community to see the political sphere or public life as something to avoid at all costs. But the this-worldliness of the cross and of Christian spirituality will not let us draw that conclusion. Members of the new-covenant community are still to seek the welfare of the city in which they reside, as Jeremiah told the exiles (Jer 29:7). But this must be a good they seek in *cruciform* mode. Their lives should be a living presence and voice that reflect the cross of the crucified Messiah. This is not, I would submit, the way that most discussions of Christians and politics (or public witness) proceed. If politics as it is normally understood and practiced is at least in part about the exercise of power, Christians have far too often sought to share that secular power, to control the political and/or public realm, and even to participate in the exercise of power in ways that are antithetical to the cross. As we all know, in fact, at times the cross has ironically and idolatrously become the symbol of such un-cruciform power, whether in the execution of medieval crusades, or in so-called "cross-lightings" by the KKK, or in contemporary popular war propaganda in which crosses and American flags are merged into a single blasphemous icon.

So what is an appropriate politic for those who claim allegiance to the crucified Messiah? It is the task of every Christian community, in each and every time and place, to seek the will of God, the mind of Christ, and the guidance of the Spirit in discerning how to be such a community of the new covenant within the host culture, which is to say in the "world." That world, is both the object of God's love and the locus of human rebellion against God. The church's presence in the world, as an alter-culture, including its alternative politics, is thus grounded in the twin realities of divine love, on the one hand, and human sin and need, on the other. The world, or the human city (in Augustine's words), is therefore both the focus of the church's cross-shaped mission and the source of the church's cross-shaped suffering, its temptations and trials. The church is salt and light. Its cruciform voice will be double-edged, like that of the prophets, offering both critique and hope, judgment and salvation, with both aspects of its message shaped by the cross. As N. T. Wright has written with respect to the book of Revelation, in which pagan culture and politics are so thoroughly critiqued, "The church is to live as the alternative *polis*, not by separating itself into sectarian isolation but by bearing witness . . . The aim is not to damn, but to redeem; the leaves on the tree [Rev 22:2] are for the healing of the nations, and the gates stand open for the kings of the earth to bring their treasures."[25] Yet this witness may be costly, Wright says, because although the world needs structures of power, "power corrupts and the church must bear witness against that corruption, by critique, by non-collaboration, by witness, and if need be by martyrdom."[26]

Thus the cruciform political life will resemble—in fact, it will be a continuation of—the cruciform spirituality we have already examined. To be more specific, we can briefly review the practices we have discussed throughout the book.

First, new-covenant politics will be a politics of truthful witness: speaking and embodying the truth in love. It will be a be a prophetic presence and voice willing to speak gospel truth to power and even to suffer for truthful witness to the gospel. But it will do so only out of love. As Pastor André Trocmé of LeChambon in south central France said in resisting the Nazis and hiding thousands of Jews: What we do, we will do "without fear and without hate." That is speaking and embodying the truth in love.[27]

Second, new-covenant politics will be a politics of servanthood rather than power and control. For those who live in the world's only super-power, there are special un-cruciform temptations to avoid and special cruciform tasks to embrace.

Third, new-covenant politics will be a politics of hospitality and solidarity rather than exclusion and rejection, especially with the vulnerable and the suffering. When the community of LeChambon was asked by the authorities, "Do you have any Jews living among you? We know you do!" Pastor Trocmé replied, "Nous ne connaissons que des hommes": "we know only human beings."[28]

Finally, new-covenant politics will be a politics of forgiveness, reconciliation, and *shalom* rather than revenge. The church has witnessed some incredible recent embodiments of this politics: the Truth and Reconciliation commissions, for instance, and the Amish community of Nickel Mines, Pennsylvania after the horrific 2006 school shooting. These sorts of cruciform practices both instruct fellow Christians and bear witness to the world.

25. Wright, "Revelation and Christian Hope," 121.

26. Ibid., 121.

27. As documented in Sauvage, *Weapons of the Spirit*; for the full story, see Hallie, *Lest Innocent Blood*.

28. As documented in Sauvage, *Weapons of the Spirit*; Hallie, *Lest Innocent Blood*, 103.

In sum: Christian political judgments—discernment and decisions about how the church is to live in the public square—are to be made with a cruciform hermeneutic within the community of the new covenant, shaped by the Spirit of the crucified and resurrected Jesus into a life-giving presence of faithful witness, love, service, and reconciliation.

From the many specific examples of what this means concretely, I wish to focus briefly on just one: Christians and war. I do so not only because the new covenant means the inauguration of the age of messianic peace, as we saw especially in chapters 6 and 7, but also because, theologically, the cross and war are antithetical to each other, yet many Christians fail to think about this antithesis. What most Christians do, instead, is to think about the necessity of war because, they say, the age of messianic peace has not really arrived or, more often, has not arrived in its fullness.

While the latter claim (that the age of messianic peace has not arrived in its fullness) is, in one sense, patently obvious, it is, in another sense, quite wrong. When Jesus confronted the Roman imperial powers and those assisting them with a different, messianic, cruciform politic of enemy-love and forgiveness, of resistance to empire by non-imperial means, had the messianic age of peace arrived in its fullness? To say "no" would be to state the obvious; Rome executed Jesus and, from one perspective, "won." The military-industrial complex (so to speak), rather than the way of messianic peace, carried the day. Yet to say "no" would also be to open a door that Christians do not, or should not, want to open: the door leading to the implication that there was something less than complete, less than perfect, less than messianic, and less than incarnate (divine) about the way Jesus lived and died.

Stanley Hauerwas has written that "in the cross of Christ war has already been abolished . . . The world has already been saved from war. The question is how Christians can and should live in a world of war as a people who believe that war has been abolished."[29] That is, the church's mission, as the people of the new covenant brought into existence by the peacemaking death and resurrection of Jesus, is to be an *alternative* to violence, including war.[30] As such, the church can, and hopefully will, influence others to believe that war is neither desirable nor inevitable. But there can be no such witness without the prior conviction that this is in fact the reality that Jesus'

---

29. Hauerwas, *War and the American Difference*, xi.

30. See also ibid., xiii, and the entire argument of the book, as well as additional bibliography included there.

new-covenant-creating death has accomplished. This conviction, in turn, requires a politics (in the sense we are using it here) to embody it, and both the conviction and the politics require an appropriate liturgy, or worship (in the sense described below), to sustain them.

ULTIMATE AND PENULTIMATE MODELS OF THE ATONEMENT: WHY WE HAVE AND NEED OTHER MODELS

Having concluded our proposal for the new-covenant model of the atonement, including further reflections on its spirituality and politics, we may briefly consider the relationship of this model to some other models of the atonement, both traditional and more recent. The third advantage and implication of our study noted above was that the new-covenant model also incorporates and integrates the various aspects of other models of the atonement, those we have labeled "penultimate." It is not my intent to offer an in-depth review of any of these, but rather to hint at how each might contribute to a broader, more comprehensive model of the atonement.

Christus Victor/Apocalyptic Interpretations

The *Christus Victor* model of the atonement popularized by Gustaf Aulén nearly a century ago as the retrieval of patristic atonement theology has recently been revived, thanks especially to the work of N. T. Wright and the concerns of those opposed to "violent" interpretations of Jesus' death (see below on the nonviolent atonement).[31] We have seen from the discussion of Jeremiah that the new covenant will be the result, like the Mosaic covenant, of a victory and thus a liberation; it will be a new Exodus. No doubt this is implied in the Last Supper, and it is of course present in New Testament texts that speak of God's victory over (and thus the liberation of human beings from) the powers, from Sin and Death, and from the devil. This theme is therefore inherently part of the new-covenant model. Its presence implies that covenantal and apocalyptic understandings of atonement can—indeed, must—co-exist.

---

31. See, e.g., Jersak and Hardin, *Stricken by God?*, which includes a long excerpt from Wright's *Jesus and the Victory of God* (78–149) as well as several other essays in the spirit of *Christus Victor*.

The promise of the new covenant is ultimately to deliver people into a form of covenantal life that the Mosaic covenant prescribed but did not fully provide. New Testament writers, especially Paul, attribute this, not to some inherent flaw in the first covenant, but to the power of the forces arrayed against humanity. Christ's victory in his death and resurrection provides the liberation from these powers that humans need in order to start afresh and to live in the new age of the new covenant by the power of the indwelling Spirit. Christ's victory over the powers, and its application to those who embrace the gospel, enable humans to enter the new covenant as redeemed people.

Satisfaction/Sacrificial/Penal Interpretations

The new-covenant model can also incorporate a sacrificial model of the atonement, carefully articulated, as a partial explanation of what Christ's death effects and how it effects it. Christians can, with Paul, affirm that Christ "loved me and gave himself for me" (Gal 2:20), and that he "died for our sins" (1 Cor 15:3). As sinners, humans need not only incorporation into God's new-covenant people; they need the forgiveness of their sins. Indeed, the former is impossible without the latter, as even Jeremiah and Ezekiel insisted. All this is true for at least three reasons.[32]

First, the same New Testament writers who use new-covenant language also use the language of sacrifice. Forgiveness of sins via the sacrifice of Christ is an essential, but not a sufficient, dimension of an atonement model rooted in the New Testament texts. To suggest that the new-covenant model and the sacrificial model are mutually exclusive would be to ignore the evidence of the New Testament itself. The prophetic promise of a forgiven covenantal people is realized in the sacrificial death of Christ.

Second, as T. F. Torrance (among others) points out, the sacrificial system in the Old Testament is itself an emblem of God's covenantal faithfulness and mercy, an expression of God's hospitality, in the apt phraseology of Hans Boersma.[33] The sacrifice of Christ, therefore, must be viewed by us as it is viewed by the New Testament writers: as the ultimate expression of God's covenantal love. Now, however, the reach of that love extends beyond Israel to all peoples; this is part of the newness of the new covenant as it

---

32. See also the discussion of nonviolent atonement interpretations below.

33. See, e.g., Torrance, *Atonement*, 38–39; Boersma, *Violence, Hospitality, and the Cross*.

is articulated in the writings of the New Testament. The death of Christ should not be seen as the expression of divine anger or even wrath, but as the expression of divine love. It is the gift of God's Son and, at least in some sense, the gift of God's own self: "God was in Christ . . ." (2 Cor 5:19; MJG). If that is the major emphasis from the satisfaction/sacrificial/penal kind of atonement models, then there may also be room for the satisfaction and penal components as minor sub-plots in the atonement narrative, but only if they can be clearly found in New Testament texts, and only if they retain their minor role in relation to divine, covenantal love. Barth certainly attempted to keep divine love and wrath together, but that has not always been the case.[34] Vanhoozer, for his part, puts divine punishment together with restorative justice in the context of God's covenantal, relational desires.[35] Whether or not any of these approaches (especially those involving punishment) is fully satisfactory, their coherence is increased to the degree that they are part of a larger approach to atonement.

Third, the death of Christ is also the manifestation of Christ's own love, an act of self-giving and self-sacrifice. Whatever we make of the various New Testament references to sacrifice and the sacrificial systems behind them, the central truth is the reality that Jesus the Messiah self-sacrificially offered himself. Christ is both the gift and the giver, the one who gives himself in covenant love.[36] Beneficiaries of the new covenant who receive this gift are also participants in it. The recipients of the gift become like the gift and the giver.

34. See, e.g., Barth, CD IV/1, 254: "For the sake of this best [God's plan for us], the worst had to happen to sinful man: not out of any desire for vengeance and retribution on the part of God, but because of the radical nature of the divine love, which could 'satisfy' itself only by killing him [sinful man], extinguishing him, removing him." Barth grounded this and his entire doctrine of reconciliation in the covenant; the covenant is the "presupposition" of reconciliation, which is, in turn, the fulfillment of humanity's broken covenant (CD IV/1, para. 57) as the judge is judged in our place (CD IV/1, para. 59, part 2). From a different perspective, Dietrich Bonhoeffer could argue that Jesus lived and died vicariously, including becoming guilty and sharing our punishment, in a way that also makes him the truest human being and thus the one to be imitated as well as the one who conveys the true life of God. See the analysis in Lawrence, *Bonhoeffer*, 29–33. And Hauerwas, in a sermon called "The End of Sacrifice"—on Christ's death as the one true sacrifice—claims that "Christ's sacrifice is the one true sacrifice calling into question all the sacrifices asked on behalf of lesser causes, and lesser gods" (*Cross-Shattered Church*, 72).

35. Vanhoozer, "Atonement in Postmodernity," esp. 380–82, 396–401.

36. In fact, Christ is the gift in two ways: as gift from God the Father as giver and as gift from himself as giver.

This line of thinking leads us naturally to the question of participation and theosis, for theosis is the consequence of a divine act of giving and self-giving that manifests the very character of God and draws people into it.

Incarnational/Theosis/Participation

A number of recent proposals for new (and ancient) models of the atonement have stressed its connection to the incarnation, and therefore its participatory character, even to the point of theosis, or deification: becoming like God, sharing in God's holiness and immortality, by participating in the life of God, or "becom[ing] participants in the divine nature" (2 Pet 1:4, MJG; one of the classic biblical texts). In my own work on Paul I have defined theosis as follows: "transformative participation in the kenotic, cruciform character of God through Spirit-enabled conformity to the incarnate, crucified, and resurrected/glorified Christ."[37] Similar approaches to justification and atonement in Paul have recently appeared (or been rediscovered), including especially the work of Morna Hooker, Douglas Campbell, Udo Schnelle, David Litwa, and Ben Blackwell, not to mention their patristic predecessors, especially Irenaeus and Athanasius.[38]

The new-covenant model proposed here, with its emphasis on participation and the "birth" of a new community, resonates deeply with these new directions. At times, in fact, we have suggested that the language and theo-logic of the New Testament are highly consonant with the soteriological tradition of theosis. In becoming part of the new-covenant community, human beings takes on the Christlike holiness of God by the work of the Spirit, and specifically the divine character traits of faithfulness, love, and peace (as in "the God of peace"). They are drawn into the life of the Triune God. They participate in God's being-expressed-in-acts, God's narrative identity, God's very life.

37. Gorman, *Inhabiting the Cruciform God*, 7.

38. See especially Hooker, *From Adam to Christ*; Campbell, *Deliverance of God*; Schnelle, *Apostle Paul*; Litwa, "2 Corinthians 3:18" and *We are Being Transformed*; and Blackwell, *Christosis*, who reads Paul in light of patristic interpretations. For treatments of the topic more broadly than Paul, see the articles on "Atonement, Rebirth, and Deification" in Jersak and Hardin, *Stricken by God?* (406–518).

Moral-Influence Interpretations

The moral-influence model of the atonement is the weakest of the traditional models. Nonetheless, the new-covenant model clearly includes the best of the moral-influence model. In our proposal, the cross is the quintessential act of covenant fulfillment, and particularly of love of neighbor, even of enemy. By the work of the Spirit within—though not merely by inspiration or imitation—the community of the new covenant is able to re-instantiate, even if imperfectly, the divine love and hospitality that are the motivation behind and the substance of the cross.

Nonviolent-Atonement Interpretations

Recently, some interpreters of the atonement have stressed its nonviolent character, often as a reaction against the sacrificial, satisfaction, and/or especially penal interpretations of the atonement.[39] This reaction can lead in several different directions: an emphasis on atonement as victory, as nonpenal forgiveness, as rebirth, and so on.[40]

As noted above, the new-covenant model emphasizes Jesus' death as an act of divine, self-giving love. It is not an act of violence but of love, a love that generates a covenant community of faithfulness, love, and nonviolence. This is one of the new developments in the New Testament's appropriation of the new-covenant tradition: the emphasis on nonviolence and reconciliation. There is not a scrap of evidence that the images of sacrifice and ransom in the New Testament created a violent people among the original recipients of the various writings. If it is true that "by their [first] fruits you shall know them," then perhaps calling atonement by sacrifice inherently violent is a grave error. On the other hand, if we include the long-term reception history and impact history of such biblical images among their "fruits," as indeed we must, then we will rightly come to the conclusion that those images, when wrongly interpreted and appropriated, have the potential to inspire or underwrite violence. It is tempting, therefore, to completely disassociate God from the cross of Christ.

It is insufficient, however, from the perspective of the New Testament, simply to say that the cross "happened," that it was the culmination of human evil against Jesus' prophetic stance, or something like that. Neither will

39. E.g., Heim, *Saved from Sacrifice* (using the work of René Girard); Weaver, *Nonviolent Atonement*.

40. See the variety of proposals in Jersak and Hardin, *Stricken by God?*

it do to link God only to the resurrection. As Thomas Yoder Neufeld puts it in his book on the New Testament and nonviolence, the New Testament writers cannot tell the story of the cross without telling it not only as the death of an innocent man but also "as the story of *God's* initiative." He also stresses, however, that this initiative is one of love—"the ingenuity of love the evangelists saw in the cross."[41] Once again, the new-covenant model embraces the nonviolent model inasmuch as the cross is the manifestation of God's self-giving, life-giving, peacemaking love.

Restorative-Justice and Reconciliation Interpretations

One of the most critical and yet constructive reactions to theories of penal substitution, and to the corollary charges of violence in those sorts of theories, has been the interpretation of the atonement as God's act of *restorative* rather than *retributive* justice.[42] This approach to the atonement agrees strongly that the cross is not an act of violence, but it focuses attention positively on the redemptive or healing aspect of the cross. Darrin Belousek, for instance, speaks of the cross in terms of "redemption beyond retribution," and he is able to connect the ministry of Jesus as one of justice-doing and peacemaking directly to the cross and then to the church, the cross as the culmination of Jesus' work of justice and peace, and the church as the continuation of that work.[43] Derek Flood, from another perspective, interprets sin fundamentally as sickness and the cross as Christ's act of healing.[44] With a broad definition of both sickness and healing, Flood creatively incorporates many of the metaphors and models of atonement into his proposal. His interpretation of the atonement, like that of the present book, includes a strong element of participation, including especially enemy-love.

---

41. Yoder Neufeld, *Killing Enmity*, 94, 95. His whole chapter on the atonement and violence (73–96) is worthy of careful reading. Willard Swartley allows for divine judgment but calls the attribution of "violence" to God as judge a "category fallacy," a "misnomer" (*Covenant of Peace*, 394–95). Though Swartley is not there speaking about the atonement, the point would apply to the cross even if it were interpreted in some sense as an act of judgment.

42. See, e.g., Belousek, *Atonement, Justice, and Peace*; Flood, *Healing the Gospel*; and the essays in Jersak and Hardin, *Stricken by God?* in the section entitled "The Atonement and Justice."

43. Belousek, *Atonement, Justice, and Peace*.

44. Flood, *Healing the Gospel*.

Similarly, Alan Spence argues for mediation, or reconciliation, as the normative theory of the atonement that incorporates the best aspects of other theories: "*The Son became as we are so that he might, on our behalf, make peace with God*."[45] For Spence, this reconciliation "has to do with God, with one another and with all of creation."[46]

Clearly this sort of interpretation of the atonement resonates deeply with what we have been saying throughout the chapters of this book. The death of Jesus is not an isolated act but part of an entire way of being in the world. The new covenant is not merely an end in itself, but part of a larger divine plan, which is why the new-covenant community is inherently a missional community, with justice and reconciliation integral to its identity. Moreover, as we have indicated at various points, *shalom* means peace or reconciliation, but also wholeness, and it includes justice. For this reason the new-covenant model of the atonement can certainly be interpreted to include both restorative justice and healing, in addition to reconciliation.

Feminist Interpretations

Feminist (including womanist) approaches to the atonement have been both critical and constructive. On the critical side, some feminists have argued against the possibility of suffering and sacrifice being redemptive and/or blamed traditional atonement theories for justifying violence against women and others. Some have famously referred to the cross, or at least certain interpretations of it, as "divine child abuse."[47] This has often led to an emphasis on aspects of Jesus other than his death (e.g., his earthly ministry, his victory over death) as that which is salvific.[48] Not every feminist theologian, however, agrees with these critiques, and some have specifically rejected the accusation of divine child abuse and the non-salvific value of the cross and suffering. Susan Wood has made the following important point in interpreting Philippians 2, though it has significance more broadly:

---

45. Spence, *Promise of Peace*, 17, 19, *et passim*. The final formulation of his thesis reads as follows: "*The Father gave his only Son to become as we are so that, in offering up himself on our behalf through the Spirit, he might reconcile us to with God*" (118).

46. Ibid., 115, commenting on Colossians but indicating its more general theological significance.

47. For example, Brown and Parker, "For God So Loved the World?," 2.

48. See, e.g., Williams, *Sisters in the Wilderness*, from a womanist perspective.

> Women [and, we should add, men] reject images of service and *kenosis* [self-emptying] only with great peril. Either the entire Christian community follows the model that Jesus sets for us, or we are doomed to struggle for positions of honor and elitism, domination and power. We cannot have it both ways. We serve one another or we dominate one another. There is no middle ground.[49]

Also on the constructive side, some feminists have highlighted the atonement as community-creating love rather than punishment; Jesus' identification with the suffering; the need for our subjective appropriation of the cross; and—with liberationist approaches more generally—atonement as liberation. Feminist theological approaches also remind us of the importance of social context in the interpretation and performance of Scripture and doctrine. These aspects of feminist interpretations of the atonement can contribute to the new-covenant model. In Christ's death, we have argued, human beings are being liberated and transferred into a new people, a new humanity—a humanity actually *freed* from violence. What this nonviolent new humanity specifically looks like "on the ground" is necessarily going to vary from place to place and time to time. Feminist approaches to the atonement keep that contextual reality in front of us. Furthermore, they remind us that Jesus suffered *with* humanity (as well as *for* humanity), and that we cannot separate Jesus' death from his life and his resurrection.

Summary

We have now surveyed certain models of the atonement and made some comments about how they may be incorporated into the new-covenant model of the atonement proposed in this book. This short survey cannot address all the issues raised by these various models or by the possible tensions among the various models. Nonetheless, it is important that the plurality of images, metaphors, and models of the atonement be kept in conversation, so to speak, with one another. To put it a bit differently:

> *Christian theology has developed, and continues to need, multiple models of the atonement because the ultimate goal of Jesus' death— the formation of the new-covenant community—is a multi-dimensional reality that is the soteriological result of a multi-dimensional reality—the human condition—within which human beings need salvation.*

49. Wood, "Philippians 2:5–11," 183.

In other words, human beings, both individually and corporately, are in need of forgiveness, liberation, empowerment, instruction, and so on, and this is what Christ's death (as well as his life and his resurrection), according to the New Testament, offers humanity as God's way of constituting a new-covenant people, a new humanity. In this sense, the new-covenant model is the "umbrella model" that includes all the others.

At the same time, there can be no "umbrella" or ultimate model without the various penultimate models that contribute to and help define the ultimate model, the creation of a new-covenant people. Accordingly, research, study, and reflection about *all* the various models of the atonement is necessary.

THE NEW-COVENANT MODEL: PARTICIPATION, PERFORMANCE, AND LITURGY

I have argued that the new-covenant model is more comprehensive, integrated, participatory, communal, and missional than any of the major models in the tradition, traditional or recent. The New Testament writers apparently were far less concerned about the mechanics of the atonement than about the results, but the new-covenant model can incorporate other, penultimate models of the atonement that do depict the mechanics, some of which are hinted at in the prophetic promises themselves, and some of which we have just discussed.

But our primary goal in this book, as said in the conclusion to chapter 3, has been to rediscover the features of a new-covenant model of the atonement from various parts of the New Testament. We have argued that the New Testament writers viewed the several aspects of the promised new covenant as having been effected by the death of Jesus. This new covenant was to be expressed in concrete practices of faithfulness, love, and peace. Once again, this is not to assert that any or all of these writers had articulated, or could have articulated (if asked), a systematic doctrine of the atonement that they would have labeled "the new-covenant model of the atonement." Rather, we have found several converging patterns and an emerging, remarkable consistency on some fundamental aspects of the New Testament writers' views on the ways in which Christ's death has effected this new covenant, this covenant of peace.

In various ways—sometimes deliberately, sometimes perhaps not—the New Testament writers interpreted the death of Jesus in ways that correspond to the various dimensions of the new covenant and the covenant of peace promised by the prophets. The hope for a new-covenant people who would be liberated, restored, forgiven, sanctified, covenantally faithful, empowered, missional, and permanent has been fulfilled by virtue of the work of Christ. To repeat the overview of our proposal from the conclusion to chapter 3:

> *Christ's death effected the new covenant, meaning specifically the creation of a new-covenant community of forgiven and reconciled disciples, inhabited and empowered by the Spirit to embody a new-covenant spirituality of cruciform loyalty to God and love for others, thereby participating in the life of God and in God's forgiving, reconciling, and covenanting mission to the world.*

In other words, the church and all who are part of it—that is, the community of the new covenant—is not merely a *beneficiary* of Christ's atoning death, but a *participant* in it and thus, to use once again the words of Kevin Vanhoozer, a *performer* of the atonement. This is not to attribute to the church a salvific role that only the crucified Messiah has, but rather to reinforce the claim that participation means concrete practices. Nor it is to attribute to the church a self-generated power to participate in Christ's death by means of these practices. Rather, the church relies fully on the power of the indwelling Spirit, on the reality that the crucified Messiah Jesus is also the resurrected Messiah Jesus, and on the truth that since God was in Christ to reconcile the world, now we are in Christ so that God's reconciling work can be known throughout the world.

This brings us back to the ultimate implications of the participatory language we have found in the New Testament and used throughout this book: that by participating in the work of God we actually participate in the very life of God, in the story of God. We become partakers of the divine character. And in so doing—in becoming Godlike by becoming Christlike by the power of the Spirit—we also become most fully human, for ultimately the new covenant is about a new humanity, even a new creation, and it is our privilege to be beneficiaries of and participants in that reality.[50] That benefit and that participation are most fully realized, not in isolation, but in community; not in withdrawal from the world, but in mission.

---

50. We should recall from chapter 3 the notion of the cross as ecclesiophany (revelation of the church's identity) and, in Brent Laytham's words, anthrophany (revelation of true humanity).

The church's participatory and missional identity, as the "community called atonement,"[51] is revealed, named, embraced, and practiced in liturgy—in worship. At least three aspects of liturgy are important to note.

First, we saw in chapter 6 that the New Testament's "epistolary flourishes" about "grace and peace" are much more substantive than they might at first appear. So too the simple exchange of peace within liturgy.[52] This brief ritual reminds us that in Christ God has made peace with us and among us, and that God sends us forth to participate in that ministry of reconciliation in the world. It even reminds us, in the memorable words of John Howard Yoder, that "I and my enemy are united, through no merit or work of my own, in a new humanity that forbids henceforth my ever taking his life in my hands."[53] This kind of "reminder" is not the mundane sort, but rather the biblical "remembering" that allows us to participate in past events (such as the exodus) and that brings past events into present experiential reality.

Second, then, this sort of participatory liturgical remembering is practiced also in the sacraments (or "ordinances," in some traditions), especially baptism and the Lord's Supper, or Eucharist. These liturgical, participatory events are the first and foundational ways in which individuals and the church as a whole share in the atonement. In an initial way, people die and rise with Christ in the unified act of faith-and-baptism.[54] In an ongoing way, believers implicitly or explicitly reaffirm their own death and resurrection with Christ when they are in the presence of others who are being baptized. Thus even to witness a baptism is to be invited, once again, to participate in the atonement and to be renewed in the baptismal vows of cruciform faithfulness, love, and hopeful peacemaking.

This ongoing participatory remembrance of the atonement comes to fullest liturgical expression in the Lord's Supper, the Eucharist, or—appropriately—communion, *koinōnia*. It is here that the church remembers—in the robust, biblical sense—what God in Christ has done for us, making us the new-covenant people of God through liberation from Sin, forgiveness of sins, deliverance from the devil, the gift of the Spirit, the writing

51. The title of Scot McKnight's book.

52. See especially Wadell, "Sharing Peace."

53. Yoder, *Politics of Jesus*, 224. Yoder's comment is actually about justification as "the Good News that I and my enemy are united," but it is no less true of the liturgical practices that flow from justification/reconciliation.

54. That is, the faith of the baptized or of the parents on behalf of the baptized.

of the Law in our hearts, and so on. In short, we remember, as noted in the introduction to this book, that "By the baptism of his suffering, death, and resurrection, you [God] gave birth to your church, delivered us from slavery to sin and death, and made with us a new covenant by water and the Spirit."[55] Moreover, in remembering the atonement, the church as a body and each individual member in it embraces Christ's death once again, not merely as beneficiaries but as participants and performers.

To "take communion," or to "receive," then, is not merely to ingest elements made by human hands, and not only to take in the body and blood of the Lord, but also to be marked by the sign of the cross. It is to be consumed as well as to consume—to be drawn into the ongoing life of the crucified and resurrected Messiah, in whom true life remains always in the shape of the cross: the cross of faith, love, and hope/peace. It is, therefore, to offer our individual bodies as well as our corporate, ecclesial body in loving, covenantal service to the one who offered his body and blood for us. *Worship in general, and specifically participation in the Eucharist, is the church's alternative to the world's liturgy of domination and violence.* Because the church is the transnational community of the new covenant that transcends all political divisions and all other political allegiances, the church at worship says that we will no longer sacrifice our bodies on the altar of violence and war. "If Christians leave the Eucharistic table ready to kill one another, we not only eat and drink judgment on ourselves, but we rob the world of the witness it needs in order to know that there is an alternative to the sacrifices of war."[56]

Third and finally with respect to liturgy, a comment about the meaning of the other major elements of liturgy (music, preaching, prayers) from the perspective of participation and atonement is in order. In worship there is a natural rhythm of speaking (including singing) and listening, but one is not active and the other passive. Rather, both are active, both participatory. Whether we are listening to a choral anthem or singing a hymn, whether we are reading a unison prayer aloud or listening to a preacher proclaim the word of God, these activities summon us to pay attention, to listen for what God has done and is doing, to offer praise and renewed love to the Triune God. Because Christians gather together believing that Jesus is God the Father's only Son, the crucified and resurrected Lord who is present by the Spirit in the assembly, the entire liturgical event is an event of communion

---

55. From the United Methodist services of Word and Table I and II.

56. Hauerwas, *War and the American Difference*, 69.

with Jesus and with his body, the church. To pay attention in this context is to hope, to expect, that the church will hear from and speak to the God revealed in Jesus, and thus be re-formed week in and week out in his image. This re-formation culminates each week in the final benediction, which is both a blessing and a commission, a reminder of what God has done and a summons to participate in it day by day. It is an invitation to make the sign of the cross (whether literally or not) the way to leave the assembly, just as it is, for many Christians, the way to enter it.[57]

Worship, then, is the event in which the new-covenant people remember who they are; they praise, thank, and listen to the One who called them into being; and they re-commit to the way of the cross—the self-revelation of God and the salvific means of their new birth, both as individuals and as the community of the new covenant. Liturgy is that which fosters the practical integration of this integrated model of the atonement, merging forgiveness received and forgiveness extended, communion with God and communion with others, faithfulness and love, spirituality and politics, worship and mission, cross as gift and cross as summons. The death of the Messiah and the birth of the new covenant are celebrated and practiced so that they can be performed in the world.

CONCLUDING REFLECTIONS

What final conclusions may we offer about the new-covenant model of the atonement? The new-covenant model is above all integrative, joining various significant realities that are often inappropriately separated. Atonement in this model is about the creation of a liberated, forgiven, Spirit-infused, and transformed people, the people of the new covenant. The new-covenant model has a this-worldly spirituality; we might refer to it as the *exteriority of interiority*. It is therefore also a kind of politics, a way of being *in* the world but not *of* the world that is shaped by the truth-telling (faithful), hospitable, others-serving, *shalom*-making death of the Messiah on a Roman cross. The corollary practices that emerge from that death are not arbitrary additions to a saving event but, rather, the appropriate, Spirit-empowered expressions of its significance for and in human life. Ultimately, to return to a question raised in the introduction, for Christians the significance of the cross, as well

57. I of course recognize that many Christians do not make the sign of the cross at all. It may be time to renew that practice ecumenically while stressing its utmost seriousness among those for whom it may have become too routine.

as the non-arbitrariness of the practices associated with it, is due to the fact that *God was in Christ; that is, it is due to the incarnation.* The incarnation, Christians assert, means that Jesus of Nazareth, fully God and fully human, reveals both true divinity and true humanity. This revelation occurs both in Jesus' earthly ministry and in his death. Finally, and most importantly, then, in the new-covenant model the atonement produces not merely *beneficiaries* but *participants*: participants in the cross and therefore also participants in the life-giving self-giving of God. This participation is made possible by God's prior participation in our situation, that is, by Christ's incarnation, life, and death among us and for us.[58] The polyvalent cross is not only the source, but also the shape, of salvation; it is the means of, and the pattern for, becoming most fully human, most fully Christlike, most fully Godlike. The cross is remembered, celebrated, and performed as the work of Christ but also, ultimately, as the work of God and now, by the power of the Spirit, the ongoing work of the church. All of this is so because, and only because, God has raised to life the crucified Jesus. Now death—his—has become the means of birth—ours, both individually and corporately.

These concluding observations, reflecting the entire book, make certain theological claims in the language of academic theology. It is certainly my hope that this book will contribute to the academic discussion of the atonement. But I also have other, greater hopes. Perhaps this book will help some people negotiate the "atonement wars" and move beyond some of the old, tired ways of speaking about the atonement in narrow rather than in generative, creative, life-giving modes. It is my strong conviction that the kind of holistic, communal, participatory, missional model of the atonement that we have called the "new-covenant" model is precisely what the church needs to appropriate, articulate, and actualize today. I look forward to others joining the conversation and, more importantly, putting this model and its participatory practices into practice.

---

58. On participation being dependent on Christ's prior participation, see esp. Eastman, "Apocalypse and Incarnation." Although her article is about Paul, I would contend that its basic principle applies across the New Testament. It is also at the heart of the patristic contention about salvation as theosis: He became what we are so that we could become what he is. Eastman therefore rightly refers to Morna Hooker's work on "interchange texts" (168–69, 172). I am less convinced, however, that Eastman's term "participatory rectification [justification]" (176), as a reference to justification by God's and Christ's movement toward us (divine participation), rather than justification by our transfer into Christ, is an adequate account of soteriology for Paul or for us. Both Christ's movement toward us and our movement into Christ are required.

Works Cited

Anderson, Gary A. *Charity: The Place of the Poor in the Biblical Tradition*. New Haven: Yale University Press, 2013.

Attridge, Harold W. *Hebrews*. Hermeneia. Philadelphia: Fortress, 1989.

Aulén, Gustaf. *Christus Victor: An Historical Study of the Three Main Types of the Idea of the Atonement*. Translated by A. G. Herbert. New York: Macmillan, 1931.

Aune, David E. "Following the Lamb: Discipleship in the Apocalypse." In *Patterns of Discipleship in the New Testament*, edited by Richard N. Longenecker, 269–84. Grand Rapids: Eerdmans, 1996.

Baker, Mark D., and Joel B. Green. *Recovering the Scandal of the Cross: Atonement in New Testament and Contemporary Contexts*. 2nd ed. Downers Grove, IL: InterVarsity, 2011.

Bakke, Odd Magne. *When Children Became People: The Birth of Childhood in Early Christianity*. Translated by Brian McNeil. Minneapolis: Fortress, 2005.

Barth, Karl. *Church Dogmatics*. 4/1: *The Doctrine of Reconciliation*. Edited by G. W. Bromiley and T. F. Torrance. Translated by G. W. Bromiley. 1956. Peabody, MA: Hendrickson, 2010.

———. *Church Dogmatics*. 4/3.2: *The Doctrine of Reconciliation*. Edited by G. W. Bromiley and T. F. Torrance. Translated by G. W. Bromiley. 1961. Peabody, MA: Hendrickson, 2010.

Bauckham, Richard. *The Theology of the Book of Revelation*. New Testament Theology. Cambridge: Cambridge University Press, 1993.

Bayne, Tim, and Greg Restall. "A Participatory Theory of the Atonement." In *New Waves in Philosophy of Religion*, edited by Yujin Nagasawa and Erik Wielenberg, 150–66. Hampshire, UK: Palgrave, 2008.

Belcher, J. David. "In Christ, There Is No Opposition: Cross, Resurrection, and Baptism in the Apocalyptic Paul." In *Apocalyptic and the Future of Theology: With and Beyond J. Louis Martyn*, edited by Joshua B. Davis and Douglas Harink, 264–93. Eugene, OR: Cascade, 2012.

Belousek, Darrin W. Snyder. *Atonement, Justice, and Peace: The Message of the Cross and the Mission of the Church*. Grand Rapids: Eerdmans, 2012.

Bird, Michael F., and Joel Willitts, eds. *Paul and the Gospels: Christologies, Conflicts and Convergences*. LNTS 411. London: T. & T. Clark, 2011.

Blackwell, Ben. *Christosis: Pauline Soteriology in Light of Deification in Irenaeus and Cyril of Alexandria*. WUNT 2/314. Tübingen: Mohr/Siebeck, 2011.

Bock, Darrell L. *A Theology of Luke and Acts: God's Promised Program, Realized for All Nations*. Biblical Theology of the New Testament. Grand Rapids: Zondervan, 2012.

Bøe, Sverre. *Cross-Bearing in Luke*. WUNT 2/278. Tübingen: Mohr/Siebeck, 2010.

Boersma, Hans. *Violence, Hospitality, and the Cross: Reappropriating the Atonement Tradition*. Grand Rapids: Baker Academic, 2004.

Borgman, Paul. *The Way according to Luke: Hearing the Whole Story of Luke-Acts*. Grand Rapids: Eerdmans, 2006.

Boring, M. Eugene. *Mark: A Commentary*. NTL. Louisville: Westminster John Knox, 2006.

Bovon, François. *Luke the Theologian*. 2nd rev. ed. Waco: Baylor University Press, 2006.

Brenneman, Laura L., and Brad D. Schantz, eds. *Struggles for Shalom: Peace and Violence across the Testaments*. Eugene, OR: Pickwick, 2014.

Brondos, David. *Fortress Introduction to Salvation and the Cross*. Minneapolis: Fortress, 2007.

Brown, Joanne Carlson, and Rebecca Parker. "For God So Loved the World?" In *Christianity, Patriarchy and Abuse*, edited by Joanne Carlson Brown and Carole R. Bohn, 1–30. New York: Pilgrim, 1989.

Brown, Raymond E. *A Crucified Christ in Holy Week*. Collegeville, MN: Liturgical, 1986.

———. *The Death of the Messiah: From Gethsemane to the Grave; A Commentary on the Passion Narratives in the Four Gospels*. Vol. 2. Anchor Bible Reference Library. New York: Doubleday, 1994.

———. *The Gospel According to John XIII—XXI*. AB 29a. New York: Doubleday, 1970.

Brueggemann, Walter. *Isaiah 1–39*. Westminster Bible Companion. Louisville: Westminster John Knox, 1998.

———. *Peace*. Understanding Biblical Themes. St. Louis: Chalice, 2001.

———. *Theology of The Old Testament: Testimony, Dispute, Advocacy*. Minneapolis: Fortress, 1997.

Bultmann, Rudolf. *Theology of the New Testament*. Vol. 1. Translated by Kendrick Grobel. New York: Charles Scribner's Sons, 1951.

Burridge, Richard A. *Imitating Jesus: An Inclusive Approach to New Testament Ethics*. Grand Rapids: Eerdmans, 2007.

Campbell, Douglas A. *The Deliverance of God: An Apocalyptic Rereading of Justification in Paul*. Grand Rapids: Eerdmans, 2009.

Campbell, W. Gordon. *Reading Revelation: A Thematic Approach*. Cambridge: Clarke, 2012.

Campbell, William S. *Unity and Diversity in Christ: Interpreting Paul in Context—Collected Essays*. Eugene, OR: Cascade, 2013.

Carroll, John T. *Luke: A Commentary*. NTL. Louisville: Westminster John Knox, 2012.

Carroll, John T., and Joel B. Green. *The Death of Jesus in Early Christianity*. Peabody, MA: Hendrickson, 1995.

Chennattu, Rekha M. *Johannine Discipleship as a Covenant Relationship*. Peabody, MA: Hendrickson, 2006.

Clark-Soles, Jaime. "John 13: Of Footwashing and History." In *John, Jesus, and History*, edited by Paul N. Anderson, Felix Just, and Tom Thatcher, 2:255–69. Atlanta: SBL, 2009.

Coloe, Mary L. "Welcome into the Household of God: The Foot Washing in John 13." *CBQ* 66 (2004) 400–415.

Culpepper, R. Alan. "The Johannine *Hypodeigma*: A Reading of John 13." *Semeia* 53 (1991) 133–52.

Danker, Frederick. *Benefactor: Epigraphic Study of a Graeco-Roman and New Testament Semantic Field*. St. Louis: Clayton, 1982.

Deidun, T. J. *New Covenant Morality in Paul*. Analecta Biblica 89. Rome: Biblical Institute Press, 1981.

De Villiers, Pieter G. R. "Peace in Luke and Acts: A Perspective on Biblical Spirituality." *Acta Patristica et Byzantina* 19 (2008) 110–34.

———. "Peace in the Pauline Letters: A Perspective on Biblical Spirituality." *Neotestamentica* 43 (2009) 1–26.

Donahue, John R., and Daniel J. Harrington. *The Gospel of Mark*. SP 2. Collegeville, MN: Liturgical, 2002.

Dunn, James D. G. "Did Paul Have a Covenant Theology?" In *Celebrating Romans: Template for Pauline Theology*, edited by Sheila E. McGinn, 3–19. Grand Rapids: Eerdmans, 2004.

———. *Jesus, Paul, and the Gospels*. Grand Rapids: Eerdmans, 2011.

———. *Jesus Remembered*. Grand Rapids: Eerdmans, 2003.

———. *The Oral Gospel Tradition*. Grand Rapids: Eerdmans, 2013.

———. *The Theology of Paul the Apostle*. Grand Rapids: Eerdmans, 1998.

Eastman, Susan Grove. "Apocalypse and Incarnation: The Participatory Logic of Paul's Gospel." In *Apocalyptic and the Future of Theology: With and Beyond J. Louis Martyn*, edited by Joshua B. Davis and Douglas Harink, 165–82. Eugene, OR: Cascade, 2012.

Elliott, Neil. *The Arrogance of Nations: Reading Romans in the Shadow of Empire*. Minneapolis: Fortress, 2008.

Elliott, Neil, and Mark Reasoner, eds. *Documents and Images for the Study of Paul*. Minneapolis: Fortress, 2011.

Evans, Craig A. "Did Jesus Predict His Death and Resurrection?" In *Resurrection*, edited by Stanley E. Porter, Michael A. Hayes, and David Tombs, 82–97. JSNTSup 186, RILP 5. Sheffield: Sheffield Academic, 1999.

———. "King Jesus and his Ambassadors: Empire and Luke-Acts." In *Empire in the New Testament*, edited by Stanley E. Porter and Cynthia Long Westfall, 120–39. McMaster New Testament Studies. Eugene, OR: Wipf and Stock, 2011.

Evans, Craig A., and James A. Sanders. *Luke and Scripture: The Function of Sacred Tradition in Luke-Acts*. Minneapolis: Fortress, 1993.

Farmer, William R., and Denis Farkasfalvy. *The Formation of the New Testament Canon: An Ecumenical Approach*. New York: Paulist, 1983.

Feldmeier, Reinhard. *Power, Service, Humility*. Waco: Baylor University Press, 2014.

Fiddes, Paul S. *Past Event and Present Salvation: The Christian Idea of Atonement*. Louisville: Westminster John Knox, 1989.

Finger, Reta Halteman. "'Reconciled to God through the Death of His Son.'" In *Beautiful upon the Mountains: Biblical Essays on Mission, Peace, and the Reign of God*, edited by Mary H. Schertz and Ivan Friesen, 183–96. Elkhart, IN: Institute of Mennonite Studies/Scottdale, PA: Herald, 2003.

Finlan, Stephen. *Options on Atonement in Christian Thought*. Collegeville, MN: Liturgical, 2007.

Fitzmyer, Joseph A. *The Gospel according to Luke X—XXIV*. AB 28a. New York: Doubleday, 1985.

Flood, Derek. *Healing the Gospel: A Radical Vision for Grace, Justice, and the Cross*. Eugene, OR: Cascade, 2012.

Foster, Paul. "Who Wrote 2 Thessalonians? A Fresh Look at an Old Problem." *JSNT* 35 (2012) 150–75.

Fowl, Stephen. *God's Beautiful City: Christian Mission after Christendom.* The Ekklesia Project Pamphlet #4. Eugene, OR: Wipf and Stock, 2001.

Francis, James. "Children and Childhood in the New Testament." In *The Family in Theological Perspective*, edited by Stephen C. Barton, 65–85. Edinburgh: T. & T. Clark, 1996.

Gabrielson, Jeremy. *Paul's Non-Violent Gospel: The Theological Politics of Peace in Paul's Life and Letters.* Eugene, OR: Pickwick, 2013.

Gamel, Brian K. "Salvation in a Sentence: Mark 15:39 as Markan Soteriology." *JTI* 6 (2012) 65–78.

Gibson, Jeffrey B. "Paul's Dying Formula: Prolegomena to an Understanding of Its Import and Significance." In *Celebrating Romans: Template for Pauline Theology*, edited by Sheila E. McGinn, 20–41. Grand Rapids: Eerdmans, 2004.

Gorman, Mark C. "On the Love of God." ThD diss., Duke Divinity School, forthcoming.

Gorman, Michael J. *Apostle of the Crucified Lord: A Theological Introduction to Paul and His Letters.* Grand Rapids: Eerdmans, 2004.

———. *Becoming the Gospel: Paul, Participation, and Mission.* Grand Rapids: Eerdmans, forthcoming.

———. "The Cross in Paul: Christophany, Theophany, Ecclesiophany." Forthcoming in *Ecclesia and Ethics*, edited by Allen Jones et al. London: T. & T. Clark, 2014.

———. "Cruciformity according to Jesus and Paul." In *Unity and Diversity in the Gospels and Paul: Essays in Honor of Frank J. Matera*, edited by Christopher W. Skinner and Kelly R. Iverson, 173–201. SBLECL 7. Atlanta: SBL, 2012.

———. *Cruciformity: Paul's Narrative Spirituality of the Cross.* Grand Rapids: Eerdmans, 2001.

———. "The Death of the Messiah: Theology, Spirituality, Politics." Lecture at St. Mary's Seminary & University, Baltimore, MD, November 8, 2012.

———. "Effecting the New Covenant: A (Not So) New, New Testament Model for the Atonement." *Ex Auditu* 26 (2011) 26–59.

———. *Inhabiting the Cruciform God: Kenosis, Justification, and Theosis in Paul's Narrative Soteriology.* Grand Rapids: Eerdmans, 2009.

———. "Justification and Justice in Paul, with Special Reference to the Corinthians." *JSPL* 1 (2011) 23–40.

———. "The Lord of Peace: Christ our Peace in Pauline Theology." *JSPL* 3 (2013) 219–53.

———. "Paul's Corporate, Cruciform, Missional Theosis in Second Corinthians." Forthcoming in *"In Christ" in Paul: Explorations in Paul's Theology of Union and Participation*, edited by Kevin J. Vanhoozer, Constantine R. Campbell, and Michael J. Thate. WUNT 2. Tübingen: Mohr/Siebeck, 2014.

———. *Reading Revelation Responsibly: Uncivil Worship and Witness; Following the Lamb into the New Creation.* Eugene, OR: Cascade, 2011.

———. "Romans: The First Christian Treatise on Theosis." *JTI* 5 (2011) 13–34.

———. "*Shalom* in the Book of Revelation: God, Church, Judgment, New Creation." In *Struggles for Shalom: Peace and Violence across the Testaments*, edited by Laura L. Brenneman and Brad D. Schantz, 279–90. Eugene, OR: Pickwick, 2014.

———. "The This-Worldliness of the New Testament's Other-Worldly Spirituality." In *The Bible and Spirituality: Exploratory Essays in Reading Scripture Spiritually*, edited by Andrew T. Lincoln et al., 151–70. Eugene, OR: Cascade, 2013.

———. "The Work of Christ in the New Testament." Forthcoming in *The Oxford Handbook of Christology*, edited by Francesca Aran Murphy. Oxford: Oxford University Press, 2014.

Green, Joel B. *1 Peter*. THNTC. Grand Rapids: Eerdmans, 2007.

———. *The Gospel of Luke*. NICNT. Grand Rapids: Eerdmans, 1997.

———. "Kaleidoscopic View." In *The Nature of the Atonement: Four Views*, edited by James Beilby et al., 157–85. Downers Grove, IL: InterVarsity, 2006.

———. "Must We Imagine the Atonement in Penal Substitutionary Terms? Questions, Caveats, and a Plea." In *The Atonement Debate: Papers from the London Symposium on the Theology of Atonement*, edited by Derek Tidball et al., 153–71. Grand Rapids: Zondervan, 2008.

———. *The Theology of the Gospel of Luke*. New Testament Theology. Cambridge: Cambridge University Press, 1995.

Grieb, A. Katherine. "'So That in Him We Might Become the Righteousness of God' (2 Cor 5:21): Some Theological Reflections on the Church Becoming Justice." *Ex Auditu* 22 (2006) 58–80.

Grimsrud, Ted. *Instead of Atonement: The Bible's Salvation Story and Our Hope for Wholeness*. Eugene, OR: Cascade, 2013.

Gunton, Colin E. *The Actuality of Atonement: A Study of Metaphor, Rationality, and the Christian Tradition*. Grand Rapids: Eerdmans, 1989.

Hahn, Scott W. *Kinship by Covenant: A Canonical Approach to the Fulfillment of God's Saving Promises*. New Haven: Yale University Press, 2009.

Hallie, Philip. *Lest Innocent Blood Be Shed: The Story of the Village of Le Chambon and How Goodness Happened There*. New York: Harper & Row, 1979.

Hannah, Darrell D. "Isaiah within Judaism of the Second Temple Period." In *Isaiah in the New Testament*, edited by Steve Moyise and Maarten J. J. Menken, 7–34. London: T. & T. Clark, 2005.

Harrisville, Roy A. *Fracture: The Cross as Irreconcilable in the Language and Thought of the Biblical Writers*. Grand Rapids: Eerdmans, 2006.

Hauerwas, Stanley. *A Cross-Shattered Church: Reclaiming the Theological Heart of Preaching*. Grand Rapids: Brazos, 2009.

———. *War and the American Difference: Theological Reflections on Violence and National Identity*. Grand Rapids: Baker Academic, 2011.

Hauerwas, Stanley, and William H. Willimon. *Resident Aliens: Life in the Christian Colony*. Nashville: Abingdon, 1989.

Hays, Richard B. *The Conversion of the Imagination: Paul as Interpreter of Israel's Scripture*. Grand Rapids: Eerdmans, 2005.

———. *Echoes of Scripture in the Letters of Paul*. New Haven: Yale University Press, 1989.

———. "Faithful Witness, Alpha and Omega." In *Revelation and the Politics of Apocalyptic Interpretation*, edited by Richard B. Hays and Stefan Alkier, 69–83. Waco: Baylor University Press, 2012.

———. "'Here We Have No Lasting City': New Covenantalism in Hebrews." In *The Epistle to the Hebrews and Christian Theology*, edited by Richard Bauckham et al., 151–73. Grand Rapids: Eerdmans, 2009.

———. *The Moral Vision of the New Testament: Community, Cross, New Creation; A Contemporary Introduction to New Testament Ethics*. San Francisco: HarperCollins, 1996.

————. "The Word of Reconciliation." http://www.faithandleadership.com/sermons/the-word-reconciliation.

Heim, S. Mark. *Saved from Sacrifice: A Theology of the Cross.* Grand Rapids: Eerdmans, 2006.

Heppner, Caleb F. "A Covenantal View of the Atonement." http://www.thepaulpage.com/a-covenantal-view-of-atonement/.

Holder, Arthur. "Introduction." In *The Blackwell Companion to Christian Spirituality*, edited by Arthur Holder, 1–11. Malden, MA: Wiley-Blackwell, 2005.

Hooker, Morna D. *From Adam to Christ: Essays on Paul.* Cambridge: Cambridge University Press, 1990.

————. *Not Ashamed of the Gospel: New Testament Interpretations of the Death of Christ.* Grand Rapids: Eerdmans, 1994.

Horrell, David G., et al. *Greening Paul: Rereading the Apostle in a Time of Ecological Crisis.* Waco: Baylor University Press, 2010.

Hurtado, Larry W. "Jesus as Lordly Example in Philippians 2:5–11." In *From Jesus to Paul: Studies in Honour of Francis Wright Beare*, edited by Peter Richardson and John C. Hurd, 113–26. Waterloo, OT: Wilfred Laurier University Press, 1984.

Jersak, Brad, and Michael Hardin, eds. *Stricken by God? Nonviolent Identification and the Victory of Christ.* Grand Rapids: Eerdmans, 2007.

Jewett, Robert. *Romans.* Hermeneia. Minneapolis: Fortress, 2007.

Johns, Loren L. "Leaning toward consummation: Mission and peace in the rhetoric of Revelation." In *Beautiful Upon the Mountains: Biblical Essays on Mission, Peace, and the Reign of God*, edited by Mary H. Schertz and Ivan Friesen, 249–68. Elkhart, IN: Institute of Mennonite Studies/Scottdale, PA: Herald, 2003.

Johnson, Adam. "The Crucified Bridegroom: Christ's Atoning Death in St. John of the Cross and Spiritual Formation Today." *Pro Ecclesia* 21 (2012) 392–408.

Johnson, Luke Timothy. *The Acts of the Apostles.* SP 5. Collegeville, MN: Liturgical, 1992.

————. *The Gospel of Luke.* SP 3. Collegeville, MN: Liturgical, 1991.

————. *Hebrews.* NTL. Louisville: Westminster John Knox, 2006.

————. *The Letter of James.* AB 37a. New York: Doubleday, 1995.

————. *The Literary Function of Possessions in Luke-Acts.* SBLDS 39. Missoula, MT: Scholars, 1977.

Kaylor, R. David. *Paul's Covenant Community: Jew and Gentile in Romans.* Atlanta: John Knox, 1988.

Keazirian, Edward M. *Peace and Peacemaking in Paul and the Greco-Roman World.* Studies in Biblical Literature 145. New York: Peter Lang, 2014.

Keener, Craig S. *Acts: An Exegetical Commentary.* Vol. 2, *3:1—14:28.* Grand Rapids: Baker Academic, 2013.

————. *Romans.* NCCS. Eugene, OR: Cascade, 2009.

Kilgallen, John. "'Peace' in the Gospel of Luke and Acts of the Apostles." *Studia Missionalia* 38 (1989) 55–79.

Kim, Jintae. "The Concept of Atonement in the Qumran Literature and the New Covenant." *Journal of Greco-Roman Christianity and Judaism* 7 (2010) 98–111.

Kim, Yung Suk. *A Theological Introduction to Paul's Letters: Exploring a Threefold Theology of Paul.* Eugene, OR: Cascade, 2011.

Kirk, J. R. Daniel. *Jesus Have I Loved, but Paul? A Narrative Approach to the Problem of Pauline Christianity.* Grand Rapids: Baker Academic, 2012.

Koester, Craig R. *Hebrews: A New Translation with Introduction and Commentary.* AB 36. New York: Doubleday, 2001.

———. *The Word of Life: A Theology of John's Gospel.* Grand Rapids: Eerdmans, 2008.

Lawrence, Joel. *Bonhoeffer: A Guide for the Perplexed.* London: T. & T. Clark, 2010.

Lincoln, Andrew T. *Hebrews: A Guide.* London: T. & T. Clark, 2006.

———. "The Letter to the Colossians: Introduction, Commentary, and Reflections." In the *New Interpreter's Bible*, 11:551—669. Nashville: Abingdon, 2000.

Litwa, M. David. "2 Corinthians 3:18 and Its Implications for Theosis." *JTI* 2 (2008) 117–33.

———. *We are Being Transformed: Deification in Paul's Soteriology.* BZNW 187. Berlin: de Gruyter, 2012.

Lundbom, Jack R. *Jeremiah 21–36.* AB 21b. New York: Doubleday, 2004.

Macaskill, Grant. *Union with Christ in the New Testament.* Oxford: Oxford University Press, 2013.

Macchia, Frank D. *Justified in the Spirit: Creation, Redemption, and the Triune God.* Grand Rapids: Eerdmans, 2010.

Mallen, Peter. *The Reading and Transformation of Isaiah in Luke-Acts.* LNTS 367. London: T. & T. Clark, 2008.

Marcus, Joel. *Mark 8–16.* AB 27a. New Haven: Yale University Press, 2009.

Marohl, Matthew J. *Faithfulness and the Purpose of Hebrews: A Social Identity Approach.* Princeton Theological Monograph Series. Eugene, OR: Pickwick, 2008.

Marshall, I. H. "The Place of Acts 20.28 in Luke's Theology of the Cross." In *Reading Acts Today: Essays in Honour of Loveday C. A. Alexander*, edited by Steve Walton et al., 154–70. LNTS 427. London: T. & T. Clark, 2011.

Martin, Ralph P. *Reconciliation: A Study of Paul's Theology.* 1981. Eugene, OR: Wipf and Stock, 1997.

———. *2 Corinthians.* WBC 40. Dallas: Word, 1986.

Martin, Troy. "Response to Gorman." *Ex Auditu* 26 (2011) 60–66.

Matera, Frank J. *God's Saving Grace: A Pauline Theology.* Grand Rapids: Eerdmans, 2012.

———. *New Testament Ethics: The Legacies of Jesus and Paul.* Louisville: Westminster John Knox, 1996.

———. *New Testament Theology: Exploring Diversity and Unity.* Louisville: Westminster John Knox, 2007.

Mauser, Ulrich. *The Gospel of Peace: A Scriptural Message for Today's World.* Louisville: Westminster John Knox, 1992.

McGinn, Bernard, et al., eds. *Christian Spirituality.* Vol. 1, *Origins to the Twelfth Century.* New York: Crossroad, 1987.

McKnight, Scot. *A Community Called Atonement.* Nashville: Abingdon, 2007.

———. *Jesus and His Death: Historiography, the Historical Jesus, and Atonement Theory.* Waco: Baylor University Press, 2005.

McRae, Rachel M. "Eating with Honor: The Corinthian Lord's Supper in Light of Voluntary Association Meal Practices." *JBL* 130 (2011) 165–81.

Meyer, Paul W. "The This-Worldliness of the New Testament." In *The Word in this World: Essays in New Testament Exegesis and Theology*, edited by John T. Carroll, 5–18. NTL. Louisville: Westminster John Knox, 2004 (orig. published in The *Princeton Seminary Bulletin* 2, no. 3 [1979] 219–30).

Moffitt, David M. *Atonement and the Logic of Resurrection in the Epistle to the Hebrews.* Supplements to Novum Testamentum 14. Leiden: Brill, 2011.

Works Cited

―――. "Blood, Life, and Atonement: Reassessing Hebrews' Christological Appropriation of Yom Kippur." In *The Day of Atonement: Its Interpretation in Early Jewish and Christian Traditions*, edited by Thomas Hueke and Tobias Nicklas, 211–24. Themes in Biblical Narrative: Jewish and Christian Traditions 15. Leiden: Brill, 2012.

Moloney, Francis J. *Love in the Gospel of John: An Exegetical, Theological, and Literary Study*. Grand Rapids: Baker Academic, 2013.

Moyise, Steve. *Evoking Scripture: Seeing the Old Testament in the New*. London: T. & T. Clark, 2008.

―――. *Paul and Scripture: Studying the New Testament Use of the Old Testament*. Grand Rapids: Baker, 2010.

Myers, Ben. "How Does Jesus Save? An Alternative Typology (Against Gustaf Aulén)." http://www.faith-theology.com/2013/09/how-does-jesus-save-alternative.html.

Nanos, Mark D. "To the Churches within the Synagogues of Rome." In *Reading Paul's Letter to the Romans*, edited by Jerry L. Sumney, 11–28. SBLRBS 73. Atlanta: SBL, 2012.

Neville, David J. *A Peaceable Hope: Contesting Violent Eschatology in New Testament Narratives*. Grand Rapids: Baker Academic, 2013.

Nordling, Cherith Fee. "Resurrection." In *Prophetic Evangelicals: Envisioning a Just and Peaceable Kingdom*, edited by Bruce Ellis Benson et al., 178–90. Grand Rapids: Eerdmans, 2012.

Pao, David W. *Acts and the Isaianic New Exodus*. Biblical Studies Library. Grand Rapids: Baker Academic, 2002.

Park, Andrew Sung. *Triune Atonement: Christ's Healing for Sinners, Victims, and the Whole Creation*. Louisville: Westminster John Knox, 2009.

Parsons, Mikeal. *Acts*. Paideia. Grand Rapids: Baker Academic, 2008.

―――. *Luke: Storyteller, Interpreter, Evangelist*. Peabody, MA: Hendrickson, 2007.

Paul, Shalom. *Isaiah 40–66: Translation and Commentary*. ECC. Grand Rapids: Eerdmans, 2012.

Peterson, David G. *Transformed by God: New Covenant Life and Ministry*. Downers Grove, IL: InterVarsity, 2012.

Pietersma, Albert, and Benjamin G. Wright, eds. *A New English Translation of the Septuagint*. New York: Oxford University Press, 2007.

Powers, Daniel G. *Salvation through Participation: An Examination of the Notion of the Believers' Corporate Unity with Christ in Early Christian Soteriology*. Contributions to Biblical Exegesis and Theology. Leuven: Peeters, 2001.

Reardon, Timothy W. "Recent Trajectories and Themes in Lukan Soteriology." *Currents in Biblical Research* 11 (2013) 77–95.

Roukema, Riemer. "The Good Samaritan in Ancient Christianity." *VC* 58 (2004) 56–74.

Rowe, C. Kavin. *World Upside Down: Reading Acts in the Graeco-Roman Age*. Oxford: Oxford University Press, 2009.

Santos, Narry F. *Slave of All: The Paradox of Authority and Servanthood in the Gospel of Mark*. JSNTSup 237. Sheffield: Sheffield Academic, 2003.

Sauvage, Pierre. *The Weapons of the Spirit* [documentary]. 1989.

Schertz, Mary H., and Ivan Friesen, eds. *Beautiful upon the Mountains: Biblical Essays on Mission, Peace, and the Reign of God*. Elkhart, IN: Institute of Mennonite Studies/ Scottdale, PA: Herald, 2003.

Schmiechen, Peter. *Saving Power: Theories of Atonement and Forms of the Church*. Grand Rapids: Eerdmans, 2005.

Schneiders, Sandra. "Biblical Spirituality." *Interpretation* 56 (2002) 133–42.

Schnelle, Udo. *Apostle Paul: His Life and Theology*. Translated by M. Eugene Boring. Grand Rapids: Baker Academic, 2005.

———. *Theology of the New Testament*. Translated by M. Eugene Boring. Grand Rapids: Baker Academic, 2009.

Shaw, David A. "Apocalyptic and Covenant: Perspectives on Paul or Antinomies at War?" *JSNT* 36 (2013) 155–71.

Shelton, R. Larry. "A Covenant Concept of the Atonement." *Wesleyan Theological Journal* 19 (1984) 91–108.

———. *Cross and Covenant: Interpreting the Atonement for 21st Century Mission*. Tyrone, GA: Paternoster, 2006.

———. "Relational Atonement: Covenant Renewal as a Wesleyan Integrating Motif." Paper presented at the annual meeting of the AAR, November 2008. Pages 1–24. http://www.ctr4process.org/affiliations/ort/2008/SheltonL-Relational Atonement.pdf.

Skinner, Christopher W. "Virtue in the New Testament: The Legacies of John and Paul in Comparative Perspective." In *Unity and Diversity in the Gospels and Paul: Essays in Honor of Frank J. Matera*, edited by Christopher W. Skinner and Kelly R. Iverson, 301–24. SBLECL 7. Atlanta: SBL, 2012.

Snodgrass, Klyne. *The NIV Application Commentary: Ephesians*. Grand Rapids: Zondervan, 1996.

Spence, Alan. *The Promise of Peace: A Unified Theory of Atonement*. London: T. & T. Clark, 2006.

Still, Todd D., ed. *Jesus and Paul Reconnected: Fresh Pathways into an Old Debate*. Grand Rapids: Eerdmans, 2007.

Stockhausen, Carol Kern. *Moses' Veil and the Glory of the New Covenant*. An Bib 116. Rome: Pontifical Biblical Institute, 1989.

Swanson, Dennis M. "Introduction to New Covenant Theology." *Master's Seminary Journal* 18 (2007) 149–63.

Swartley, Willard M. *Covenant of Peace: The Missing Peace in New Testament Theology and Ethics*. Grand Rapids: Eerdmans, 2006.

Talbert, Charles H. *The Apocalypse: A Reading of the Revelation of John*. Louisville: Westminster John Knox, 1994.

———. *Reading Acts: A Literary and Theological Commentary*. Rev. ed. Macon, GA: Smyth & Helwys, 2005.

Tannehill, Robert C. *Dying and Rising with Christ: A Study in Pauline Theology*. Berlin: Töpelmann, 1966.

———. *The Narrative Unity of Luke-Acts: A Literary Interpretation*. 2 vols. Philadelphia: Fortress, 1986.

———. "Participation in Christ: A Central Theme in Pauline Soteriology." In *The Shape of the Gospel: New Testament Essays*, 223–37. Eugene, OR: Cascade, 2007.

Thatcher, Tom. *Greater than Caesar: Christology and Empire in the Fourth Gospel*. Minneapolis: Fortress, 2009.

Thompson, Alan J. *The Acts of the Risen Lord Jesus: Luke's Account of God's Unfolding Plan*. Downers Grove, IL: InterVarsity, 2011.

Thompson, Michael. *Clothed with Christ: The Example and Teaching of Jesus in Romans 12.1—15:13*. JSNTSup 59. Sheffield: JSOT Press, 1991.

Torrance, Thomas F. *Atonement: The Person and Work of Christ*. Edited by Robert T. Walker. Milton Keynes, UK: Paternoster.

Trelstad, Marit. "Atonement through Covenant: A Feminist, Process Approach." Pages 1–9. http://www.ctr4process.org/affiliations/ort/2008/TrelstadM-Atonement through Covenant.pdf.

Vanhoozer, Kevin J. "The Atonement in Postmodernity: Guilt, Goats, and Gifts." In *The Glory of the Atonement: Biblical, Theological, and Practical Perspectives*, edited by Charles E. Hill and Frank A. James III, 367–404. Downers Grove, IL: InterVarsity, 2004.

———. *The Drama of Doctrine: A Canonical Linguistic Approach to Christian Doctrine.* Louisville: Westminster John Knox, 2005.

Waaijman, Kees. *Spirituality: Forms, Foundations, Methods.* Leuven: Peeters, 2002.

Wadell, Paul. "Sharing Peace: Discipline and Trust." In *The Blackwell Companion to Christian* Ethics, edited by Stanley Hauerwas and Samuel Wells, 289–301. Oxford: Blackwell, 2006.

Wagner, J. Ross. *Heralds of the Good News: Isaiah and Paul in Concert in the Letter to the Romans.* Leiden/Boston: Brill, 2003.

———. "Isaiah in Romans and Galatians." In *Isaiah in the New Testament*, edited by Steve Moyise and Maarten J. J. Menken, 117–32. London: T. & T. Clark, 2005.

Ware, James P. *Paul and the Mission of the Church: Philippians in Ancient Jewish Context.* Grand Rapids: Baker Academic, 2011.

Watson, David. *Honor among Christians: The Cultural Key to the Messianic Secret.* Minneapolis: Fortress, 2010.

Weaver, J. Denny. *The Nonviolent Atonement.* 2nd ed. Grand Rapids: Eerdmans, 2011.

Wengst, Klaus. *Pax Romana and the Peace of Jesus Christ.* Translated by John Bowden. Philadelphia: Fortress, 1987.

Whittle, Sarah K. *Covenant Renewal and the Consecration of the Gentiles in Romans.* SNTMS. Cambridge: Cambridge University Press, forthcoming.

Williams, Delores S. *Sisters in the Wilderness: The Challenge of Womanist God-Talk.* Maryknoll, NY: Orbis, 1993.

Wood, Susan. "Is Philippians 2:5–11 Incompatible with Feminist Concerns?" *Pro Ecclesia* 6 (1997) 172–83.

Wright, N. T. "The Letter to the Romans: Introduction, Commentary, and Reflections." In the *New Interpreters Bible*, 10:393–770. Nashville: Abingdon, 2002.

———. *Paul: In Fresh Perspective.* Minneapolis: Fortress, 2005.

———. *Paul and the Faithfulness of God.* Christian Origins and the Question of God, vol. 4. Minneapolis: Fortress, 2013.

———. "Revelation and Christian Hope." In *Revelation and the Politics of Apocalyptic Interpretation*, edited by Richard B. Hays and Stefan Alkier, 105–24. Waco: Baylor University Press, 2012.

Yoder, John Howard. *The Politics of Jesus.* 2nd ed. Grand Rapids: Eerdmans, 1994.

Yoder Neufeld, Thomas R. *Killing Enmity: Violence and the New Testament.* Grand Rapids: Baker Academic, 2011.

Yoder, Perry. *Shalom: The Bible's Word for Salvation, Justice, and Peace.* Nappanee, IN: Evangel, 1987.

York, Tripp, and Justin Bronson Barringer, eds. *A Faith Not Worth Fighting For: Addressing Commonly Asked Questions about Christian Nonviolence.* Eugene, OR: Cascade, 2012.

Zerbe, Gordon Mark. *Citizenship: Paul on Peace and Politics.* Winnipeg, MB: CMU Press, 2012.

————. "Paul's Ethic of Nonretaliation and Peace." In *The Love of Enemy and Nonretaliation in the New Testament*, edited by Willard M. Swartley, 177–222. Louisville: Westminster John Knox, 1992.

Subject Index

atonement,
    as theological problem, 17–19
    ethics and. *See* covenant of peace,
        practices of; cruciformity;
        demands of covenant/new
        covenant; discipleship; faith/
        faithfulness, and works/love;
        forgiveness; justice; love; non-
        violence; passion predictions,
        as summonses; servanthood/
        service, cruciform.
    justice and, 10n3, 17–18, 21n42,
        68n46, 229–30. *See also* justice.
    "mechanics" of, 1–2, 4, 33, 39, 42, 44,
        63, 68n45, 75, 170, 204, 210,
        232
    mission and. *See* mission, atonement
        and.
    participation in. *See* participation.
    peacemaking and. *See* covenant of
        peace, practices of; love, of en-
        emies; nonviolence
    performance of, 217, 232–36
    refocusing, 1–8
    transformation and. *See* transfor-
        mation.
    See also atonement, models of.
atonement, models of, 1–8, 9–17,
    203–37
    Christus victor, 10–11, 224–25
    feminist, 230–31
    incarnational, 227
    moral influence, 10, 228
    new-covenant, 1–8, 9–31, 38, 75–76,
        133, 203–37

    absence of, 9–23, 133
    advantages of, 208–15
    as "umbrella" model, 232
    ethics and. *See* covenant of peace,
        practices of; cruciformity;
        demands of covenant/new cov-
        enant; discipleship; faith/
        faithfulness, and works/love;
        forgiveness; justice; love; non-
        violence; passion predictions,
        as summonses; servanthood/
        service, cruciform.
    implications of, 208–15
    liturgy and, 232–36
    mission and, 4, 13–14, 22, 28,
        236–37. *See also* mission.
    other models and, 224–32
    participation and. *See* participa-
        tion, in Jesus' death (atonement).
    politics and, 219–24
    spirituality of, 216–24
    nonviolent, 17–19, 228–29
    penal, 10–11, 20, 21n41, 225–27, 229
    problems with, 19–23
    recent, 10–19, 224–32
    sacrificial, 10, 19, 225–27
    satisfaction, 10, 225–27

baptism. *See* participation, baptism and.

covenant, new. *See* new covenant.
covenant of peace, 5, 25, 30–31, 36,
    43n34, 131, 132–202, 203,
    207–8, 232–33
    dimensions of, 147–60, 165–68

Name Index

Scripture and Other Ancient Sources Index

1 Thessalonians

	90
1:6	90
2:2	90
2:5–9	42n33, 121
2:5–6a	122
2:6	121
2:6b	122
2:7–9	122
2:8	121, 122
2:9	122
2:14–16	90
3:3–4	90
3:12	189
4:1–12	189n44
4:5	116
4:8–9	53
5:3	154
5:8	151
5:11	189n44
5:13	138n16, 152
5:13b	189
5:14	109
5:15	113n15, 151, 152, 153, 189
5:23	150, 152

2 Thessalonians

	139n20, 170
3:7–9	42n33
3:16	139, 150, 154

1 Timothy

1:13	193n55
1:14	125n43

2 Timothy

	94
1:8–12	93
1:8	94
1:12	94
1:13	125n43
2:3	94

2:8–13	94
2:22	153
3:10	125n43
3:11	94
3:12	91n38, 94
4:5	94
4:6–7	94
4:16–18	94

Titus

2:14	3

Philemon

	15–16, 152, 177

Hebrews

	16–17, 69–72, 100–102, 111, 199–201
1:3	200n70
1:8	200n70
1:13	200n70
2:9	101, 200n70
2:10	101
2:17–18	70, 101
2:17	71, 101
2:18	101
3:1–6	71, 101
4:14–16	70, 101
4:14	200n70
4:15	101
5:6	70
5:7–10	101
5:7–9	101
5:7	200n70
5:8	101, 200
6:1–8	69, 102
6:20	70, 200n70
7:1–3	171, 199, 201n72
7:3	70
7:17–28	70
7:26	200n70
7:27	69, 101

DEAD SEA SCROLLS

CD (Cairo Damascus Document)

1QM (War Scroll)

1QpHab (Commentary on Habakkuk)

1QSb (1Q28b) (Rule of the Blessings)

4Q285 (War Rule)

RABBINIC WRITINGS

Isaiah Targum

EARLY CHRISTIAN WRITINGS

Didache

Epistle to Diognetus

Justin Martyr, *Dialogue with Trypho*

Theophilus, *Ad Autolycum*

Lightning Source UK Ltd.
Milton Keynes UK
UKOW04f1132160415

249749UK00002B/56/P